T0291212

WHAT SPONSORS WANT

An Inspirational Guide
for Event Marketers

EMERGING ISSUES AND TRENDS IN SPORT BUSINESS

Series Editor: Norman O'Reilly *(University of Guelph, Canada)*

Published

Vol. 1   *What Sponsors Want: An Inspirational Guide for Event Marketers*
         by Mark Harrison

Emerging Issues and Trends in Sport Business - Vol. 1

WHAT SPONSORS WANT

An Inspirational Guide for Event Marketers

Mark Harrison

The T1 Agency, Canada

World Scientific

NEW JERSEY · LONDON · SINGAPORE · BEIJING · SHANGHAI · HONG KONG · TAIPEI · CHENNAI · TOKYO

Published by

World Scientific Publishing Co. Pte. Ltd.

5 Toh Tuck Link, Singapore 596224

USA office: 27 Warren Street, Suite 401-402, Hackensack, NJ 07601

UK office: 57 Shelton Street, Covent Garden, London WC2H 9HE

British Library Cataloguing-in-Publication Data
A catalogue record for this book is available from the British Library.

Emerging Issues and Trends in Sport Business — Vol. 1
WHAT SPONSORS WANT
An Inspirational Guide for Event Marketers

ISBN 978-981-121-901-6 (hardcover)
ISBN 978-981-121-902-3 (ebook for institutions)
ISBN 978-981-121-903-0 (ebook for individuals)

For any available supplementary material, please visit
https://www.worldscientific.com/worldscibooks/10.1142/11789#t=suppl

Desk Editor: Sandhya Venkatesh

Typeset by Stallion Press
Email: enquiries@stallionpress.com

PREFACE

I love sponsorship. I have always loved sponsorship. Well, almost always.

When I played quarterback for my community football team, our team was led by a devoted guy named Kenny. He was the coach, manager, and franchise owner, and he held a passion for football that I not only admired but came to mirror for my entire life. He launched community football in my hometown of Orillia, Ontario and for that he deserved a lot of credit.

Unfortunately, Coach Kenny didn't know much about sponsorship, but he did understand leverage. When it came time to finding a company to pay for our team uniforms, he immediately targeted the two places where he personally spent the most money — The Beer Store and Kentucky Fried Chicken (KFC). Despite his passionate pitch, The Beer Store Management convinced him they could not sponsor a youth football team, so off he headed to the local KFC.

To this day, I don't know if it was his passion, the appeal of giving back to youth, or the threat of Coach Kenny's fervent pleas, but KFC decided to underwrite our team. Coach Kenny was ecstatic and made sure that every player, parent, and half the town knew about his coup. The teenage marketer in me was half impressed and more than half amazed. I was starting to think Coach Kenny had more to offer than just his ability to slap me on the back and reminisce about his own, often mythical, high school football experiences.

My one request was to ensure that I received the number 10 on my uniform, given my worship of a certain Alabama quarterback of the day, Walter Lewis. In hindsight, I should have added some more details to my request. On uniform day, the large, sealed cardboard boxes had all of us players jumping with excitement. Kenny teased the reveal. He started with the socks: bright red with white stripes, fashionable for the time. Matching white pants with big red pipping down the legs were handed out. Then came the jerseys. Oh, the jerseys! I couldn't wait!

If nothing else, Coach Kenny had a flair for the dramatic. He pulled my buddy's out first. He was number one, so it was fitting. We couldn't believe they were of such high quality, which was the only aspect that was going to give us pause before we cropped them at the belly button. The big bold "1" on the back screamed power, talent, and victory. We were thrilled, until Coach Kenny flipped the jersey around to show us the front.

It wasn't our team name. I understand now that the sponsor needed value, so, it was okay to be the "Orillia Kentucky Colonels". However, it was the number or rather the lack of a number, that was the problem Right where the numeral was supposed to reside was a line art drawing of... Colonel Sanders' face. "Okay, deep breaths", I remember thinking. "We can get through this." We would be the only team in a football league wearing what were essentially hockey jerseys. How bad could that be?

Teenagers are two things if anything; they are very creative, and they are cruel. Our opponents let us have it in every game we played. They clucked. They did the chicken walk. They ordered lunch. They had more jabs and jokes than I can remember. Coach Kenny had sold us out. Every-time I saw him with a bucket or barrel of fried chicken, I was convinced he had taken a kickback along with the deal.

At that time, I had no idea my career would be anchored in sponsorship marketing. What has happened to me since those teenage years drove me to write what you're currently reading.

I launched a highly regarded sponsorship marketing agency, along with three other businesses — one of which failed dramatically. I have launched one of the most admired sponsorship marketing conferences in the world. I launched a promotional marketing conference, which died after just two years. I have spoken more than 100 times across North America and Europe. I have worked with brands such as The Red Cross, Nike, Coca-Cola, The Canadian Olympic Committee, and Fruit of the Loom. I have attended and worked at a bucket list full of events.

I've been an industry mentor and helped spawn the careers of countless sponsorship marketers. I have been an industry friend, promoter, adviser, and ringleader for thousands of professionals. My proudest accomplishment is that I have taught part–time at two universities and given countless speeches at countless colleges and universities.

My passion for sponsorship is rooted in the people I have come to know, love, and admire. This is a people business, and a business with the best people. I wrote this to share one person's ethos; if you are going to be successful, you need to get to know the people you are dealing with. That is the most important aspect of this industry.

I have spent my career working both sides of the sponsorship equation. I have been a buyer, a seller, a builder, and an adviser. This is written for the seller from the buyer's perspective. This is my best stab at taking all the things I've learned from working with sponsors and packaging them in a way that helps sellers do their jobs more effectively. You don't have to be a property to get something from these lessons. I suspect any brand–side sponsor will be inspired to reframe how they deal with their properties after reading and consideration. I chose the perspective I did to make it easier to read.

If you are new to sponsorship, I hope I will add to your excitement about entering a new field. I am not suggesting that everything will be easy. Not at all, this is a tough, competitive, "numbers don't lie" business. However, if you like people, if you like trying to figure people out, if you like working hard at building relationships, and if you like a personal challenge, then this business is for you.

So is this book.

CONTENTS

Preface   v

Endorsements   xiii

**Chapter 1   The Business of Sponsorship —
                    It's the Greatest Magic in Marketing**   **1**

I Love What I Do   1
No More Gold–Silver–Bronze   8
Where is the Buried Treasure?   12
Sponsorship is a People Business   19
Power of Shared Goals   20
What Sponsors Need   24

**Chapter 2   What Sponsors Want from You and
                    Your Property**   **27**

A Potential Shortcut   27
Sponsorship Strategy   32
Matthew Leopold   33
Norm O'Reilly   36

**Chapter 3   To Borrow Equity — The Definition of
                    Sponsorship**   **39**

Borrowing Equity   39
Performance Equity   42

Legitimizing Equity   45
Positioning Equity   47
Community Equity   49
Emotional Equity   50
Tim Dignard   52
John Vidalin   56

Chapter 4   To Tell Stories — A Sponsor's Tale   59

Marketing is Storytelling   59
Writing the Script   60
Writing Great Stories   62
Finding their Pain   63
Searching for A Cure   66
The Story   69
Using the Story to Engage   73
Jacquie Ryan   75
Florian Riepe   78

**Chapter 5   To Engage Stakeholders — Activate.
Activate. Activate   83**

Flashback   83
Why Engagement?   84
Activation   84
The Activation Ratio Fallacy   86
Stakeholder Groups   88
The Stakeholder Orbit   91
The Activation Cycle   93
Benefits of the Activation Cycle   115
Engagement Beyond Activation   116
Brad Sims   119
Kim McConnie   123

**Chapter 6   To See Proof — Don't Be Afraid
            of the Truth   127**

It Shall Set You Free   127
Valuation   129
Self-Assessment   131
Invaluable Numbers   134
Value of Equity   136
Evaluation   139
Yoeri Geerits   161
Zaileen Janmohamed   165

Chapter 7   To Get Promoted ... Not Fired   169

Getting Your Sponsor Promoted   169
Overpaid for Over-delivering   171
It's a People Business   174
Stop Selling, Start Helping   179
Handbook for Success   181
Diarmaid Murphy   188
Patrick O'Brien   193

Chapter 8   Building A Strategy — Planning for Success 199

What is Strategy?   199
The T180 Process   200
Phase I – Outcome Alignment   201
Phase II – Internal Assessment   208
Phase III – External Assessment   218
Phase IV – Benchmarking Analysis   227
Phase V – Distill Findings   233
Phase VI – Strategic Plan   236
OGSM Development   237
Phase VII – Develop the Implementation Plan   241

The What Sponsors' Want (WSW) Proposal Deck   243
Sean Goodall   245
Don Mayo   248

**Chapter 9   The Future of Sponsorship —
Is it already here?**   **251**

Predictions Are Dangerous   251
What Will Sponsors Want?   254
What Will Your Sponsors Want?   256

Scenarios   **259**

Golf Property Sponsorship Offering Scenario   259
Losing Title Sponsor Scenario   263
Arts Festival Scenario   268
Local Cause Property Scenario   275
Music Property Scenario   280

ENDORSEMENTS

"This book's concentration on the human condition reminds us that successful sponsorship models embody the promise of mutual support, partnership, and trust. In a moment where we are quick to reduce the industry to flashy pitch decks and fast cash, Harrison provides a viable framework for building a future that is both sustainable and personal."

— Becca Higgins
Talen Buyer at Blue Note Entertainment Group

"Mark Harrison has written possibly the best sponsorship book and one that will continue to teach, inspire and guide for many years to come. It is part guidebook, part operations manual and 100% inspirational. It is a must have for anyone that works in the sponsorship industry."

— Brandon Tosti
Manager, Corporate Partnerships & Activation Denver,
Arts & Venues, Author

"With 30 years in experiential marketing, Mark Harrison is a sponsorship hall of famer. The common threads in Mark's businesses are unmatched client service, brilliant creative applications, and a laser focus on execution. This book thoughtfully reveals the important perspectives and motivations for both sponsors and properties, and their supporting agencies, partners and stakeholders. The book is written with the industry's voice, and includes important planning and valuation tools. With experiential marketing ready to take off in 2021, this is an important book."

— Jeff Corcoran
Founder of Kinwood, former Marketing Executive,
Ontario Lottery & Gaming

"Mark has captured the essence of sponsorship through engaging anecdotes from personal experiences combined with exclusive interviews with sponsorship experts that provide compelling insight and enjoyment. A worthy read for anyone currently in or pondering to get into the sponsorship game."

— Peter Cosentino
President, DEC Sports & Entertainment

"Done poorly, sponsorship is a fool's errand of ego and wasted resources. Done right, it's one of the most powerful forces in marketing, uniquely able to capture imaginations. This book — from one of the lions of the industry — is for anyone interested in doing sponsorship right. Practical, engaging, and witty, Mark synthesizes the lessons of his storied career into helpful ways to make sponsorships shine in the modern marketing era."

— Raymond Ludwin
Senior Director, Marketing, Air Canada

Chapter 1

THE BUSINESS OF SPONSORSHIP — IT'S THE GREATEST MAGIC IN MARKETING

I LOVE WHAT I DO

It would not be possible for me to overstate my love of sponsorship marketing. I truly believe it is the greatest marketing discipline in the world. It combines art, science, emotion, entertainment, live experiences, and business into one magically explosive formula. It is a discipline that touches all other disciplines. Moreover, it should not be considered a discipline like any other, but a holistic marketing platform. At its most powerful, sponsorship marketing is central to an effective marketing strategy.

I know that thousands and thousands of marketers around the world share my passion. Each and every day, people are sharing their expertise through social platforms, industry workshops, on-the-job mentorship, conferences, and content exchanges. Every minute of every day, these professionals are practicing their craft, developing partnerships and crafting strategies, building activation plans and designing evaluation systems, creating assets and engaging consumers, influencing influencers and delighting new prospects, opening new markets and raising funds for charity, motivating children and inspiring their parents. Sponsorship advertisers are building new communities.

The sponsorship community is vibrant and exciting. It features the most passionate and talented individuals you could ever meet. Many who toil in this business want to lend a hand, provide advice, or pay it forward, and many people who have contributed to my learning share those drivers with me. People I have known and worked with for decades, others with whom I have only connected in the past few years, and individuals who I have only met in recent pursuits. There are even more who I have yet to meet personally, but who have contributed content in support of my ethos. Safe to say, they are all as passionate as I am.

We agree that the stronger the individuals in the sponsorship industry are, the stronger we all are. There is a bond in sponsorship that extends across industries, agencies, territories, and geographic boundaries. As you read this, you will feel the passion of the people in the industry leap off the page, and you will start to understand the unique dynamic at work in this form of marketing. It is a dynamic driven by the one of the most fundamental aspects of the sponsorship industry — relationships.

The commercial relationship that results in a sponsorship partner-ship between a corporation and a property, regardless of size, is a living, breathing entity. Designing and agreeing to the relationship is only the beginning. The real magic of this industry is the lifespan of the relationship as two and often more parties work together to maximize their individual and mutual returns from the relation-ship. Sponsorship partnerships are often referred to as marriages; they involve the long-term commitment of two individuals who really do not know each other that well, and usually, the creation of offspring in the form of campaigns, programs, and initiatives.

This very human dimension of the industry can often be over-looked. Yet many of my colleagues share my belief that it is the most important aspect of the industry. To understand how to build sponsorship programs for your organization or how to sell sponsor-ships, the participants need to be front and centre. That is not to suggest that the human element is not a key part of developing other forms of marketing such as advertising or content, because it is, but unlike those activities, a brand rarely embarks on a multi-year, multifaceted journey with the director of a video or the copy-writer of an advertisement.

Everyone involved in sponsorship will confirm that the stakes are high. Sponsorship marketing is big business around the world, and it is growing faster than most other marketing disciplines. In the past ten years, global sponsorship spending has risen from $34 bil-lion to $58 billion. The Canadian Industry alone is worth $1.74 bil-lion. However, it is not the enormity of the industry that drives its significance in the marketing world. It is sponsorship's impact.

Sponsorship has a tremendous impact on the many organizations and stakeholders who are involved. For a high-performance ath-lete, sponsorship can mean the difference between having to work instead of being able to train. For a local charity, it can mean the difference between being able to feed homeless families or turning them away. For a stadium operator, it can mean the ability to attract government funding, or not. For a brand, it can be the dif-ference between a successful campaign launch or a failed one. This industry can appear to be glamorous, exciting, and full of rich expe-riences. It is all of those things — and a big business.

Jobs are at stake. Businesses are at stake. The livelihoods of artists and entertainers are at stake. Thus, the focus of this book is the human side of the equation. More specifically, it is about understanding the corporate sponsor; the people who own the brand and getting inside their heads to understand what they want from sponsorship. As a 'property', you will have to assess their wants and needs. To do that successfully, it is fundamental to understand the potential of the partnership and develop a cohesive approach.

Fortunately, you are learning about an aspect of marketing that has unlimited potential and power for any business or entity. Sponsorship is a tool that builds love for brands among consumers, that can have a direct impact on distribution and supply chains, that can produce content and assets to be leveraged online and offline, and that taps the passions of all involved like no other.

With sponsorship at the core of an idea or campaign, other related disciplines benefit from its power and critical importance. That is because sponsorship provides tangible and intangible assets that can establish the legitimacy of messaging, create a point of view for a brand, capture the attention of consumers, and provide engaging touchpoints to engage them. A well constructed sponsorship campaign includes: mass communications, peer–to–peer communications, live experiences, promotional elements, media relations, product innovation, digital amplification, advertising, transactional activities, government relations, employee engagement, and collaboration among multiple partners. Sponsorship's proven ability to increase the effectiveness of all other marketing tools sets it apart.

In this era of digital advertising, internet of things, viral social media, and unmitigated, altered states of reality, it is reasonable to ask why a discipline that is over 50 years old would stand out. I am not suggesting that sponsorship is more powerful than online videos or traditional advertising or experiential marketing. Each and every type of marketing tool can be the best choice when the business situation and market dynamics call for it. There is no black and white, cookie cutter solution to what is best. It is entirely situational.

Unlike other marketing tools, sponsorship is versatile. It can be used in digital, in experiences, in virtual reality, in social media, in public relations, in government relations, in sales promotion etc. This ability to be the ideal marketing tourist should exempt sponsorship from being called a discipline. If you picture a traditional marketing blocking chart, the various forms of communication are listed on their own, without interaction or exchanges between them (Table 1).

This is not a realistic dynamic for sponsorship. Your marketing activities are often integrated with each of the other activities on the blocking chart. A sponsorship campaign often has its own unique integrated marketing communications plan that identifies how other marketing disciplines will support the central sponsorship marketing platform. The blocking chart above may not appear

Table 1:   Traditional Marketing Blocking Chart

TIMING	JANUARY	FEBRUARY	MARCH	APRIL
Contest Live	▓	▓	▓	▓
Promoted Social Posts	▓	▓		
Influencer Support		▓	▓	▓
UGC	▓	▓	▓	▓
SM Community Management	▓	▓	▓	▓
30 Second Ads		▓		▓
PR Launch	▓	▓		
Activation			▓	▓
POS Promo		▓	▓	
Cinema Pre-Show Banners		▓	▓	

dramatically different in its structure than a traditional approach, but in fabric it is much different. Each activity is depicted to show its contribution to amplifying the sponsorship platform.

Sponsorship is not listed as a separate discipline because in and of itself, sponsorship is not an activity — it is content that needs to be distributed through various activities. Think of sponsorship as the heart, pumping blood to all parts of the body. Without blood, the rest of the body would not feel, function, or move. Clearly, I am no doctor, but you get the point. Sponsorship is the emotional fuel for all other marketing actions.

Perhaps we need a new form of marketing blocking chart to illustrate this dynamic better, an infographic that can paint a new vision of how sponsorship interacts with each of the other components. This new approach would need to come to life to reflect the emotion, engage-ment, and experiences that sponsorship provides (Figure 1).

I do not want you to take my passionate point of view as the last word on why sponsorship is so powerful. That would be counter-productive to the spirit of learning and discovery that inspired me to write this for you. If anything, I want you to read these words, digest my comments, and challenge them with your own thoughts, your own biases, your own assumptions, and your own filters. Before you do that, I would ask that you learn and absorb even more than the information and intelligence provided on these pages. Ask people who work in the industry, subscribe to blogs, discussion groups, and industry newsletters that discuss the topic. Witness sponsorship in action at your favourite local event or through the lens of an international property. Seek out as many points of view as you can.

As you drop in and discuss events, I am certain you will find that this is a people driven industry. Human beings make decisions

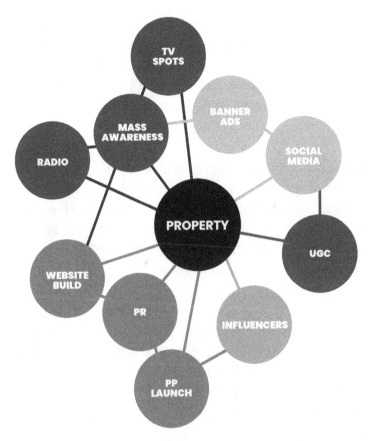

Figure 1:   Marketing Blocking Chart Infographic

every day about what to sponsor, what not to sponsor, why to invest, why not to invest. In short, companies do not decide what to sponsor. People do. Yes, I understand that businesses build strategies, frameworks, and criteria for investing their resources, but software, ad servers, or programmatic buying systems do not influence sponsorship decision–making, even at the highest levels. Gross rating points, financial yields, or algorithms do not determine the investment levels. What science that does exist in the industry is ultimately developed by a human mind. A mind that has feelings, emotions, needs, desires, insecurities, and ambition.

While other sponsorship marketing texts address the trends, tools, and technologies of the business, this book focuses on the people behind those things. While an understanding of the tools is incredibly important, I believe that understanding how people use the tools is even more important. Beyond the "how" is the "why," and beyond the "why" is the "what."

Why do sponsors make certain decisions for their companies? Why do they post a specific policy on their website, even though a mapping of their investments demonstrates a different path? What were the elements of a specific sponsorship opportunity that motivated the final decision–maker to approve it? Who are those decision makers?

Helping you understand what sponsors want and how you can deliver it to them is the crux of this book. Peel back the brick or cyber walls of the companies you do business with and understand the people inside. It is an understanding I will share with you from my three decades of travel through this industry, and it is an understanding that I have translated for you into an actionable business plan.

NO MORE GOLD–SILVER–BRONZE

Somewhere along the way someone decided that sponsorship should be sold like wedding cake. The more tiers you wanted, the more you paid. Then somebody else decided to name the tiers:

- Major–Minor–Official.
- Gold–Silver–Bronze–Diamond–Platinum.
- Premium–Premier–Prime.

All of it seemed logical and efficient. Sponsorship packages became as easy to communicate as the trim packages on a car. The top trim checks off every box and gives more of what you wanted. Lower tiers require compromise and trade–offs. The presentation of these options even mirrored a spec sheet in a car brochure.

I understand the tidiness of all this. I like organization and simplicity. Tiered sponsorship packages simplify the buying process for the seller and the prospect. Remember, a confused buyer doesn't buy. Tiers make sense. Tiers are easy. Tiers are understandable. Slap Gold–Silver–Bronze (GSB) on them and this sponsorship stuff practically sells itself!

However, there is a significant flaw in this thinking. It is in the way the tiers are traditionally packaged; their value is based on tangible items such as number of assets. I may be oversimplifying the concept, but tiers are generally priced at various levels based on the number of items they offer. For example, the Bronze tier may provide one onsite banner, while the Gold tier provides four. The Gold tier is subsequently priced three to four times higher than the Bronze, following the ratio of assets.

Gold–Silver–Bronze (GSB) Example

Table 2 above assumes that value in sponsorship is driven by impressions, and the belief that the more logos, the better. This is somewhat valid, if for no other reason than you want to ensure your stakeholders understand you are affiliated with the property, but a straight–line approach assumes that sponsorship is simply a form of out–of–home (OOH) or online advertising, where benefits such as digital presence are valued in the same manner as the one or four banners example. In many cases, companies buy sponsorships purely for visibility; at the venue; on the athlete; or during the broadcast. Their decision might have been driven by their need for awareness or desire to be present during key moments in their consumers' lives, but this is not really integrated sponsorship.

Table 2:   Gold–Silver–Bronze (GSB) Tiered Sponsorship Packages

SPONSORSHIP RIGHT	GOLD	SILVER	BRONZE
VIP Passes	10	6	4
Acknowledgment on Website	✓	✓	✓
Opportunity to set up a promotional booth	✓	✓	✓
Logo on newsletter	✓	✓	✓
Logo on main banner	✓	✓	
Logo on promotional material	✓	✓	
Right to tie-in special promotions	✓		
Naming rights	✓		
On-site promotional giveaway	✓		
Total Cost	50,000	25,000	10,000

There is much more to a strategic and integrated sponsorship program than simply logo exposure. The best partnerships include the sharing of values, joint initiatives, combined intellectual property, pursuit of a common goal, transference of brand equity, and the building of communities. The most strategic sponsorship programs are far more complex than a piece of creative stuck on a sign. That complexity is hard to box up, harder to sell, and even harder to value, but that complexity is what properties need to embrace if they want to be successful in the modern sponsorship marketing world.

I like to rant on this topic when I make speeches at industry events. Usually, I set–up my discussion by asking the audience if they use the GSB approach to their decks. Most are honest and confess. A few deniers are betrayed by their facial expressions. The odd attention seeker replies that they also have a "platinum" level, but as crude as this science is, the show of hands proves that the GSB method still has a lot of currency.

It confuses people when I say I am not condemning the use of tiers or levels in a sponsorship. There is no question that a partner who invests more, not just financially, should be more deeply involved with your property. What I am attacking is the formulaic use of physical assets to develop those tiers, and more vigorously, the false belief that they represent the value in your sponsorship property. This belief belies everything that is powerful about sponsorship; it reduces it to an impression–based monetization of eyeballs, effectively boxing sponsorship in the field of media advertising, which in turn reduces the true value of the strategy far beneath its potential.

A GSB approach assumes that if one consumer sees a sponsor's banner, that banner is worth one unit of currency. If two consumers see that banner, or if a consumer sees two sponsor banners, then it is now worth two units. The property then assembles their sponsorship package based on the number of impressions. The more signs, the more people will see them, the more valuable the package. That is advertising in my book, and that approach does not consider sponsorship's centrality to the marketing mix.

How important is the property in the eyes of the consumer? How important is your support of that property to consumers? How are you engaging with the consumer? How much value are you adding to their lives? It is ironic that so many properties brag about customizing packages for sponsors, even though they still use the "eyeballs" approach as their base.

Two issues. First, everybody customizes their packages. This is not new. I was in a meeting recently with one of the big four sports leagues, and one of their senior sales reps must have repeated "customization" five times like he was some sort of guru. The tepid response from the other side of the table was seemingly lost on him.

Second, the seller adopts the mindset that views customization as horse–trading. What assets will be added or removed to achieve a package structure that will generate the dollar amount they hope to secure? In essence, customization of the GSB approach benefits the property, not the sponsor!

Tiering works when you are selling a tangible product, but not when you are selling a particular affiliation and the intangible benefits that are accrued from that affiliation. Sponsorship is for the obsessive, not the enthusiast. The property needs to become an empathetic server who learns from the guests how to anticipate their needs, what their guests crave, what their guests want to experience, and what would best serve that craving. The property needs to understand the emotions of the meal experience. They need to realize that merely piling more food on the plate is not going to add value. In many situations, more can be less.

WHERE IS THE BURIED TREASURE?

Now that I have crushed the dreams of all sponsorship prospectors, you are probably asking where does one find the buried treasure? To begin your journey, I am going to first ask that you walk in my shoes. Travelling together will make the concepts I am about to share easier to understand and hopefully appear more logical.

Before we begin, I have a confession to make. When I first launched my sports marketing agency, I knew nothing about sports marketing, sponsorship marketing, or event marketing. I launched my company because I knew three things for certain:

- How to discover and fulfil clients' needs;
- That I wanted to control my destiny and own my future;
- And that I loved sports.

I knew there was a gap in the market; an opportunity I might seize. To oversimplify, I watched the big brands work with big agencies on big events in big cities. Having grown up in a small, but not tiny, community of 25,000 people, I felt there was a lot of business opportunities in those communities for big brands. I quickly discovered that those brands had no idea how to reach the smaller markets. Those that did were convinced it was tedious to do so. My pitch was to bring big brands to smaller events in smaller markets. *That* I knew how to do.

Beyond that, I knew little of the industry that is the subject of this book. I began my self–education. To be frank it was a matter of survival. No knowledge meant no clients, which would mean no business, which would mean no revenue. I had some experience from my previous life — I was with a top–tier consumer promotions agency. We had conducted many promotions and activations with sponsorships our clients had taken on, so by the time I had launched my company, I had already worked with festivals, professional sports, multinational events, amateur athletes, community events, and charities, but I had never been central in the creation of those partnerships.

To keep the few lights I had on at my small company, I focused on my strengths. I pursued promotional work with brands in sports partnerships. I decided to work both sides of the fence and sell sponsorships for a few promising properties. Trying my hat at selling for the first time in my life taught me new lessons, but if I was going to be successful as a hunter — when I had been a farmer for all of my career — I would need new wiring.

I quickly learned the hardest part of sales is finding a person with a need. I thought that selling was about mass cold calling, lots of lunches, a bit of golf, and slick presentations. I was very wrong.

Companies only buy sponsorships when they have a business need. Being there when they decide to fix that need — especially if you have pointed it out to them — is the mark of a great salesperson. Many of the people that mentored me early on taught me how to identify when those needs became apparent. They taught me how to monitor companies and industries that were being proactive, to spot signals that might indicate that change is coming. Change often drives need. New senior leaders, new competitors in the market, new channels of distribution, new products coming down the pipeline. All of these changes will soon grow into business needs.

Mentors — these were one of the first sources of education early in my career. You need mentors. You need to have mentors in your organization and on the outside. Whether they are formal or informal, your relationship should be explicit. Communicate what you want from your mentor. Explain how they can best help you. Be clear about how often you would like to meet and how. I did not realize that the three wise men coaching me in my 20s were mentoring me and perhaps if I had, my pig headed stubbornness would have likely rejected them. These three men were key suppliers to the promotional marketing agency that employed me. One was a print broker. Another owned the graphics studio we used. The third was in the creative production business as well.

My educational sessions were never announced as such, nor were they scheduled. Rather, I taught myself by participating in meetings, attending late night press approvals, doing weekend deliveries, and over countless coffees and beers. I asked lots of questions and received equal amounts of wisdom. How do I deal with difficult clients? What is the best way to discuss cost overages? Should I trust people at their face value? These discussions often left me confused but willing to try new approaches when I dealt with people. I was in a foggy haze, but often, it would lift, and I could think and see clearly. Some of the hypothetical situations my mentors described over coffee came to materialize in my work, and when they did, I was ready to manage them.

When I launched my company, I was pleasantly surprised to find a new set of mentors and supporters — some of my clients. It seemed that many a corporate soldier privately held the dream of sharing their legacy with the generation that followed them. Perhaps I was their proxy in their minds. Having their support did not mean that business flowed in endlessly, but their advice and counsel certainly did. They were a much–needed source of motivation and information. Often, I would take my former clients through pitches or approaches I had thought up for new prospects. Their feedback was incredible, informed by their own experiences of being pitched to. It was especially valuable to me; the proverbial one–man band; I lacked even a single associate with whom to brainstorm.

Mentors have played a large part in my education. The model and advice contained in your hands represents many people's thoughts. I have never stopped seeking mentors. Today, I have mentors that probably do not know they are filling such a role. Some of them are competitors, others are industry colleagues, suppliers, and a few former employees. Some have nothing to do with my industry, but their brains are too big to ignore.

In addition to having mentors, I resolved early in my career to get to know as many people in this industry as I possibly could. I quickly learned that media events were a great place to network and meet people. I looked for ways to be added to mailing and invitation lists as an industry observer. Call me a professional room filler, but it was a great opportunity to meet people and start a relationship. This was before social media: you could not just develop an online network with a few keystrokes. Every time I added a new person to my circle, I immediately and persistently probed them for information. People love to talk about what they do, and they were soon to meet a good listener in me.

It was not long before the information that they shared with me became more valuable; the best conferences to attend; the best newsletters or magazines to subscribe and receive; the best associations to join. I took all of their inputs and acted on them. I particularly love attending conferences. My business, speeches, blogs, and theories are all based on ideas learned from others. Most have come from lessons learned at conferences, each supplying its own nugget of information to be added to another that helped to form my ideas.

Industry publications may seem like propaganda to some, but they can educate you if you are disciplined in mining them. No one article or issue is going to provide a total picture, but you are seeking useful ingredients and recipes, not an entire meal. I have done more than my part in keeping many industry publications afloat for the past quarter century, and they have served me well inspiring new ideas, revealing best practices, and providing critical data. I am so addicted to publications that, to this day, they hold a regular place on my Daily Task app.

As my business grew and people began to know me, I began to get asked to write for publications and to speak at conferences. That was a time of trial and error. I have to admit that my first few attempts were horrible. At one conference, I could tell I was falling on my face, and while some people left, I adored the others who willed their way through my presentation and even applauded at the end. I quickly realized that my failures were due to my speeches being more science fiction than fact-based stories. In other words, I knew more than enough about the topics from my work, my learning, and my industry sleuthing, but instead I attempted to create some new take on the topic that had no basis in fact. This insight inspired all future speaking occasions and for me to create new sources of information, which in turn yielded new insights and knowledge. In addition to being a conference groupie, which I was and still am, I launched my own. After reading industry research reports, I began commissioning some of my own. Beyond surmising what was happening in the industry, I started interviewing industry colleagues. All of these initiatives yielded useful content.

At our Sponsorship Forum event (started in 2005), we had speakers from Space X, Pepsi USA, Visa USA, FC Barcelona, UFC (Dana White himself), Movember, WE (formerly Free the Children), Nike, Coca–Cola, The International Paralympic Committee, and more. Our delegates have come from every sector of sponsorship, from every continent in the world. On paper, I am the Founder and Chairperson, but in my mind, I am still a delegate, soaking up their every word. As an added perk, I often have a privileged behind the scenes opportunity to pick their brains.

One outcome of my conferences are the proprietary research studies, such as the Most Valuable Property project, which we worked on with Ipsos Reid and the Canadian Sponsorship Landscape Study. These initiatives have given me access to information about what consumers look for in the properties that they sponsor. These reports provide data on what consumers believe brands should support, empirical evidence in what sectors brands are investing, and measured feedback from sponsors on what they need from properties. Since this is not meant to be a textbook, I will not be citing statistics, but the data and insights I gained from this research over the years have all been accounted for in the theories I am sharing.

In addition to formal studies, I often leverage my industry network for insights. I was presenting at a not–for–profit conference recently and wanted to provide a deeper dive into what sponsors want. To prepare, I conducted a quick and easy online Q&A with about 20 corporate partners. The objective was to add colour and context to the presentation, rather than gathering statistics. This type of input for a conference presentation is powerful for the audience and for the speaker. As the speaker, you are even more comfortable with the slant you are taking. As the audience, you end up benefitting from the opinions of many, not just your presenter. In this case, the feedback from my small poll inspired me to think about changing the presentation title from *What Sponsors Want* to *Why Your Sponsors Hate You*. I did joke about this during the presentation, and the audience's nervous laughter convinced me that they knew this truth as well; most properties do not do a great job of working with their partners. I will do my best to illuminate that problem even further and provide a thorough plan of attack to solve it.

My first piece of advice would probably echo that of the many who have directly and indirectly contributed to this book; you need to want to be *great*. Not just good. Not just different. Not committed, but great. I work really well with people who want to be great and not so well with people who do not. Being great means working at it every day. Trying and trying again. Being great means having a plan. Let us be great together!

SPONSORSHIP IS A PEOPLE BUSINESS

First and foremost, sponsorship marketing is a people business. Early in my career, an older businessperson, not someone whom I particularly respected to be candid, told me that it was not what you know in business, it is who you know. I can vividly remember how offended I was by that comment. My massive ego had told me that I would wow the business world with my skills and prowess, and that old world connections and private school networks would mean nothing, especially when pitted against my enormous talent. I looked at him like he was a corporate dinosaur whose shoddy advice and flawed wisdom gave him zero credibility. Unfortunately, I was wrong, and he was dead right.

Throughout my career, I have come to understand what he meant. He was not referring to privilege. He was not referring to secret handshakes. He was not referring to private clubs. He was referring to the fact that sponsorship marketing is really a people business. It is about who you know and who knows you.

To advance his point, he could have elaborated that the "who" has a strong companion word, "what." It is not just who you know, it is what you know about them. Similarly, it is not just who knows you, but what they know about you. People do business with people they trust.

I understand your scepticism if you believe that all of this sounds fundamental to any business and not necessarily unique to sponsorship. There is no disputing the fact that most businesses are people businesses. However, in sponsorship marketing, there is an important nuance in the relationship dynamic between sponsors (buyers) and properties (sellers). The nuance resides in the fact that the relationship does not begin in earnest until the contract is signed.

By way of comparison, consider a programmatic digital media campaign. With programmatic buying, a brand (buyer/sponsor) can purchase and sell advertising space in real time. Through the use of algorithms, software automates the buying, placement, and optimization of media inventory via a bidding system. In this case, the relationship is at its most intense during the negotiating phase; it is then briefly rekindled during the reporting phase. The relationship has only periodic intensity. Not so with a sponsorship marketing partnership.

POWER OF SHARED GOALS

A sponsorship marketing partnership is more akin to the relationship between a marketer and an agency or consulting firm. It is always-on, 24/7/365 for the duration of the agreement. It is characterized by a wide variety of interactions, including opportunity seeking, research, strategizing, creative development, asset development, resource deployment, infield execution, media fulfilment, and evaluation. There are peaks and valleys of engagement, ebbs and flows of activity, and periods of ramping up and winding down.

In a sponsorship marketing partnership, you need to stop selling and start helping. You should strive to be the best part of your sponsor's day, week, or year. When the sponsor interacts with you, they should expect passion, conviction, and dedication. They should feel like the most important person in your world. They should be telling everybody in their organization, if not anyone who will listen, how amazing you are.

Think of the fundamental shift this will create in your approach and that of your organization. The best sponsorship properties have airtight relationships with their contacts. That should be a tantalizing prospect for you.

It is an amazing opportunity. Do you want your personal brand to be that of someone who is trusted, sought after, and well respected? Or would you prefer to be known as a smooth–talking huckster? The latter is someone who will pitch anything to anyone. The former is a person who people seek out. You will probably not spend your career in just one organization. You should get out of the Sales or Business Development function immediately and jump headfirst into the Department of Helping.

A great many stakeholders on both sides are involved in the relationship, as are a myriad of departments in each entity. This too represents a difference from many other types of marketing relationships. Other vendors in the marketing ecosystem often deal with an end user and a purchasing department representative. Even advertising or other communications agencies often only have a few key contacts with whom they deal with consistent frequency. With sponsorship marketing, you have fulfilment managers, communications personnel, programmers, officials, talent, operations, board members, volunteer committees, and salespeople all involved on the property side. On the client side, you have sponsorship experts, marketing communications staff, product development, sales and account people, public relations, and digital departments. Sponsors and their partner properties become joined at multiple points across their respective entities. The multitude and diversity of connections influence the dynamic relationship between the organizations.

Perhaps the most powerful aspect of a sponsorship marketing relationship, however, is goal sharing with the partner organizations. Each partner is substantially vested in the growth of the sponsorship property. The property is vested because it is their livelihood, their mission, or their responsibility to ensure that the property grows and prospers. The sponsor is vested, because as the property grows, so does the value and return on their investment. When you consider that the original premise of sponsorship was based on a company investing money in something that would not exist or exist in the same way without the sponsor's support, you can understand how the shared goal concept is foundational.

The sponsor–property relationship is much more similar to a relationship between business partners or co–investors than to the deal mindset that prevails in a one–way commercial transaction. If you think of a property as having clear and measurable mandates such as raising funds, selling tickets, generating exposure, providing services, offering programming, or training talent, it becomes clear why the property would want sponsors to support them. It is clear that the property recognizes that the more tickets they sell, communities they service, participants they engage, or eyeballs they attract, the more attractive they become to sponsors, and the more they can raise the price of tickets. This starts to create a flywheel effect where success begets success.

Correspondingly, the sponsor wants the property to succeed. In addition to their rights fee, they are investing termed resources in activation budgets, organizational time, volunteerism, and amplification programs. If their property partner can meet or exceed their projections for consumer or corporate engagement, attendance, media exposure, likability, licensed goods sales, or ticket purchases, the more valuable they become. The sponsor will have immediate, positive business outcomes, because their original investment will automatically become more valuable. The positive movement of the majority of such metrics will impact the emotional value of the property, once again improving Return on Investment (ROI) for the sponsor. It is ironic that accomplishing these goals together can result in higher costs for the sponsor, but that is a meaty topic for another day.

A substantial amount of the sponsor–property partnership is spent working together to ensure the property's success. This extends far beyond the financial investment, although it is an important component. At a minimum, properties expect that beyond the rights fee, the sponsor will activate the property. Activation can include promotions, experiences, or use of content to name a few high–level tactics. The property covets each of these tactics, as they understand the impact of sponsors' expenditures. Properties work with their sponsors to get additional support and benefits such as volunteers, networking, access to vendors, preferred media rates, usage of physical assets, deployment of fundraising campaigns, product donations, and even product innovation that can improve the property. Sponsors and properties end up working together hosting retreats, off sites, planning meetings, venue inspections, FAM trips, and workshops. They quickly become united on meeting their goal; that the property succeeds. The sponsor is not paying a property as they would pay a digital network for click–throughs or a media outlet for Gross Rating Points (GRPs). The sponsor is helping the property. This type of business relationship can only exist when both sides understand that it is a people business. It is not a transaction, and though it requires a contract, the agreement is a secondary factor in guiding the behaviour of the two parties. It produces a more complex situation, yet one that is much more rewarding. The relationship requires the property to understand not just what the corporation wants, but more importantly, what their sponsor contact wants. It requires the property to employ a sales team that can go beyond espousing the fit of the property, or the reach, or the fact that they will customize the offering. Those elements are the price of entry and do not imply uniqueness or originality.

It is interesting to me how property salespeople spend the majority of their time pitching to partners using the same quantitative dialogue that they would use when selling someone a water treatment solution. They focus on metrics, reach, impressions, eyeballs, ticket allocations, signage commitments, logo mentions, attendance numbers, tour stops, economic impact, onsite sales, promotional rights, and value banks.

In addition to providing the quantitative measures and statistics, the property offers to customize the package for the sponsor, to be willing to try new things, to be open to a first year trial, to come and meet your CEO. The property seems to be excited about their willingness to do these things, yet they are unfortunately misguided in thinking that they are differentiating themselves by these offers. As I have already mentioned, every property in the world offers customization. Every property in the world offers exclusivity. Every property in the world offers to host your CEO.

WHAT SPONSORS NEED

The best properties in the world understand that this is a people business. They understand that in order to pitch, secure, and fulfil an amazing relationship with an attractive sponsor, they need to understand more than presented; they need to understand what their sponsors need as well as want.

There is tremendous power in understanding what people want in any sales situation. When you couple that with the fact that a sponsor–property partnership represents much more than a transaction — that it represents a business marriage — the need to understand is amplified. This is not to suggest that building sponsorship partnerships is based on psychological profiling, emotional manipulation, or some other form of mind games. It is more subtle. In order to unleash the true magic of sponsorship, you first and foremost must remember that you are dealing with human beings. Corporations do not make decisions about what to sponsor. People do.

The decision–makers in sponsorship have business challenges, professional challenges, and personal challenges, just like you do. In addition, they personify the challenges of their boss, their department, their peers, and their internal and external clients. Rarely will you meet a prospect without any needs. I would suggest that if you do, selling your property to them would be the hardest task of your life.

Fortunately, people with needs are people looking for solutions. This is Sales 101. Understanding your prospects' needs will allow you to develop a relationship that is irresistible. Making those needs explicit will allow a corporate sponsor to sell the initiative internally. Management consultants are infamous for asking their clients what keeps them up at night, but it is an invaluable question, and one of several that a sponsorship property should be prepared to ask when they visit a prospect. Instead of launching into a pitch about their property, their other sponsors, or their proposal, the property should demonstrate that they understand what their sponsors want. Or at the very least, they should want to understand.

If a property sales representative does not understand the needs of the person across from them, they are merely pushing media, not building a sponsorship partnership. They should understand how their prospect is evaluated, how they are awarded bonuses, how they work with their bosses, peers, and stakeholders. The property needs to understand how the prospect's company makes money, how they go to market, and how they choose their innovation priorities. The property needs to understand what impact current market dynamics are having and how their employees and customers are feeling.

Here below, I provide you a model for addressing what sponsors want. I have collected years of experience, pages of research, volumes of insights, and troves of testimonials, but this model is just that, a model. It has worked for many and will work for many more, but it does not have to be your model. It could inform or be a component of your model, or even become your model in complete form. It could inspire you to create an entirely different model. None of those outcomes is more desirable for me than any other, unless the outcome is no outcome. I am providing you with a compass for navigating the sponsorship marketing landscape, and to see it through the same lens as the partner with whom you are going to work. It is my belief that by understanding what sponsors want to achieve, you can better understand the magic of sponsorship marketing. If you do not understand their desires, you are simply building and selling one-way transactional advertising that is dressed up to look like sponsorship.

The sponsors or potential sponsors reading this will be able to provide a map of where you want to travel for your property partners. So too will potential properties who are soliciting you. The "understanding the wants" approach will allow a sponsor to frame a strategy that ensures internal support for a planned sponsorship initiative. It will provide a framework you can use to build your asset and activation plans. It will enable you to educate your partners on how to work better with you, as your partnership works together to maximize returns.

Chapter 2

WHAT SPONSORS WANT FROM YOU AND YOUR PROPERTY

A POTENTIAL SHORTCUT

I have a simple goal when I give a speech, write a blog, post on social media, or provide live mentoring: leave my audience with one key learning outcome, one nugget, one morsel of information that will make their time investment worthwhile. Whether it is a question, a recommendation, or a story, my goal is to help that person and provide them with something highly tangible and actionable.

The same holds true here where I describe my core theory of sponsorship.

Let us jump into the model! It is quite simple and provides you with five key elements that, when combined, will provide a powerful sponsorship marketing program, no matter the type or size of the property, the sponsoring brand's industry, the partner's homeland, or the budget available. There is a vast range of opportunities you will be able to pursue as you apply the model's elements.

The What Sponsors Want (WSW) model has substantial impact because I believe it can be used to write a more effective and

<u>What Sponsors Want</u>

1. To Borrow Equity
2. To Tell Stories
3. To Engage Stakeholders
4. To See Proof
5. To Get Promoted

Figure 1:   The What Sponsors Want Model

affective sponsorship proposal or sponsorship sales letter, to better value potential opportunities and evaluate programs, and to build consistently successful strategies. The WSW model is a framework that rests on a solid foundation — sponsorship marketing is not a discipline, but a holistic marketing platform. It works because each component is programmed to recognize that this is a people business, one where the relationships are mutually dependent and striving to grow a shared interest over time — the sponsorship property.

If your property can fulfill these five key deliverables, you will find success. If your brand has a sponsorship strategy that incorporates all five of these elements, you will have a great marketing campaign. If you are a new student of sponsorship, it will provide you with a lens to view and understand the critical components of a sponsor-property relationship.

The five key deliverables are listed in an order designed to influence how a sponsorship property would be packaged for sale, or how it would be valued by a brand sponsor. In simpler terms, the five are listed in chronological order. While you can certainly change or alter the order when you finalize your own model, I like to precede one through five. The deliverables are essentially building blocks for one another, and they require input from the previous stage to shape the design of the next. Additionally, I strongly believe that using consistent processes are an effective way to help people and groups become more creative. Process is like practice for an athlete. It is like a skills drill. By repeating it over and over, you develop muscle memory, so that when it comes time to execute in a high-pressure situation, the steps become automatic and don't have to be thought through. Your mind can focus exclusively on problem solving.

1. To Borrow Equity

Great sponsorship marketing is entirely dependent on a great affiliation. Brands and companies become affiliated with strategic partners who have substantial goodwill with stakeholder groups that are important to the sponsor. As a part of this affiliation, the brand seeks to share in some of the property's halo in order to impact the perception among stakeholders. If a property can be seen as a bar of gold, the brand's aim is to bask in its reflection. The positively perceived elements that make up the property are sought after by the brand. This is the borrowing of equity.

2. To Tell Stories

I will not be the first person to tell you that marketing is storytelling. Marketers want to tell stories about their brands, their companies, their consumers, their products, their founders, and their origins. They want to connect with consumers, and other important stakeholder groups in a compelling manner, and storytelling is one of the most powerful ways to accomplish this purpose. Sponsorship partnerships are great subject matter for storytelling by their very nature. All the elements of a great story exist in the most intriguing sponsorship properties. The stage is set, you just need to develop the script and turn on the lights and camera.

3. To Engage Stakeholders

This is more than just activation, and it is more than just reaching consumers. That is why stakeholders are so important. The tentacles of a great sponsorship marketing program can reach many internal groups, a wide variety of consumer groups, and an even broader net of industry participants. Engagement is central to making sponsorship marketing so powerful.

Traditional sponsorship focuses on engaging consumers by aligning with something they are passionate about, and on VIP hosting by providing trade customers with unbelievable experiences. Those activities are important and can generate significant returns for a company, but there is so much more potential in a sponsorship program. A powerful and effective sponsorship program expands its stakeholder reach beyond consumers and trade customers to three important groups: internal stakeholders, B2B stakeholders, and B2C stakeholders.

4. To See Proof

Let us dispel one myth. Not every property provides results — this applies to some of the biggest and most expensive properties. This does not mean that properties are not providing results for their brands. Most are, but are they providing proof? Are they providing real results? The best approach is to not be afraid of the truth. Sponsors want to see two types of proof: societal proof and business proof. Societal proof is a demonstration that their investment in your organization allowed you to further your mission. Business proof answers the question, "Did the sponsorship work?"

The most important aspect in fulfilling the proof element is to develop your plan before the sponsorship program begins.

Ultimately, you will prepare a capture plan that will provide the details and data your sponsor will relish. This plan will:

- identify key metrics, which are composed of performance metrics, efficiency metrics, and behavioural metrics;
- determine report timing, which is a sound strategy to plan for more reporting windows than less in a relationship;
- identify sources, namely the many participants who need to be briefed and coordinated by a central coordinator throughout the process;
- establish collection timing, which should identify if and when you want to be sourcing results prior to the partnership, during the partnership period, and after; and
- build report structure, which will determine what your reports will look like, what information they will contain, and how they will be delivered.

5. To Get Promoted

This is the element of the model that always throws people for a curve. Most audiences assume I am referring to the sponsor's brand or product. Logically, the words lead you to think about how to generate exposure, awareness, or recognition for the sponsor's brand. That is not what this is about.

Remember, this is a people business. Number Five refers wholeheartedly to the person across the desk from you. Your sponsor, your partner, your champion. It is your job to help them do their job better. It is the job of your entire organization and everyone involved to help them, and all their associates improve at their jobs. This is a central underpinning of all service businesses, and it is much more fundamental to sponsorship marketing than most people realize.

Most people in business want to do a job well. Most of them want to advance in their careers. Most have ambitions. A person working for a sponsorship property needs to understand that. They need to understand that after all the due diligence, fact finding, and valuation, the person on the sponsor side is going to look at you and your organization and ask a simple question: "Will I get fired if I work with you?" Or if we want it to be more positive, "Will I get promoted if I work with you?"

SPONSORSHIP STRATEGY

Developing a strategy is essential. Strategy is often a misused word, but it is far simpler than what people think it is. It means a plan. For you to adopt a new approach to marketing and managing your sponsorship portfolio, you need to conduct a thorough planning process. At our agency, we utilize a process entitled the T180, which is comprised of the following seven steps:

1. Alignment on Objectives: ensuring that all internal stakeholders are aligned with the future that the sponsorship has within the property.
2. Internal Assessment: thoroughly reviewing all historical results, strategic plans, interviews with key stakeholders, including current and lapsed sponsors.
3. External Assessment: developing an overview of the industry, competitors, sponsorship landscape, and best-in-class properties to ensure that your property understands the market.
4. Benchmarking: conducting a financial exercise to determine your total sponsorship potential, assess your current pricing versus competitors, and to use facts to inform decision making.
5. Distilling Findings: providing an in-depth opportunity to focus on the key information uncovered in the first four phases, and to determine your value proposition.
6. Developing a Strategic Plan: building on the foundation of an Objectives, Goals, Strategies, Measures (OGSM) tool to

secure alignment on the most significant aspects of your new approach.

7. Develop Implementation Plan: executing the roadmap to turn words into actions, plans into protocols, and ideas into reality.

You will know you have been successful in your planning process when all of your touch points begin to reflect the WSW model, whether it is by ensuring you are communicating your equity to all stakeholders, or designing your organizational structure to maximize your ability to service sponsors. You will know when your pitch deck is entitled *A Discussion on Building our Community Together* and no longer says *Sponsorship* or *Partnership Proposal*. You will know when your next proposal is built on a daylong brainstorming session with your prospect. You will know when volunteers are asking your sponsors how their work life is going.

You will most definitely know when you start answering all sponsorship inquiries with a five-sentence reply that talks about:

- How the sponsor can borrow your equity
- What great stories you can tell together.
- When you ask which stakeholders, they would like to engage.
- If you share with them how you have been able to prove that partnering with your property will produce business and societal results.
- When you invite them to a discussion to understand how the sponsor likes to work best with properties, leading to promotion on all sides.

MATTHEW LEOPOLD

To call Matthew the ultimate team player would be an understatement. He has spent his career living by the credo of a former boss who told him, "If the team wins, we all win", words that guide him in his approach to every aspect of his life. Matthew's dedication to the sponsorship industry is exemplary; he is a volunteer with the European Sponsorship Association, a frequent speaker and content creator. He is personally concerned about the lack of strategy and insight in sponsorship marketing and predicts that it will harm our industry for years to come. His words are not meant to be critical, but as a wake-up call for us all. In a world where actions speak louder than words, Matthew dedicates much of his personal time to helping others. He is a volunteer for the London Ambulance Service, bringing calm and reassurances to patients during the most traumatic moments of their lives. His public service is only matched by his humility in serving the many industry people, athletes, volunteers, and media members he encounters.

How long have you been working with British Gas (BG)?
I started my career at British Gas almost eight years ago.

Tell us about your current role with BG and the path you took to get there.
As with most things in life, I was in the right place at the right time! I started my career on the British Gas graduate program, working in general management. I then chose to move into marketing and started to specialize in brand marketing. As the London Olympic Games got closer, I was asked to lead the brand's sponsorship of British Swimming.

I had no experience in sports marketing or sponsorship, so it was a tough learning curve. However, by bringing general management's value focus and marketing's focus on the customer, I was able to make a big impact on the brand and sponsorship.

My role is now much broader. I sit in our Corporate Affairs team with a remit that includes the management and activation of our Corporate Social Responsibility agenda.

How does British Gas leverage the power of sponsorship?
Sponsorship can be really powerful, or it can be a waste of money. It all comes down to the insight used to identify the partnership. British Gas has very high brand awareness, so we did not need high profile rights to grow awareness.

We wanted to create a stronger and more meaningful connection with our customers. If we had sponsored football, we would have been one of many brands sponsoring a team or league. This would have done very little to create a meaningful connection.

By sponsoring British Swimming, we were one of very few partners. We could develop a deep and significant connection with the sport. We could be creative with our segmentation and activation — there was much more freedom without the clutter and complexity of working with other brands. Of course, my budget could stretch further too!

The British Gas and British Swimming partnership was a six-year relationship. When signed, it was the biggest partnership deal in the history of aquatics. Swimming is the UK's biggest participation sport. More people swim than participate in any other sport. As one of Britain's biggest energy suppliers, this had huge appeal for us. We could support a sport enjoyed by a huge number of our customers. Our sponsorship could add value to them and reward them for their custom.

Swimming is the only sport that can save your life. It is brilliant for your health, as it is low impact on your bones and joints. It is also recreation — almost everyone, even non-swimmers, jump in the pool or sea when on holiday. There were so many positive reasons to get involved. Our sponsorship focused on helping to grow participation and 'fanship' for this brilliant, popular and healthy sport. By getting more people to love the sport and to participate, I was increasing the pool (pun intentional!) of people who would be aware of our sponsorship and grateful for our investment. Sports organizations have the most amazing asset available: 'fanship'. Fans are passionate. Fans care. If a sponsoring brand can tap even 0.1% of that passion, it has huge value.

What do you think is the most common misunderstanding when it comes to sponsorship?
Sponsorship is marketing! That means we need to treat it as you would any other element of marketing.

At the time of this interview, Matthew worked for British Gas as the Head of Brand, Sponsorship and CRS. Matthew has worked for British Gas since 2011 as the Head of the Brand Sponsorship Department and the Propositions Manager and Sponsorship Head. Matthew is currently a Non-Executive Director at the European Sponsorship Association.

NORM O'REILLY

Seven books. Two Masters Degrees. One PhD. 300 triathlons completed. Over 100 conference presentations. Four children. 80 journal articles. Two jobs. Numbers do not lie, and to call Norm a work hard/play hard sort of man would be an understatement. He has taught at Stanford, Ohio University, Laurentian, Ryerson, University of Ottawa, and Syracuse. He has been on the Board of Triathlon Canada, Assistant Chef de Mission for Team Canada at 2016 Paralympics in Rio, and is the North American Editor of Sport, Business and Management: An International Journal. There is nothing that can slow Norm down and nothing for which he wants to slow down.

When is sponsorship the answer?
Sponsorship is the answer when you need to cut through a cluttered marketplace trying to reach very specific segments of the population that have an affinity for a specific property. In this case, if done right, sponsorship can be very effective.

When is sponsorship not the answer?
Sponsorship is not the answer when you are seeking awareness only in large markets. Just use advertising.

How important is sponsorship within the marketing communication mix?
The Canadian Sponsorship Landscape Study shows that about 25% of spending in marcom budgets for those who sponsor is on sponsorship. This for me indicates its importance.

Where do you see flaws in using sponsorship, or how are brands/properties misusing sponsorship?
Not activating enough, not doing proper evaluation and not doing a very deep analysis before selecting their properties to invest in. Also, not considering owned properties as an alternative.

How has sponsorship evolved over the past few years?
Impressively. It is growing, formalizing, and sophisticating — not sure if that last one is a word!

Where do you see sponsorship heading in the next five, 10, and 25 years? What is the future of sponsorship?
I think the future is bright as the marketplace gets more and more cluttered, broken, and convoluted. As TV (traditional) declines, it will be more important than ever.

At the time of this interview, Norm was a partner consultant at the T1 Agency and the Chair of the Department of Sport Administration within the College of Business at Ohio University. Prior to these positions, Norm worked for several educational institutes including Laurentian University, Stanford University and Syracuse University.

Chapter 3

TO BORROW EQUITY — THE DEFINITION OF SPONSORSHIP

BORROWING EQUITY

A product that is trusted, recognized, and has integrity is a product that has brand equity. So too does a property. Imagine then that a trusted brand or organization decides to sponsor the event or property. They want to leverage the property's assets, to bask in its glow, to reinforce the favourable perception that people have of it, and to increase the number of stakeholders who are already engaged with the best of the assets. The brand wants to borrow equity. There are many definitions of sponsorship circling this global industry, but this is my favourite. I do not think you have to adopt just one (although I am pleased I did), nor do you have to adopt somebody else's definition. You could very well create your own, but if you look at the definitions of sponsorship since it became a discipline, you will understand more clearly why I am so satisfied with "borrowing equity".

Sponsorship in its most archaic form meant the contribution of funds to an activity or event that would not take place without the support of the partner. Sponsorship meant a donation. Today, a great many properties are in this exact predicament, and it is a predicament. Think of nice cultural events all the way up to high-performance auto racing: No logo on the car, no race on Sunday.

Sponsorship in that earlier era was like sponsoring an immigrant. Without your funds and your guarantee, the individual would not be able to move. Another early form of sponsorship, which still exists, is the widespread use of the very word in fundraising. Participants in charity runs or walks ask their network to "sponsor" them to help them reach a financial goal. In theory, the walker will still participate if you turn her down. That same theory would apply even if every potential donor declined. The walker would still participate even if she had zero sponsorship. Zero sponsorship used to mean the activity did not get off the ground. Today, the show goes on.

Over time, the definition of sponsorship was highly focused on a patron's support of the property. Without that support, the property would not exist, but over the years, as additional revenue streams emerged, the role of the sponsor changed. A "sponsor" became "sponsors", and they provided financial support for the property in exchange for marketing assets. Sponsor funding would no longer make or break the property. Certain properties today still do not have multiple revenue streams, largely due to the nature of the property, such as its extreme physical challenges, but in general, these are exceptions.

I cannot live with a definition of sponsorship that is framed by the terms of a transaction, specifically the outcome of a transaction. One party provides money, value, goods, services, and intellectual property, and the other party provides exposure, assets, intellectual property, star power, and trademarks in exchange. This definition of sponsorship should be labeled "brandvertising." It is not a term I created, nor one whose origins I understand, but it is a term I love.

I use the improvised expression "brandvertising" to refer to signage and logo-impression sponsorships. Field signs, event banners, apparel logos, vehicle stickers, and on-air graphics all fall into this category. On its own, "brandvertising" is not sponsorship but a form of out-of-home advertising. It can be an effective form of advertising as often as it can be ineffective. While it may seem old news to harp on about logo slapping, the unfortunate reality is that it still represents a significant percentage of what is presented as sponsorship.

"Brandvertising" reinforces the misconception that sponsorship is about driving awareness or exposure for a brand. Most brands do not need awareness or exposure. Some do, and when a property can help deliver that, there is a tremendous financial return, but overall most major brands do not lack exposure. Properties seem to think that they do, and so they sell brands on the opportunity to raise awareness and exposure. I am unsure why they are not listening, but that is the case time and again.

Brands want relevance, consideration, increased followers, shelf offtake, motivated consumers, and engaged stakeholders. Brands already have awareness; what they want is comprehension. Brands already have exposure; what they want is favourability. They want a little love. Brands already have advertising channels; what they want is influencer networks.

This is the "borrowing of equity". The equity of the property is by far its most valuable asset. It is often its most overlooked asset as well. For example, consider the Olympics. When you buy an Olympic sponsorship, you are buying the right to utilize the rings. Those five rings stand for something in the minds of consumers around the world. Despite the many trials and tribulations, the Olympic Movement has had, you could argue that its ability to withstand those trials proves their value as a brand. It demonstrates the strength, value, equity and essence of the movement.

I like to say that the Olympics sells only two assets. The first is the right to use the rings, the second is the right to spend more money. Facetious, yes, but close to the truth. More importantly, it is a compliment. The Olympics are the ultimate example of "borrowing equity".

This is where great sponsorship starts and stops. Think about how a sponsorship proposal is created. Most proposals immediately jump into the background of the property by discussing its size, history, participants, geographic reach, schedule, media coverage, etc. Some communicate their mission, vision, and programming priorities, primarily in the not-for-profit space. Others will tell a story of key individuals or founders, but very few identify the elements of the property's DNA the sponsor could leverage. Very few properties figure out their brand positioning and declare it as the core value proposition for partners. The sponsorship properties who do understand what they stand for tend to be exciting opportunities for brands, because this understanding often permeates the organization and is not restricted to the sponsorship offering.

Properties that anchor their sponsorship offering in the "borrowing of equity", understand that sponsors are seeking to align themselves for different reasons. There are several different types of equity that a sponsor can deliver to a brand.

PERFORMANCE EQUITY

Performance equity is typically utilized by businesses who want to substantiate the performance claims of their product or service.

This is a very functional equity affiliation, directly related to the brand's features and benefits. It is less related to its image, although the features are often strong contributors to a brand's profile.

If a brand wishes to claim an enduring legacy, an affiliation with a marathon race or an ultra athlete would help communicate that impression. Similarly, a brand that wants to promote its agility could align with sports that are based on speed. A brand that wants to tout its durability may align itself with a veteran in a certain field.

The brand fit for performance equity is very linear. It needs to find a property that can indeed fulfill the performance claims you are making, because the relationship is fact based. For example, if a company claims to be able to provide tax returns quickly, and they sponsor the slowest car in the race, the equity transfer will clearly be damaging.

To balance the risk, a brand may want to consider a portfolio approach when it comes to choosing performance partners or look at affiliating with an organizing body and not individual competitors. Keep in mind that an affiliation with an organizing body may not work when a brand seeks emotional equity. However, it will provide the accomplishments the brand is looking for.

Performance equity is a powerful source of content for advertising and promotional or media materials. Affiliations usually provide a third party endorsement that will be a convincing message and messenger. A short-term partnership will not provide the platform required for ingraining a message. The sponsor should develop long-term affiliations to be able to make their claims over a sustained period.

How often have you, as a property, asked your sponsors what sort of equity they seek from your property? Many brands have multiple strategies for achieving goals, so do not be surprised if their reply applies to several different categories. Sometimes there are multiple brands in your sponsor's portfolio or multiple objectives for the corporation. Correspondingly, your property may possess substantial equity across various segments. It would be unusual, and a little unwise, to suggest that you have an abundance of each type of equity, though a strong property will have more than a median amount of each type.

As a property, your challenge is to uncover your organization's equity, articulate its value, and promote it in the best light possible. You need to understand that equity is the most valuable asset you have to offer a sponsor. Most properties significantly undervalues your equity by articulating the benefits of their use of logos or marks. Your logo and marks are not the asset. The asset is what they symbolize. The asset is the message they send to their audience and the public. The asset is the goodwill they will transfer to your sponsor partners.

Think of a multinational corporation and the elements that determine its market value. Apple, Coca-Cola, Netflix, and Google have technology, distribution, secret recipe, and intellectual property assets, yet their most valuable asset is their brand. In 2017, Fortune reported that Apple's brand represented 15% of the company's USD$700 billion market cap, representing over USD$107 billion of the company's total market cap.

Here is a simple game you can play. Imagine two different, black midsize cars, one from a luxury auto maker and the other from a value brand. Now imagine swapping their hood badges, steering wheel logos, and wheel hubs. Now draw a mental picture of the value brand with the luxury logo. Would you price this car higher? Yes, it is that obvious. Consumers believe in brands. The logo is merely a symbol, because after driving the value brand vehicle for three weeks, in all likelihood you would be hard pressed to mask your disappointment in its performance.

As you develop a "What's Sponsorship Worth" (WSW) oriented strategy for your sponsorship program, you will be challenged to answer critical questions. What is the equity in your property? What is its value proposition? What is its true worth to a sponsor?

Once your organization has adopted the adage that sponsorship is the "borrowing of equity", you will have a much easier time delivering what your sponsors want. You will have a clearer value proposition to pitch. You will have a much stronger sense of your self-worth. You will attract better sponsors. You will become more sought after. In short, you will be wanted.

LEGITIMIZING EQUITY

The marketing world always wants to be seen as authentic, however, being authentic is an overused word in social media, public relations, influencer marketing, and beyond. Legitimizing equity could be confused as "being authentic," but the process is slightly different.

Brands legitimize their equity to validate their stance or actions in society, usually by tuning their company's messaging and the role they seek to play. By legitimizing equity, the brand can speak on a subject in a more personable voice.

If a brand wants to appear environmentally conscious or sensitive then it might seek legitimacy from partnerships with park groups, water protection agencies, environmental advocates, or climate change organizations. If a brand wants to talk about equality, rights, or freedoms, it could partner with their local Pride parades, LGBTQ2IA+ organizations, or milestones honouring pioneering individuals. If a brand wants to promote its commitment to a cause, an affiliation with key players who promote that cause is vital.

Your brand has a lot to gain from partnering with a property that can provide legitimizing equity. In order to benefit from the affiliation, it is important for you to understand how your brand will be perceived when aligned with these properties. You want to review both the positives and potential negatives that may come out of the relationship. You will need to recognize that this relationship is only one element of your total marketing mix and should not represent everything you plan to say about your brand.

Partnering with an organization with the express purpose of legitimizing equity can have positive value for a company that is deeply committed to a cause. There have been countless occasions where brands have been accused of being only superficially involved in their supposedly chosen causes. Properties, especially those in the cancer charity arena, have rightfully been accused of allowing brands to utilize their marks and affiliation to an excessive extent with only minimal resource commitment. To avoid this, both sponsor and property need to research the issue thoroughly and understand what their respective stakeholders would see as significant. They should gain insights from key influencers in the market and follow their guidance.

A sponsor and a property entering a new relationship to deliver legitimizing equity may want to consider some unorthodox strategies. One may be to invert the classic model of; Announce, Do, Celebrate, and Report Impact. Instead of first profiling the relationship, the partners might consider working together to create impact for a significant period. That may be a tough request in this quarterly results driven business world, but we are trying to create legitimacy, and legitimacy is not earned overnight. The brand should consider allowing all communication on the topic to be disseminated by their property partners. This would remove bias or appearances of over-commercialization in the partnership. A third strategy would be to allow and encourage dissenting opinions from your various stakeholder groups, with the partners acting as conversation facilitators.

POSITIONING EQUITY

You may feel that there is significant overlap between legitimizing and positioning equity, but there are differences and it is very worthwhile to describe positioning equity separately.

Positioning equity is used to reinforce the image and perception of your brand. Having this kind of equity contributes to your day-in, day-out brand profile, and it is crucial to how you are perceived. A brand needs to work incredibly hard to determine who they would partner with, as changes in the partner-property's positioning equity will impact perceptions of their brand. Therefore, the importance of this type of equity cannot be overstated.

Brands that are seeking to be relevant to youth may associate with online celebrities, musicians, or actors who have a strong, positive image. A brand that is edgy will be more comfortable partnering with a sport or individuals who are seen to be pushing societal boundaries.

To ensure that its image is consistent and well understood, the brand needs to portray itself in the same way all the time. When partnering with a property, the brand manager automatically becomes the steward of two brands — the corporate brand and the property brand. It is important for both the brand and the property to feel that their affiliation is one that is natural, as it benefits neither if the public feels the arrangement is only about money. Brands, rightfully so, should seek brand ambassadors who use their product or can be seen using their product. The property should be aligned with brands that they champion.

There is some value in the sponsor aligning itself with one of the property's assets, because then they cannot exert absolute control over the entire property. For example, rather than partner with an edgy actor, the brand could support the actor's annual charity event. By taking a slice of the entire property, the brand can limit its downside in case the property is devalued in some way. Another good strategy for a brand in this situation is to align itself with several properties, whether organizations or individuals. The benefit of this approach is that it will provide a more robust equity alignment and broaden the appeal of the association, while minimizing risk if an issue arises with one of the properties.

Positioning equity properly is a powerful approach for new brands or businesses, as partnering can accelerate consumer comprehension of your brand's platform. Positioning equity can work very well for a brand attempting to change its image and profile. However, aligning with a property or portfolio of properties should not be the only tactic for a repositioning brand. The alignment should be a component of a fully integrated rebranding program, including brand assets, packaging, communications, pricing, and distribution.

COMMUNITY EQUITY

A business that wants to resonate with people in a specific region or market by showing local support will benefit from community equity. This is crucial for a regional business, as most of its customers will live in that area. For a large company or a multinational, securing recognition as a community supporter is invaluable in their attempt to appeal to local consumers. Community equity is incredibly powerful given the desire of most consumers to "give where they live" when asked about organizations they would support. Giving back to a community is not a new strategy, although technology and new marketing applications have allowed brands and savvy consumers to scale their local involvement.

Local businesses are often the first tapped for fundraisers, youth sports teams, or charity walks. They are often looked at as the first source for funding hospital expansions or new sports facilities. National brands want to be a part of those youth sports teams or local festivals. This has resulted in the recent growth of nationally coordinated grassroots strategies and an increase in travelling experiential tours. Community equity can be pursued as either standalone or as a part of a diversified strategy. In some situations, adding a community component to a national or international program can be an effective way for you to make a large-scale initiative relevant at the grassroots level.

As long as a business operates, distributes, or retails its products in a community, there is usually a solid rationale for supporting the area. The most contentious use of building community equity arises when a large organization seeking regulatory approval in a certain market is suddenly seen investing — most likely overinvesting — in a blatant effort to secure political will. Notwithstanding that sort of situation, community equity is more often a solid brand fit.

Community equity can be a very useful asset in your brand's sponsorship marketing program, and it has a dual appeal. Your brand will connect with the local community it is supporting; this can be promoted and shared with individuals in other markets, allowing community equity to serve any of the other four types of equity. The other appeal is the opportunity to engage these communities as your brand advocates, as local groups and consumers are often willing to support your campaign in return for an investment commitment.

EMOTIONAL EQUITY

You could start and stop the discussion of various types of sponsorship equity by labeling all of them as "emotional". At its core, sponsorship is all about emotions, which is why brands often use it to tap into the passions of their stakeholders. Understanding the emotional triggers of your consumers, employees, customers, and partners provides a clear pathway to develop your strategy. Emotional equity is about making a visceral connection. In simple terms, if your company supports something that your consumers love, maybe they will love you too.

The emotions of consumers range from fear to fun. Some brands partner with disease-based charities, because they know it strikes a sensitive chord with their consumers. Other brands tap into sports, as they understand their consumers' depth of loyalty for their teams. Music is one of the most powerful emotional triggers in people's lives; it is one of the best vehicles a company can use to connect with their target.

It is important to determine whether your brand has the license, or right, to be playing in certain emotional fields from the consumer's perspective. This is an important discussion for both the sponsor and the property. There have been extreme examples where a product has sponsored a property, even though the use of that product contributes to disease. Even in less obvious situations, the brand must fit. If your brand is a commodity, partnering with a charity may appear to be too commercial.

Many products sponsor sports and then force a fit. I understand the desire to reach a massive audience with sports, but when it is clear that there is no emotional fit, the brand should reposition the affili-ation. It can do so by utilizing messaging that suggests that the spon-sors' employees are big fans of the sport or team. This may have the added benefit of humanizing the employees. There is nothing wrong with utilizing a property's promotional or tactical assets, as it is often a better approach than trying to stretch your brand to fit an awk-ward partnership. A consumer is not going to get emotional enough about a fertilizer brand that is sponsoring an award show to enter a contest to win a VIP trip to the show. Attempting to manufacture a linkage would come across as inappropriate.

Sponsorship properties, like emotions, are tricky to navigate. If a sponsor conducts research that indicates music is an emotional driver for its consumers, that does not necessarily mean that all music properties will transfer emotional equity. There are many considerations for using music: artists, labels, festivals, tours, streaming, radio, video, merchandise, award shows, and more. Each element is open and available for sponsorship, but not all of them provide an opportunity for your brand to tap into emotions. Other aspects of the music industry can tap into more than one equity category for a brand. Some festivals are steeped in emotion, as the attendees view the events as an annual ritual. The same festival can provide other types of equity, such as legitimizing or positioning equity. Some properties may provide emotional equity through its components, i.e. athletes or teams as opposed to the league — leagues and their administrative leaders are often viewed as the enemy by legions of passionate fans.

Emotional equity is not something with which to be casually played. You are tapping deep into your consumers and asking them to let you share some of their most important moments. You need to understand when and how it is appropriate to do so. You need to carefully consider the aspects of the property that are important to the consumer. Is it the sport of baseball, the World Series, or the team on which their daughter plays? For those who sell sponsorships, identifying what motivates your prospect's consumers can be a powerful conversation starter in building a relationship.

TIM DIGNARD

Tim is not afraid to travel far to get what he wants, whether it be the right job or to watch his cherished Liverpool FC. Since graduating from the renowned Sport Administration program at Laurentian University in Sudbury, Canada, Tim has worked for the Vancouver Olympics, The International Olympic Committee (IOC), and The Union of European Football Associations (UEFA). His ability to speak English, French, and German have been as much of an asset to his travels and career as has been his passion for sponsorships and partnerships. Tim was recognized as a true talent at a young age. One of his university professors suggested to a colleague that Tim will someday run one of the major global sports properties. Many years later, turns out I was right.

Describe your current role with UEFA Champions League.
My current role involves oversight of the sponsorship program for the UEFA Champions League: the world's top club soccer competition. Our current structure is based on seven official sponsors and

one official supplier partner and is sold on a three-season cycle basis. Exclusivity is at the core of what we offer. At the core of our responsibilities is ensuring that our partners can fully leverage their Champions League sponsorship. Along with rights delivery this includes identifying new opportunities that can add additional value and enhancements to the partnership. Along with looking after marketing matters in the current season, we are also busy establishing the commercial framework for the future of the UEFA Champions League.

How important is the "human relationship" side of sponsorship?
If the human side was ever considered a "nice to have", it has quickly become a "must have." There was a time that sponsorship was simply a transaction: an exchange of rights for a fee or value in kind. Now, it is a partnership where both sides are helping each other to achieve shared goals. A league or team that doesn't invest time in building the relationship will never truly understand their sponsor's objectives and what they are looking to achieve from the partnership. For example: what are their objectives over the next five years, what are their priority markets, and how are they measuring success? Sponsorship is becoming more and more measurable, so if you cannot help the partner deliver on its KPIs then they will not be with you for very long.

How do partners leverage UEFA Champions League?
The UEFA Champions League provides a global platform for partners to amplify their sponsorship. Through the development of integrated marketing campaigns, our partners create a toolkit of assets that can be leveraged globally. We see our partners activating across 100+ markets through a consistent brand message. Hospitality remains a key pillar of the portfolio, providing our partners an opportunity to invite key customers and senior executives

to have positive experiences in a best-in-class hospitality environment. While there remains massive value and exposure through media assets such as perimeter boards and broadcast bumpers, digital is where we are growing the fastest. Content creation, digital and social inventory are areas where we are continuously looking to innovate and enhance the rights package. The take-up on the partner side has been tremendous. Lastly, athlete ambassadors still play a massive role in partners' campaigns. You can have the greatest story to tell, but when you couple that with the reach of a high-profile athlete or influencer, then you are setting yourself up to succeed.

Do you find that partners are expecting more and more? Give some examples of how partners' expectations are evolving.
Partners' expectations are evolving, but less is becoming more. Rather than trying to do too many things, partners want to focus on a few key initiatives and make them impactful. We work with some of the most sophisticated marketers in the world. The change of pace in sponsorship is more rapid than it was even five years ago. The challenge that we and every other rights holder is facing is adapting to and turning these evolving trends into concrete assets that can be measured, sold and leveraged by the partner. One of the most evident trends I have noticed is the increasing blurred line between sponsors and broadcasters. For sponsors, developing content around the passion and emotion of sport is a key to success. On the flipside, broadcasters are becoming more and marketing savvy, and finding unique ways to leverage their exclusive content. For any rights holder selling exclusive broadcast or marketing rights, striking the balance between these two is a challenge. At the same time, the progress made on digital means that there is an enormous opportunity. The rights holders that succeed will be those who can protect the value of their broadcast rights while offering content and digital opportunities

that complement the traditional media assets — encouraging broadcast and marketing partners to work together.

What is the future of sponsorship?
Digital, digital and more digital. Sponsors traditionally created campaigns that were then adapted for TV, out of home, social, and so on. Now we are seeing an increase in digital first campaigns. Changes in content consumption have not completely evaded the sports industry, which still benefits from the importance of live viewing. Facebook Live, Snapchat and others are completely changing the game and disrupting the landscape. The question is where do sponsors fit in this mix? Real-time marketing has become a vital way for sponsors to adapt their message and leverage those big moments. We have all seen the spikes in tweets during controversial or decisive points in a game. Partners want to be part of that conversation, but they need to find an authentic way to stand out amongst all the other noise. The traditional method of slapping a logo on a property is outdated. Sponsors need to stand out and own an exclusive asset. Look at Red Bull for example. Rather than sponsoring an event, they create and own their events and now, even teams. This has caused many leagues, teams and companies to relook at their own approach. At the core of all these efforts is data. For example, by leveraging in-depth knowledge we can deliver tailored brand experiences that will only enhance and fuel every football (soccer) fan's passion for the game they love.

At the time of this interview, Tim was the Club Competitions Sponsorship Manager for UEFA. For eight years prior to this position, Tim was heavily involved with the Olympics. Starting off as Project Coordinator of Sport Services for the Vancouver Olympics, then moving to a position within Client Services Rights Management for the London Olympics then moving to working with the IOC as the Junior Account Manager & Rights Activation and Account Manager of Partnership Marketing.

JOHN VIDALIN

Is there something ironic about the fact that a man who has landed hundreds of millions of sponsorship dollars is also an avid fisherman? John has spent his career figuring out how to fish and where the fish are. From his first job managing Key Accounts for Alberto Culver, his NHL years with the Calgary Flames and Washington Capitals, followed by a decade in the NFL with the Houston Texans and San Francisco 49ers, and now with his first foray into the NBA with the Miami Heat, John has netted plenty of fish. Along the way, this dedicated family man has always made time to help local charities, such as the Boys & Girls Club and the YMCA, perhaps tying in another life message: "If you give a hungry person a fish, you feed them for a day, but if you teach them to fish, you are feeding them for a lifetime."

How would you describe your role with the Miami Heat?

I am the Executive Vice President and Chief Revenue Officer for the Miami Heat. I am responsible for driving the club's local, regional, national, and international business opportunities, while overseeing the Corporate Sales and Service, Broadcast Sales, Digital and Content Sales, Premium Seating, Service, and Ticket Sales departments.

How do you go about hiring your team?

I think it is important to look for a premium seller. This includes attitude, approach, presentation (how they present themselves), and whether they are enthusiastic. This description is more for sales and servicing. The second piece is people who can work a room well, people who can work with senior people, networking ability, etc. On the partnership side, you need someone who is almost a consultant, who can figure out how to connect with someone and prove to them that buying tickets is beneficial to them. This person takes more of a research approach. This can be more from the agency and not necessarily the "salespeople". Other important attributes include data management, creativity, consultancy, and being a psychologist at times. In basketball or other sports, it is important for people to not be arrogant just because you are winning. You need to treat people well regardless of winning or losing.

What is more difficult, the first sponsorship deal with an organization or additional deals? Why?
The job is not easy, even if you are working with a big brand. You need to be innovative and creative, solve problems and create opportunities the partner did not know existed. Customize solutions and evolve them as needed to keep the partnership relevant and fresh. It is important not to be arrogant or dismissive, always be approachable and partner focused. Renewing deals is difficult; it could have been a great idea originally, but if it was not executed well the partner will not renew. Fulfillment, detail, consistency, and integration are so critical in making a partnership successful. You want long term relationships. It builds equity with the partner and allows the team to plan for the long term.

In sponsorship, how important are relationships and understanding the person on the other side of the table?
People tend to forget that a partnership cuts both ways. For a deal to be truly successful, both the partner and team need to be fully engaged and committed. If you walk into a company and talk about yourself and your team, you will not sell a sponsorship. Logo on a website? Who cares? In getting the deals, creativity is important, but you must get into the shoes of the other person and understand what they want to accomplish. Is B2B important? Is retail important? You need to understand what is most important to them. Getting into what matters to them does not just help do deals, it also helps build deals and renew deals. Sponsorship is a relationship business and a results business. The partnership must fulfill specific criteria in order to be successful over time. What those criteria are depends on the partner and their goals.

How important is storytelling in sponsorship?

The ability to tell a story is very important. You must make that story relevant, unique, and meaningful to the partner and their business.

How important is it for brands to leverage agencies when it comes to sponsorship fulfilment?

Agencies are certainly important. While they are usually the decision maker, you want to include them in the process as they will have valuable input on the activation, fulfillment and renewal of the agreement. Most big companies have agencies to help with creative, sponsorship fulfillment, etc.

At the time of the interview, John was the Chief Sales Officer for the San Francisco 49ers. Prior to this position, John was the Vice President for the Houston Texans for 6 years. John was also the Vice President for the Washington Capitals from 2001–2004.

Chapter 4

TO TELL STORIES — A SPONSOR'S TALE

MARKETING IS STORYTELLING

I like to tell people that my favourite book about marketing is *Story* by Robert McKee. What's amazing about *Story* is that it is not a marketing textbook or a business best seller — it is a book about screenplay writing, and McKee is one of the best screenplay educators in the world.

Building stories in a sponsorship marketing campaign is the creative parallel for the borrowing equity component, with the latter serving as the strategic platform. The affiliation with the property provides the brand with the foundation to make claims about their product or service, position themselves in a new light, and endear themselves to key target groups. Using that foundation is the first phase of storytelling.

What will the story be? What is the narrative that marketers will use to sell the brand? How will the brand affiliate itself with the property? What role will the brand assume in the property? What creative message about the brand will be shared? That is the main event in the second phase of storytelling — determining the story.

Storytelling is a complex art with a simple ambition — to bring a brand to life in the hearts and minds of the property's loyal supporters and fans. It requires the collaboration of the sponsor, the property, and their respective external, creative agency partners to craft the most compelling and sustainable messages. Storytelling can be deliberate and scripted, or it can be nuanced and organic.

Either way, it is powerful.

Storytelling is much more than simply designating a brand as "The Official X of Property Y." This is an archaic practice, and to the dismay of certain brands who think that they have suddenly earned creative honours for doing so, storytelling entails much more than changing "Official Product" to "Official Fan", or a similar label. No, storytelling is central to the development of engagement and activation programs because it is the brand's significance to them. As in a good book, the design of all other elements of the story flows from correct application and exploration of its themes.

WRITING THE SCRIPT

Think of every sponsorship story like a movie script. We are introduced to a protagonist, the hero who faces some conflict, obstacle, evil, or antagonist that they must overcome. Throughout the story, the audience identifies with the main character and cheers on their efforts to overcome their challenges. A brand marketing story, especially when affiliated with sponsorship, will convey the same rhythm. This does not mean that the brand is necessarily heroic, although its role is always evident. The brand is telling the story that the audience wants to hear. The story transforms a brand from one that is the product of choice for a certain sport to a brand that is championing a comeback. It shifts sponsorship from a brand that is seen as the technology provider for a music tour to a brand that champions creativity or innovation among groups who may face adversity — and ultimately triumph over it despite extraordinarily difficult circumstances. It shifts the perception of a brand from the official bank of a charity to a brand that champions the rights and liberties of the people engaged in the cause.

Many properties claim they have great stories, and they do, but are those stories great for an audience, greater than their competitors' stories, or so great that the world already knows about them because they heard them before, told in countries around the world and have already become planted in the minds of many? Probably not.

The great stories of the property are not what is important here. What is important is whether your property can be a great story-teller for the brand. Can your property provide the characters, the stage, the script, and the setting that will help the brand connect with its stakeholders? In many cases, the sponsor has greater reach than the property. Yes, there are situations where smaller or emerging brands bet big on a big property to generate break-through for them. That is a smart strategy and one we will discuss in more detail. However, the opposite is true in most cases.

Most often, the sponsor has more reach, budget, and avenues for connecting with consumers than the property, but the property provides an enormous blast of emotion that will amplify the sponsor's reach to a level they could never imagine. When measured by research, deftly weaving the property and the sponsor together to tell the sponsor's story produces the highest impact scores. In the end, success comes down to a great story told well.

WRITING GREAT STORIES

I was once at a conference and heard a speaker from Nike addressed the room, "What business are we in?" A question with an amazing answer. He informed the audience that Nike was not in the shoe business, nor was it in the apparel business. He said, Nike is in the storytelling business. That was over a decade ago.

Today, I would argue that many companies feel the same way about their business and their brands. Storytelling is now a foundational component of marketing. Marketers, agencies, and experts espouse the magic of storytelling in countless articles, speeches, and interviews. Despite its ubiquity, storytelling — outstanding storytelling — is not easily executed. An increase in the number of brands that wish to tell their story with inventive, striking narratives creates a perpetually rising bar. Other brands must jump a lot higher if they want to be heard.

Sponsorship marketing can provide several, powerful elements for storytelling, including settings, characters, and channels. As a property, your role is to work with your sponsors to understand what story they wish to tell, and how it can be brought to life. Storytelling provides the opportunity for the sponsor to communicate your relationship to their stakeholders and benefit from the affiliation with your property.

Writing a great story with your sponsor is a challenge. Each of your sponsors has affiliated with you for different reasons. Every one of them has a specific need they are attempting to fill by aligning with you. Each has a variety of challenges based on their position in the market, consumer demand, and competitive circumstances. Even a company that is leading its industry or sector has ongoing concerns, such as new competitors, changing regulatory environments, or difficulties in managing a highly qualified workforce. Any one of these business dynamics could be a catalyst for partnering with your property. These are circumstances you should have discovered during the solicitation process.

If not, or if due diligence was superficial, the development of the storytelling campaign is the step in the process to dive deep and try to understand the sponsor's business. As a property, it is your job to understand the challenges facing a sponsor and work with them to build a messaging platform that resonates with stakeholders and addresses the sponsor's challenges.

FINDING THEIR PAIN

Storytelling may have a happy ending, but it does not always have a happy beginning. I believe that truly great stories, like a great song, come from a place of deep, dark pain. Pain, anguish, despair, tragedy, suffering, fear, anger, and sadness all precede triumph. The darkest days of an individual, community, or country often precede the greatest victories. Insurmountable obstacles drive entrepreneurs, innovators, and experimenters to their greatest discoveries. Nothing moves a business or organization to change faster than fear of extinction.

I am not trying to drown you in despair — I am asking you to test yourself. What are the best stories you have ever told friends, classmates, or colleagues? There is probably a funny story, probably a story of unlikely coincidences, and definitely a story where something good came from bad. Even when you recall funny personal anecdotes, there is almost always a hurdle you overcame with a humorous twist. The story people will remember is the sports comeback you engineered, long odds and perseverance in school, or how you were able to emigrate to a new homeland.

A great story has a protagonist who faces a seemingly insurmountable challenge, which they eventually overcome with the help of others or newfound powers discovered within themselves. More than a happy ending, it is an amazing journey that connects with your emotions in a way that makes you empathize with the story's protagonist. A great story has a sense of relatability to it, because you have faced or witnessed a similar challenge. A great story is impactful because the outcome is plausible, realistic, and while exceptional, comprehendible.

Your consumers and customers will retain and embrace a great story over stated facts in any situation. Facts and data are important but rolling them into a script greatly increases their retention. Consumers do not care about "Official This" and "Official That". They care about a brand that resonates with their feelings. A great story begins with the pain your sponsor is experiencing and ends when it connects with the consumer.

Pain is the launching pad for a great sponsorship story. Each of your sponsors has pain they are enduring or anticipating. While it may seem counterintuitive, this is your starting point. Identifying the point of their pain is the first step in crafting a great story. Uncovering your partner's pain will allow you to help them build the messaging and elements of an amazing campaign strategy and an activation plan to generate positive business returns. Your discovery of your partners' pain is an invaluable selling tool when you are meeting with prospects. Focusing on the buyer's needs — relieving their pain — and not pitching unsold inventory that your boss wants you to monetize is the hallmark of a great approach to selling.

Before meeting with your sponsor to develop their story, prepare a list of questions you are going to ask. Think of yourself as a consultant who has been sent to investigate the problems plaguing an underperforming plant or a failing division of a large company. Think of yourself as the potential saviour of an entrepreneur or manager who faces an inbox full of problems every day and a dearth of solutions from her teammates. Think of yourself as an ally of your sponsor in their daily battle with other businesses in your market.

Your pen and paper, or your tablet or computer, is the sword that will help you defeat the enemy. Sharpen it, learn how to use it with deft skill and aplomb, and steel yourself to use it with gallant conviction. Equip it with probing, insightful questions to discuss with your sponsor:

- What is keeping you up at night?
- What are the challenges facing your company today? Tomorrow? In three years?
- How would your boss answer that question?
- What do your customers/consumers think of you?
- What does the media say?
- If I went online, what would I read about you?
- Who is your biggest competitor?
- Which competitor do you fear the most?
- What obstacles are preventing your company from being great?
- What is the best campaign your competitors execute?
- Who do you think does sponsorship really well?
- How can we at Property CYZ help you succeed?

I guarantee that you will be no more than three questions into this discussion when the ideas begin to flow. Jot them down on a separate page as you continue to probe for the challenges facing your sponsor. While you may have prepared questions for discussion that you shared in advance, you should allow the momentum of your sponsor's answers to lead the discussion to their thorniest problem areas. If your client talks about weakening sales in certain markets, ask pointed follow-up questions:

- Have they lost distribution in those markets?
- Do you have new salespeople in that region?
- Have there been significant economic changes such as mass layoffs?
- Has your competitor lowered prices or introduced new products?
- Has your competitor increased their sales coverage or gained new points of distribution?
- Do you think this decline is a blip or a trend? Has it happened in other markets? How did you address it?

Every aspect of their pain should be thoroughly investigated. It is almost like picking a scab; peeling at an existing wound provides more and more data about what caused the wound, how deep it is, whether the injury is superficial or if a bone has been injured. Hopefully, the wound is not infected or worse, has started to spread to other parts. If it has, follow the blood.

Great follow-up questions and their answers will make a huge contribution to the storytelling narrative. Do not be afraid to inflict a little more pain on your sponsor: it will lead to healing. You are not hurting to be cruel, but to help identify a cure. Your sponsor will thank you for it.

SEARCHING FOR A CURE

Now that you understand your sponsor's pain, how do you build a powerful story to help them find a cure? While sophisticated sponsors will often have marketing experts and various communication agencies helping them, you should position your property as a strategic contributor to the effort as well. Offer to take the lead on this initiative, utilizing your own internal marketing communications team or your partner agencies.

As a sponsorship agency, we often take the lead in this area for our brand clients. Many times, we are one of several outside experts working with our clients, while in other cases we are acting alone. Regardless of the situation, we appreciate properties that can contribute to the process. Demonstrating your expertise in storytelling or any area of the What Sponsors' Want (WSW) model benefits all parties, including your sponsor's agencies, which will benefit you in the short and long run, as you have now created another supporter of your property. In effect, you have expanded the WSW model to include What the Sponsor's Agencies Want. Developing storytelling skills will be invaluable for sponsors who do not have external agency partners or the internal resources — this will occur more frequently with smaller companies or regional units of larger companies. In all situations, if you volunteer to lead the charge, you cannot go wrong.

As a leader, you should develop a process for working with the key stakeholders your sponsor wishes to engage in developing the story. Your process should include determining who will provide input on the pain the sponsor wishes to address and how that input will be gathered. You should identify who will assess the sponsorship landscape to see where your sponsor can have a conversation they can own. You should include information about the target groups your sponsor wishes to reach. You effectively want to summarize the key hurdles to overcome, where an open space exists to do so, and who the messaging is addressing.

To kickstart the process, you should write a creative brief (Figure 1). A well written brief provides an inspirational roadmap for all participants in the process, and it should distill complex information

The TI Agency - Brief

Campaign/Program Name
Project #:   Prepared By:
Date: Strat. Approver:

The Ask
What we need to do for our client. In one sentence.

The Pivotal Brand Issue/Opportunity
What is the Pivotal Business Issue or Opportunity we are trying to address?

The Spark
What does the consumer need to think and feel about the brand in order to change their behaviour?

The One Thing We Need To Say
What is the single thing that we need to tell the consumer in order to spark the consumer?

The Consumer
Who is our consumer?

What is going on in their life as whole that makes them different from other consumers?

What does our client's category mean for this consumer?

The Brand & Category
What are the key insights about the brand that we need to understand?

How does the brand/category help alleviate the tensions for our consumer?

Who is the competition? How do they differ from our clients brand?

Deliverables
What are the mandatory and executional specifics required by the client?
- What languages do we need?
- What markets?
- What type of assets does the client need?
- Is there anything needed for internal (sales) meetings?
- What assets does the client already they want to be integrated?
- Key language/positioning that must be used?
- What channels are mandatory?
- For activations, the space that is secured (if already done)?
- Creative territories that we need to explore

What are the key project milestones, and when are these milestones due?

What budget are we working with (working and non-working)?

Everything Else
What is everything else that we should know about the client, the competition, the category?
- Examples of past work
- Key learnings from past work
- Existing creative assets that we can leverage
- Additional brand information
- Details on our role in an inter-agency project
- Competitive intelligence
- In market campaigns (client and competitive)

What else do we need to know about the deliverables?
- What languages do we need?
- What markets?
- What type of assets does the client need?
- Is there anything needed for internal (sales) meetings?
- What assets does the client already they want to be integrated?
- Key language/positioning that must be used?
- What channels are mandatory?
- For activations, the space that is secured (if already done)?
- Creative territories that we need to explore?

What production requirements do we have?

Key Watchouts
Is there anything additional that we should know about to make our work more effective for the client?

What other information may be helpful or important in developing the creative executions?

Figure 1:   Creative Brief Example

into digestible bits. It should be clear and direct about what is being asked, providing reliable checkpoints to ensure the storytelling is on track. You'll need to ensure that your sponsors and any internal decisionmakers are aligned with the brief before it is circulated.

The creative brief will recap the equity affiliation between you and the sponsor, which is the strategic backbone of the relationship. It should then identify the need to create a story to communicate that affiliation and the messaging the sponsor requires. Lastly, the brief should identify the potential types of engagement and activation programs that will tell this story. While engaging stakeholders is the next phase of the WSW model, the brief needs to take deployment into consideration.

A brief is invaluable whether you are working alone or with numerous individuals across multiple organizations. A great brief will make as much sense to someone who has been at arm's length from the process as it will to someone who has helped create it. If you are working solo on this task, the brief will be your best friend as you embark on a daunting assignment. You have every right to be concerned, frightened even, of being tasked to write a movie script, but I would argue that if you spend more time writing scripts, you will actually have to spend less time selling.

THE STORY

First, let us set the stage.

Your sponsor is the lead character in this movie. They have a strategic business problem. You have embraced your role as a problem solver by spending hours asking questions. You and your team have thrown every question possible their way. Are they misunderstood by consumers? Are they having problems finding key suppliers? Are they not well liked by the media? Do they lack brand awareness?

From their answers, it has become evident they are having issues in recruiting. Their most significant issue is hiring the right people, which sounds like an unlikely problem to have except when you consider their circumstances.

If you start to think of your sponsor as a character in a movie script, you will describe all the attributes they possess. You would talk about their entrepreneurial founder who built the company with his bare hands. You would describe their ground-breaking technology and how it produces products with a much more environmentally efficient process. Consumer and customer testimonials about the quality and durability of the product would be too numerous to list. Your lead character, your sponsor, sounds like somebody you would want to have as a friend, a coach, or a boss. What could possibly be wrong?

The challenge for your sponsor, a midsize technology company, is that the founder built the business in a smaller community, away from the key regional tech hubs. It is not close to a hub airport, so travel is less direct for business flights and personal vacations. While the community is a great place, it has a reputation for being sleepy, not having other technology companies, or the right infrastructure. It is a bit of a miracle that your sponsor flourishes despite the surrounding environment, yet the founder has no interest in moving the company. The offices sit on the land his grandparents settled when they immigrated, definitively ensuring that heritage is going to win the argument every time. His loyal senior executives know that moving is not an option, but they also know that sustaining their growth means more qualified staff than the local area can provide. They know that enticing people to move here is an ever-increasing challenge.

Potential employees like the technology, the product, and the company, but are lukewarm on the community. They wonder about jobs for their spouses, schools for their children, and amenities for their lifestyle. They are concerned that if they want to move in a few years, they will have taken themselves off the fast track. Does going from a big college to a big company or two, and then to this place signal a step back in their career development? Thankfully, your sponsor is an industry thought leader, so the career concerns are often solved during the recruitment process, selling the community has been a tougher task.

Your property can be the cure for the sponsor's pain. If this were a movie, your property would be the hero or the lead, but in this case, let us keep the sponsor as the hero and position your property as the relentless sidekick who enables the hero to win the ultimate battle. The battle is to overcome perceptions that they operate in a sleepy town with little to offer.

Your property is a fantastic little gem. It is an annual community fundraiser that enlists young people to participate in team-building challenges. The teams can be comprised of groups of friends, neighbours, families, or workplace groups. While your sponsor may be the only tech company in the area, many other employers in the community love your property. The team-building component is so strong that you often sell sponsorships through the human resources department heads. Other companies who do not have sponsorship budgets encourage their employees to enter teams and provide resources to help them fundraise. Community groups follow the same model.

The relationship with the technology company is a new one. Some of their employees have been involved as mentors in the program for several years, but for some reason you had not been able to create a formal sponsorship affiliation. Perhaps it was that past efforts had focused on pitching awareness to the marketing head (which is not needed in the company's hometown) or sales opportunities to the business development head (which was not realistic considering there were no customers for hundreds of miles). However, a conversation at last year's event led to an introduction to the head of recruitment and the first glimpse at their corporate pain.

It makes a lot of sense for the tech company to become a sponsor. The sponsorship is a great community builder because every year the funds raised go to a different civic project. Your property has a great reputation for integrity and strong values. And it was already attracting participants from various parts of the company. Now that recruiting top talent has become such a significant business issue, there is another strategic reason for them to be involved: sponsorship could significantly benefit talent retention and potentially talent recruitment. The opportunities are tantalizing.

The storyline is quite straightforward. The sponsor wants to tell current employees and potential recruits, plus media and influencers, that their community is a great place to live. The plan is to utilize the property as a platform for that messaging. The challenge is how to engage the primary target group — recruits — with this message, especially since they live out of town.

The strength of the storyline is too good to pass up. It is about living in a community where people care about each other. It is a return to when people worked and socialized together. It appeals to the desire to have amazing personal experiences instead of owning physical things. It appeals to people's desire to give back. The property could be positioned as the tip of the iceberg for launching many year-long, community-wide mentorship activities.

The sponsor wants to position themselves as a key enabler of the property. They could support event volunteers, provide tools for fundraising, or focus on easing transportation. Whatever role they take, their focus will be on making something good even better.

USING THE STORY TO ENGAGE

The first idea would be to hold recruitment open houses during the month leading up to the event. The beauty of the open houses is that the sponsor's story can be told by staff hosting the recruits as they tour the facilities and the community. The recruits will see signage, overhear conversations, and engage in spontaneous conversations with other staff and community members. If done properly, new recruits will find the community very, very appealing.

The sponsor should decorate its facility to promote their partnership with the property. As the property, you should ensure that the lodging and restaurants frequented by the recruits are similarly decorated. The event would be a good occasion for hosting industry media, influencers, or regulatory officials. Perhaps the event could be combined with the unveiling of a new product or research. The people involved in these initiatives could be important advisors to potential staff, so sharing the story would be a powerful tool connecting people and networking.

Beyond this recruiting window, the sponsor should generate social content that is targeted to recruits. Whether paid media or search, it will allow the sponsor to showcase their involvement on a year-round basis. The content should not focus on being the "Official" or "Title" sponsor, rather it should leverage the equity of their property and its amazing attributes. Testimonials featuring staff talking about how the property is a symbol of year-round living in the community would be powerful elements in the story.

In a similar vein, you could help your sponsor tweak their recruitment materials to ensure that the storyline of their affiliation is woven throughout their narrative. Think of their content on digital platforms, videos, and materials sent to recruiters and prospects as channels to tell the story. Eventually, developing the narrative will become natural and effortless for all involved.

It is vital that you create a story with your sponsor. You do not want to have the sponsor simply talk about being an official sponsor of the fundraiser. It is not enough to say that your sponsor is the proud supporter of the volunteers or the parking lot. Even being the title or presenting sponsor isn't enough. Those sponsorship structures are out of date, and they are not the story.

The story needs to be rooted in the community and bring home the message that future employees will be welcomed to a great community. The story needs to convince employment prospects that they can have an amazing life, a promising future for their children, and everything they want in a hometown. More than that, the story must tell these prospects that they are going to be surprised and delighted when they take a closer look at this community.

Your story could take the shape of something along the lines of discovery, opening the recruit's eyes to the beauty of the community. It could reinforce the sponsor's pride in being based in this community, and how much they are vested in helping it grow. There is a powerful angle in sharing the pride this sponsor feels in being based in such a hidden gem of a town. The story should reflect the promise of moving to this community and working for this company. You could imagine the headline of this story or the title of this script:

- Discover the beauty of Township.
- Township, as you are.
- Township, innovative as you are.

- Creating the future together.
- Designed for a better life.

None of these is meant to be a tagline or a public facing or consumer communication, but they are meant to underpin the platform in relation to your sponsor's story: the story they want to share with their key stakeholders while leveraging your property.

This story helps validate the strategic fit of your partnership. It is designed to appeal to the emotional drivers of your sponsor's key targets: recruits. The story provides a more purposeful reason for the sponsor to partner with your property. While I have taken a mostly singular tack, the opportunity exists for a sponsor to address several pain points and build an integrated communications approach to deal with each one.

The above story is one example that demonstrates that sponsors are interested in much more than brand awareness or VIP hosting. Any communication emanating from this story would be used to solve their pain. It is a story that can be easily deployed through an engagement plan and measured by the proper implementation of a capture plan. Ultimately, recruiting success increases and costs decrease. Retention is strengthened enabling the sponsor to understand their return on investment.

JACQUIE RYAN

Whether it was scooping ice cream at her first job or curating USD$800 million-dollar naming-rights deals in her current job, Jacquie has always lived by the advice she gave to her younger self, "Work hard and find ways to create your own opportunities." This approach has paid dividends for Jacquie throughout her career climbing the corporate ladder in the sponsorship industry. She has built and nurtured a strong network over *the years, with a keen understanding that successful people must pay it forward as their repayment for what they have earned. Always true to herself, Jacquie loves the Maya Angelou quote, "I've learned that people will forget what you said, people will forget what you did, but people will never forget how you made them feel."*

How would you describe your current role and responsibilities with Scotiabank?

Vice President, Sponsorship Marketing and Global Philanthropy. I am responsible for leading Scotiabank's hockey sponsorship strategy across Canada, through our relationships with the NHL, MLSE, CWHL and support of kids' community hockey. I also lead Scotiabank's robust Arts and portfolio, including: the Scotiabank Giller Prize, Scotiabank CONTACT Photography Festival and six marathon events across the country, to name a few.

As the lead of Scotiabank's Global Philanthropy strategy, I am responsible for driving the Bank's focus of supporting Young People in the Community through the areas of health, wellbeing and education. Where possible, we align and weave our philanthropy strategy into the sponsorships in which we participate, e.g. The Scotiabank Charity Challenge.

What is the motivation of Scotiabank to put so much energy and time into sponsorship?

At one time, Scotiabank focused mostly on advertising. We then asked ourselves "how do we fit into the marketplace?" Using a modest budget, we began supporting a variety of properties and used the metrics from those sponsorships to measure performance and determine where the largest impact could be made. Being an active corporate citizen is crucial to the success of any large organization. We used our learnings to now focus in on areas where we think we can make the largest impact for our customers, shareholders and communities where we do business.

With there being five major banks in Canada, can you discuss the importance of exclusivity in sponsorship?
Sponsorship can play a major role in distinction. There are times when we do join our competitors as sponsors of charitable events, however with only a limited number of competitors, it becomes important to own exclusivity to distinguish yourself. Scotiabank has unofficially become known as "The Hockey Bank", by our customers, competitors, and really the country. This tells us we are doing our job right.

How important is it for Scotiabank to continuously evaluate their sponsorships?
It is very important for Scotiabank to evaluate our own performance and not only rely on third-party data. Comparing ourselves against competitors is important in the Financial Services industry, in addition to keeping an eye on leading brands in sponsorship, marketing, and digital, and community investment. As business priorities evolve, we need to continuously ensure that our sponsorships align with the goals of not only the Bank, but also our customers, shareholders and communities where we operate.

Why did Scotiabank land on a sponsorship strategy that is so heavily reliant on the sport of hockey?
Hockey resonates with Canadians and it also resonates with Scotiabankers, it is quite frankly in our DNA. We are players, coaches, volunteers and fans. The sport of hockey is a great way to speak to Canadians without the corporate image in mind. Hockey creates the connection between Scotiabank and our

customers. It also aligns well to the Bank's philanthropic strategy of helping to support young people reach their infinite potential. This hockey season we announced that we have helped to support one million kids. And counting, through our support of community hockey across Canada. We are really proud of that milestone.

How is Scotiabank unique when it comes to sponsorship?

Scotiabank is unique in that our sponsorship strategy is very connected with our brand and very prominent in our advertising and marketing. Everything ties together — from advertising, to sponsorship, to philanthropy and customer events, we make sure that the narrative is consistent so that our customers have a clear view of who we are as a Bank and why we do what we do.

At the time of this interview, Jacquie was the Vice President of Sponsorship Marketing and Global Philanthropy at Scotiabank. Prior to this, she spent twelve years working for RBC in various positions including, Manager of Sponsorship Strategy and Sponsorship Marketing, the Director of Community Marketing and Sponsorship, Brand Management and Advertising, the Head of Olympic Marketing and the Director of Corporate Donations. Throughout the past 15 years Jacquie has worn many hats within sponsorship marketing in financial institutions.

FLORIAN RIEPE

During his time in college, Florian worked as a chauffeur for a limousine service where he met the chairman of the supervisory board of Hertha Berlin, a German Bundesliga soccer club. This encounter became his personal kickoff into the industry, as he ended up working for this club for two-and-a-half years. He was named after Saint Florian, a Christian holy man and the patron saint of firefighters, and his favourite quote is: "It's your mind that creates this world."

His advice for his younger self? "You should travel the world on a shoe-string in order to understand different perspectives of life and use public transport (occasionally) to understand your own market."

Tell us about your current role at HSV.
I have been in the sports marketing industry since 1998 in various roles. Currently, I am running the marketing department (Head of Marketing and International Markets) of my hometown soccer club HSV, one of the biggest clubs in the German Bundesliga. In my role, I am heading the departments of Marketing Operations, International Markets, Merchandise, Pre and After Sales, Kids Marketing (Kids Club/Mascot/Football School), and Arena World/ Museum/Destination Marketing.

Can you describe the large tournament HSV runs you ran in Bulgaria?
One career stage of mine was to head up the Bulgarian office for SPORFIVE in Sofia. One of our most important clients — next to the Bulgarian Football Union — was Heineken. They wanted to do something with their local beer brand, Ariana, with a focus on Bulgaria's favourite sport of soccer, involving fans and amateur soc-cer players. The challenge was to find the right topic since Heineken did not trust the national federation or anyone in the league to fulfil any kind of engagement in a proper way. Therefore, we had to come up with an independent new platform without leaving the governing bodies of soccer out.

Our pitch to Heineken/Ariana was to create a nationwide public soccer tournament, playing in Bulgaria's 10 most important cities and Ariana regions. Keeping in mind that Bulgaria is Europe's poor-est country, we tried to make everyone feel like a pro soccer player during these events. Each team received complete game gear from Ariana's co-sponsor Puma. All pitches were in proper condition and branded by Ariana. A DJ entertained the crowds between and after the games, and each team had a female "team manager" to organize the details for them. The core idea was to create local heroes in a high-scale soccer environment with a maximum of public engagement via respective digital channels. The first tournament was in 2010 when social media was rather basic (Facebook), though it already worked in regards of pictures.

In each city, we had between 800–1,200 participants, playing five against five on small pitches on weekends. The winning team of each tournament qualified for the final round in the capital city of Sofia, playing on a small pitch in the national soccer stadium. The winner of these 10 teams played the Grand Final against the reigning Bulgarian league champion. Licenced referees, a rather rare case on amateur level soccer in Bulgaria, headed all the games.

What is your approach to sponsorship with this type of tournament?

We always try to transfer the unique emotional potential of sport to a custom-made story for the partner's respective target group. Heineken/Ariana activated this event nationwide in bars, supermarkets/POS, on bottles and cans, displays and billboards all around the country with the great result that their beer sales with Ariana went up in all the focused regions, becoming Bulgaria's favourite beer around soccer!

Is it difficult to engage stakeholders?

In an ideal world, the sponsorship platform you must sell should be of national interest. In this case, it is much easier to convince the sponsor to activate the cooperation via their classical advertising and POS channels like we did with Heineken and Ariana in Bulgaria. However, most team sport platforms in Europe have only regional impact/importance. In this case, national brands are usually not able to implement regional cooperation in their national campaigns.

Do you find stakeholders are expecting more and more?
The current challenge is to find more measurable sponsorship channels based on unquestionable related KPI.

What is your advice on the best way to engage stakeholders?
Everyone is searching for relevant content, something most brands can hardly generate themselves. All that needs to be done now is to pitch the right sponsorship with a branch relevant and credible story.

At the time of this interview, Florian was the Head of Marketing for HSV, one of Germany's most popular sport clubs. Florian started off his career working for Sportfive, where over six years he held three different positions — Director of American Football, Managing Director of Sportfive Bulgaria and Senior Director of Marketing of National Football Teams.

Chapter 5

TO ENGAGE STAKEHOLDERS — ACTIVATE. ACTIVATE. ACTIVATE

FLASHBACK

My first involvement in sponsorship activation came when I worked with Eat-More candy bars at the legendary Calgary Stampede. It was a program I inherited, and I was thrilled not only about the project but about the prospect of glamourous business travel. The Calgary Stampede is a ten-day show featuring rodeo, concerts, midway, chuck wagon races, agricultural competitions, partying, pancake breakfasts, and eating everything and anything. Our activation for Eat-More fit right in. It was called the Eat-More Chew Contest. The Eat-More Chew Contest was as straightforward as it sounds. Contestants would try to chew down as many Eat-More bars as they could without damaging themselves. They competed on a rickety little stage while an overly enthusiastic host gave a play-by-play of their 60-second battle. Water and plenty of cheering inspired their jawing. Want-to-be cowboys, courageous kids, and dads who probably did not need the calories competed cheek-to-cheek for pride and a souvenir t-shirt declaring them an Eat-More fan!

It was simple, a little bit stupid, very scary at times, but it worked.

WHY ENGAGEMENT?

For sponsors to get their desired returns from their investments in properties, they must leverage the properties to engage key stakeholders like influencers, media, government, new consumers, and buying groups. They need to activate the property.

A sponsor has invested in key properties to borrow equity. They have crafted a compelling story to dramatize their involvement. Now they need to communicate that involvement to their audiences. Research has proven that unless a sponsor engages stakeholders, their partnership will not be successful. When sponsors do not engage their stakeholders, they are treating sponsorship like they would most media that are static and offer only one-way transmission of messaging. At least dynamic media, such as online videos or print advertisements, offer opportunities to include a storyline and selling messages. It is not enough to simply put up a sign at an event or run an ad on television. Sponsors need to interact with people in a meaningful way.

There are two core approaches to engagement: activation and integration. While most sponsors focus on activation, a savvy marketer will pursue integration; both are by no means mutually exclusive, but they are not dependent on one another. As a property, your objective is to satisfy the needs of sponsors with the right combination of both.

ACTIVATION

A sponsorship program is dead until it is brought to life by activation. Activation enables a sponsor to connect with stakeholders, spark a spontaneous two-way conversation, and deliver value — activation makes a sponsor stand out.

Activation is the opportunity a sponsor provides for their stakeholders to interact with a property. A simple example is a pre-event contest for consumers who can win VIP tickets by sharing content the sponsor provides on the consumer's own social media channels.

In an earlier time, activation began simply and slowly with commonly used approaches such as promotions to give away tickets, in-event giveaways, and corporate hosting. To this day, these are the underpinnings of many sponsorships, especially those that follow Gold-Silver-Bronze (GSB) models.

Yes, signage at the event or an ad in a program guide is a core benefit for the sponsor, but it is not activation. Think of a contest to attend the event with entry forms available when you purchase the sponsor's product — this is and example of activation.

Very few properties today provide the right environment for their sponsors to stand out. That is mostly because sponsorship properties are cluttered battlegrounds. Given the power of their affiliation with you, your sponsors have more to fear from your other sponsors than from industry competitors. If you have a bank sponsor, all other banks are prevented from utilizing your property in their marketing, but your other sponsors in non-competitive categories — auto, telecom, tech, pharma — have the same rights as your bank sponsor. Each sponsor wants to do a better job than the other of promoting their affiliation with your property, as each of them is essentially competing for the same audience — your loyal followers. That is why activating a property affiliation is so important; it gives the sponsor a competitive advantage over its industry rivals and provides the best mechanism for standing out from the other sponsor partners of a property.

Activation programs are generally identified as the incremental spending and activities the sponsor initiates to extend their reach and increase impact. Historically, the activation of a sponsorship was the sole responsibility of the sponsor and their communication agency partners, such as advertising, PR, sponsorship, digital, and experiential agencies. The property was responsible for the organization, staging, and marketing of its program, including the delivery of the core benefits it had promised the sponsor, but that was then. Today, incremental promotion involves a collaboration between the sponsor and the property.

Activation can include all the one-time extras that a sponsor may have to buy, such as advertising during the event broadcast or in publications, social media stunts, public relations, retail activation, employee hosting, experiential marketing, and athletes' endorsements. Many of these are often purchased from the property or its media properties, but others, such as athletes' endorsements, are negotiated with their agents.

The good news is that activation works. It works so well that a sponsorship that is not activated is almost doomed to failure — they will not achieve the same results as an activated sponsorship. IMI International, one of the leading sponsorship research firms on the planet, estimates that activation increases purchase intent by 475%. With that sort of success, you would wonder why a company would not activate. Unfortunately, it may be because activation requires resources: time, money, and partners.

THE ACTIVATION RATIO FALLACY

Far too many sponsors spend the bulk of their budget on rights fees and not enough on activation. A rights fee is the money/services a sponsor pays the property for the ability to use the latter's intellectual property, trademarks, and marketing assets for promotion and business-building. Many studies suggest there should be a rights fee ratio, i.e. one dollar of activation for every dollar of rights fee. For a long time, the industry standard has been a 3:1 ratio, but I think using a ratio presents a flawed argument: it is too reliant on the sponsorship fee paid. The ratio doesn't account for the fact you may have negotiated an excellent sponsorship deal, or that the property gave you a massive discount because of other value you bring, such as access to volunteers or fundraising skills.

Using the ratio will not work for two reasons. First, sponsorship is only one component of an integrated campaign. It is not a one-off, standalone activity that can be easily measured. Budgeting for this integrated campaign should be no different than for any other campaign a company runs. Utilize the benchmarks and financial standards that you would normally while keeping in mind that each industry and company within it has its own metrics for achieving certain results. If a company is attempting to launch a new brand, its budget would incorporate the creation of all marketing assets and the channels to distribute those assets. When it comes to sponsorship, think of the property relationship as your asset or the equivalent of your creative canvas (e.g., producing the video) then consider activation as the sharing of your creation via marketing channels. If you create a video, you need to distribute it. You can hope it will go viral, but that's unrealistic. You can invest in social platforms, influencers, media, etc. to ensure that the content engages your target audience. In either case, your budget for the investment in distribution is not based on a ratio dependent on the amount you spent creating the video.

The second argument against applying a ratio can be found in the evolution of sponsorship marketing and activation. Sponsorship marketing has evolved from a one-off tactic into a coordinated, carefully planned multimedia, multipurpose, multi-stakeholder major undertaking; it will not cut it if it is just a one-off tactic. It needs to be developed as though it is a long-term positioning campaign. This provides an exciting opportunity to use every type of marketing, communication, and promotional tactic. A well planned sponsorship campaign will include engagement and activation initiatives that impact product innovation and design, retail branding and product packaging, employee incentives and benefits, strategic partnerships and corporate alliances. As the opportunities for engagement have expanded, so too have the number of participants. Properties that embrace the What Sponsors Want (WSW) approach are active participants in the activation activities of their sponsors. They are embedding strategic engagement opportunities in their sponsorship packages. They are deploying resources and expertise to help facilitate more innovative activities by their sponsors. They are providing connections to business partners, agents, media channels, and other sponsors to create opportunistic relationships.

Sponsors are looking to their properties to facilitate engagement, and the best properties are responding. They are building or supplying expertise in areas such as creative services, staffing, event management, experiential marketing, logistics, media, and analytics. Many properties see their future as an agency helping sponsors to maximize engagement. The properties that begin to think like an agency or agency collaborator are going to be successful. Sponsors want to engage their key stakeholders, and your job is to make it easy and powerful.

STAKEHOLDER GROUPS

Using the word "activation" often implies that the focus is consumer engagement, but the opportunity to activate should extend to all groups — not just consumers — that impact a sponsor's business. Traditional sponsorship as it is still practiced focuses on delighting consumers by aligning with something about which they are passionate and by providing trade customers with unbelievable experiences, such as VIP hosting. Those activities are important and can generate significant returns for a company, but there is so much more potential in an integrated sponsorship marketing program.

A powerful sponsorship program expands its reach beyond consumers and trade customers to three important groups: Internal Stakeholders, B2B Stakeholders, and B2C Stakeholders.

Internal Stakeholders

The best advocates for any brand are the sponsor's employees. Whether they are customer service reps, warehouse staff, or assembly line workers, their passion, commitment, and support have an unbelievable impact on the business. Across the company, sponsorship can impact employee pride, create opportunities for team building, give employees a voice in their communities, and be a powerful tool in talent recruitment. Sponsorship can target stakeholders within the company, such as a specific department. If the branding team is not aligned with sales, it may use sponsorship to demonstrate its appreciation for the sales team or provide them with data or other assets that help increase their close rates. Sponsorship may be used to fuel innovation by familiarizing specific groups in the organization with new technologies, new markets, or new competitors.

B2B Stakeholders

Given the complexity of global business, the array of external stakeholders that I label as B2B is wide. It can include suppliers, distributors, resellers, retailers, wholesalers, government officials, elected officials, industry regulators, industry associations, unions, advocacy groups, and more. Understanding the food chain or spider web of these organizations in relation to your sponsor — and more importantly in relation to their corporate priorities — can produce a blueprint for a highly productive stakeholder-engagement plan.

Although smaller than any B2C group, any of the above B2B groups can have a more powerful impact on business results than any other stakeholder group. Imagine that your sponsor sells through a retail trade channel and a large chain customer decides to list or enhance their promotion of a sponsor's product, a result of their involvement with a property. A single keyboard stroke authorizing that listing can generate millions of dollars in sales for the sponsor, but it does not have to be that dramatic to have an impact. If a supply chain partner improves its performance, or an advocacy group lends its support, or a regulatory body aligns with the sponsor, the multiplier effect will generate tremendous results.

B2C Stakeholders

The largest segment of this group is the traditional target market — consumers. However, there are important subsegments that often impact your programming when talking with your target audience. These subsegments include current brand consumers, potential brand consumers, and fans of the property. There will be overlap, but you can't discount the importance of identifying subsegments.

In addition to consumers, there are other stakeholder groups that qualify for inclusion in the B2C cluster. First and foremost is the media, as reporting on the sponsorship program results in a massive reach to consumers. Another group is influencers, who have a similar ability to authenticate and scale your message. Your sponsor may be pursuing early adopters, lapsed users, or loyal customers. Whatever the group, preparing a sponsorship marketing plan requires the same rigorous approach as a product launch, a product restage, or a product offensive.

Sponsors will have more or fewer stakeholder groups depending on the complexity of their business and the objectives of their sponsorship marketing program. Your role as the property is to identify those stakeholder groups, the size and value of each, and create programming to reach those groups. These groups should have been identified during the sponsor solicitation process, as they are essential to the offerings in your proposal. The development of engagement strategies, or programming, opens the door to a deeper understanding of the stakeholder groups.

THE STAKEHOLDER ORBIT

We will use a tool called an orbit to classify and prioritize each stakeholder group, and to illustrate how your sponsor can connect with each one (Figure 1). Once they are classified, we then use a tool called the *activation cycle* to uncover opportunities to reach them.

The stakeholder orbit should identify whether the stakeholder is Internal, B2B, or B2C, and it should prioritize each segment. This can be done by a simple ranking (e.g., A, B, C), and allocating a budget amount (in dollars or percentages), which indicates priority. If it is too early in the process for ranking, provide the sponsor's objective for each segment. A combination of these indicators will be a great help in developing your activation cycle.

If you can identify all three indicators — stakeholder type, priority, and sponsor objective — you will end up with an even more powerful orbit. Over time, as you develop new stakeholder orbits for a

1. BRANCH EMPLOYEES
Promote bank branch to community

2. SHAREHOLDERS & INVESTORS
Increase net revenue

1. CURRENT CLIENTS
Increase net promoter scores

2. SUPPLIERS
Added value to relationship

3. GOVERNMENT
Implement regulatory affairs strategy

COMMUNITY BANK

2. HEAD OFFICE EMPLOYEES
Pride in their employer

3. MEDIA
To be seen as a community builder

3. COMMUNITY MEMBERS
Perceived as good corporate citizens

3. FUTURE CLIENTS
Increase net promoter scores

3. CORPORATE CLIENTS
To be seen as community builder

INTERNAL STAKEHOLDERS
B2C EXTERNAL STAKEHOLDERS
B2B EXTERNAL STAKEHOLDERS

Figure 1:   Orbit Example

wide variety of clients and sponsors, you will begin to see patterns that make developing new proposals and pursuing new prospects much easier. Many of these tools not only support your current property sponsor but provide insights and learning for your new partners.

THE ACTIVATION CYCLE

Your property probably has more opportunities for engaging stakeholders and creating activation programs for your sponsors than you realize, but I have created a tool for you to dissect your property and understand where these opportunities may be hidden. Below is the activation cycle, and it takes you on a tour of your own property in the shoes of your stakeholders. Getting to know your property this way will lead you to discover new connection points for your sponsors. Done properly, it will help you provide more novel platforms for telling your sponsors' stories, understand original ways to measure the impact you can provide a sponsor, and understand how your property can provide more support to your sponsors and improve their performance.

The activation cycle consists of five consecutive phases. There can be overlap between the phases as there is not always a firm starting and stopping point for each, and if possible, the loop is continuous and assumes the property exists over time and isn't a one-off. Each phase is named to reflect the stakeholder's perspective.

Activation Cycle Phases

- Hear
- Schedule
- Anticipate
- Experience
- Share

Hear

The Hear Phase is exactly what you would expect it to be: the first time a stakeholder hears about the property. The stakeholder could be a consumer, a business customer, a participant, or a potential donor. They would normally first hear about the property through marketing communications, word-of-mouth, or by having been a participant in similar events. In sponsorship marketing, the Hear Phase typically begins with a launch press conference or a media release to mark the start of a marketing campaign.

There are many innovative ways to launch a sponsorship marketing campaign or a property. As we investigate these ways, we will find opportunities to create activations for your sponsors, and which they can consider as integrated activation opportunities. In the Hear Phase, you can pitch a sponsor's involvement as an opportunity to be leading edge, trendy, and — here comes the most overused word in marketing — cool. As you conceptualize your launch ideas, you will quickly see that this is an exciting opportunity for a sponsor or sponsors, to leverage its affiliation. You can rejoice in the fact that it will not take a lot of imagination to conjure up impactful, powerful, and unprecedented sponsorship opportunities.

The power of the Hear Phase is clearly seen in its ability to reach multiple stakeholder groups. Imagine that your sponsor's employees are the first to know about a new property or the awarding of an event to your community. Imagine that your best customers were the first people to know, and how privileged they might feel to be "in the know."

Typically, but not always, the stakeholder group that is the primary target during the Hear Phase is B2C. When multiple groups are involved in staging the property, there is often a corporate or B2B rollout first, to align partners, secure venues, committees, and additional key stakeholders. Sponsors of a more complex or major property may find that releasing communication in stages is required. Imagine the steps of a stairwell, and waiting for you at the top of the stairs is the ultimate consumer, but along the way you gather new partners and allies who help you reach the top and lead you to your consumer stakeholders, which in turn demonstrates the power of the Hear Phase.

Sponsor integration

Let us look at how integrating a sponsor into an event can allow that sponsor or that activity to become the face of your Hear Phase. Let's imagine a community event of some sort, a 10K run, a food festival, or a fundraiser. Let us say that this community event can only afford one promotional mechanism, a poster campaign. They expect to deploy five different posters in all, one for each phase of the activation cycle. The first poster is to announce the event, which has 12 different sponsors. Five of those sponsors have paid a significant amount, four of those sponsors have paid much less, and three should really be considered official suppliers. The property wants to take care of the top sponsors.

After consulting with each sponsor, you determined that one of them was trying to position itself as innovative and groundbreaking: it wanted positioning equity. You had worked with them on a story narrative that would see it use your platform to announce news of their new products, new facilities, and new staff. It makes perfect sense to designate them as the lead partner, or the face, of the Hear Phase. They would own the announcement of the big, new, shiny event coming to town.

Now draw your poster, which could be a digital billboard, a video, or a print ad. The beautifully simple poster reads quite clearly that your property is pleased to announce the coming of this exciting event to your community.

In this phase, your other major sponsors may receive some brand recognition, though at a lower level, or you may provide exclusivity to one sponsor. In either case, you are utilizing activation effectively to help your sponsor differentiate themselves from your other sponsors while telling their story.

As you continue to lead your property through the entire activation cycle, you will bestow this lead role on different major partners in each phase. Each partner should be aligned with the phase of the cycle that is most appropriate for their business in terms of the equity they wish to borrow and the story they wish to tell.

Leverage your marketing communications assets. Cleary, you will have a larger, more integrated launch campaign than one with just a poster, pending the scale of your property, the size of your budget, and the significance of the sponsor investment. This will present you with more dynamic opportunities to profile your lead Hear Phase partner.

How else can a sponsor be involved in the Hear Phase?

Regardless of the size of your budget or the significance of your sponsor's investment, there are countless original ways to launch your property and make a splash. This will benefit your property, your sponsor, and surprisingly your stakeholders, because the perceived value of your event will increase, based on the impact of your marketing, and its ability to increase fundraising, motivation, and desire. If your event is attractive, your attendees will be more excited to attend.

Get creative and imagine a mystery launch event for your property, one that is held in the warehouse or parking lot of your leading Hear Phase's sponsor. This could be combined with the appearance of a celebrity, participants, media, staff, etc. If your property conjures up a serious image, launch events can still be created, though perhaps in a laboratory or government building. Even with a serious property, you could risk pushing boundaries by hosting your launch event at the home of a survivor, on the land site you are trying to preserve, or with a live remote broadcast feed featuring your field workers on another continent. Your launch events could lean into itself and the feeling of being an event. Metatextual imagine that your downtown core is swarming with volunteers who are distributing premiums, information, or perhaps a choir serenading people on their way to work. Ratchet it up a notch and have your music festival headliner appear as a busker on a busy street, which would be sure to create viral social media content.

Beyond the launch

The Hear Phase lasts much longer than a launch event or the impact of a press release; your lead sponsor will want to be showcased throughout the cycle. You should consistently leverage their resources and have an integrated marketing campaign that spotlights your lead sponsor and your property. The best result is you will craft a story to share with key stakeholders. Giving your Hear sponsor(s) an ongoing role as the protagonist who is bringing this great event to their wonderful community is tremendously beneficial.

The most important aspect of this, however, is the planning. You should work with your sponsor on more than just a launch event. Plan the entire marketing campaign with them, so you can leverage their channels and assets to build scale. Utilize your sponsor's assets. Do they have celebrities? Retail stores? Consumer-facing staff? Media channels? Trucks? Influencers? Billing statements? Consider how you can collaborate to market your property and activate your sponsor.

Back to the above example, you may have street teams or mall interceptors enrolling consumers beyond the launch event; these crews would be jointly branded, primarily to promote your property, but also to demonstrate your strong bond and relationship with your partner. All your launch activities would be integrated and focus on promoting the partner. If you have an out-of-home or radio partner, they can be merged with the Hear Phase sponsor.

For each phase of the activation cycle, determine how your stakeholders can interact with the property and how you can showcase your sponsor as the hero of that phase. The presenting sponsor of the Hear Phase should receive credit for informing and educating your stakeholders about the property, and in return, you should provide that presenting sponsor with a powerful platform to share their story.

This is their time to shine, so ensure that they do.

Schedule

The Schedule Phase begins when the participant or attendee commits to attend the event. Properties do not typically think about the Schedule Phase as an activation opportunity, because quite often the stakeholder experience can be less than satisfactory. However, that is the entire point of mapping their journey with the property — to identify pain points and moments for improvement.

Pain presents in the Schedule Phase. Think about long lines to register, clumsy websites that require endless entries of information with no explicit reward, and poorly described options for seating, accommodations, or attendance. All of these contribute to a negative experience, but it is one that can be made positive through the combined efforts of the property and the sponsor. The unfortunate aspect of this phase is that stakeholders are often spending a significant amount of money and perpetuating their pain. This is an experience that is begging to be improved.

Tackle the challenge to improve by thinking critically about your attendees' journey through the scheduling, purchasing, and registration processes. What opportunities exist for a sponsor to be involved in this journey, and more importantly, what opportunities exist for a sponsor to make this journey an absolutely fantastic one? How can you and your sponsors transform it into a better experience? Currently, the stakeholder is focused on the amount of money they are paying out, or their inability to get the type of ticket they want. The Schedule Phase is teeming with opportunities to transform a negative experience into a positive one that can be showcased by one of your sponsors.

Back to the example of the local community event where the organizers are going to create, produce and distribute posters reflecting each phase of the activation cycle. The Schedule Phase is now going to be allotted to one lead sponsor who is going to earn credit for delivering the mechanism enabling stakeholders to buy tickets, register for the event, or simply calendar their plans to attend. To create value for that lead sponsor, you need to ensure that the Scheduling Phase is enjoyable. I recognize that this can be easier said than done, as limited internal resources may prevent you from investing in or reimagining the way your organization registers people, sells tickets, or handles registrations. Regardless, there are many lower-cost ways to enhance the experience, even if it cannot be entirely reengineered.

Your creativity is required to imagine those ways and deliver them to your sponsor. The reality is that you should expect to allocate some of their funds to that effort. You should be able to secure them as incremental activation funds from your partner, but that may be subject to a larger overhaul of the budget.

Okay, let's get creative

One simple way may be to capitalize on the excitement and demand for tickets or access to your property. A simple, low-cost scheduling activation can be the announcement that tickets are now on sale, courtesy of your sponsor. If this feels like the Hear Phase, then that is a good thing, because done properly, it should feel like an extension of the launch marketing campaign. By announcing that registration is open and that you are switching to a new partner, you are activating the Schedule Phase and differentiating it from the Hear Phase. Take advantage of demand for an event among ardent stakeholders to create some affection for your sponsor. A similar opportunity exists when you announce the launch of the fundraising window for a not-for-profit property. This too is a simple, low-cost window for delineating phases and shining the spotlight on another sponsor.

In both cases, these announcements can be easily enhanced by improving the participant journey. Revamping scheduling can often cost significant time and money but working with your sponsor will allow you to find ways to work around these costs. What if you leveraged your sponsors' stores to sell tickets or to accept registrations? This could be done with physical stores or digital retail outlets; the tickets for your event could be listed as a specific product, complete with its own Stock Keeping Unit number. If dispensing your ticket or the registration mechanism are exclusive to your service provider, look for other ways to improve the Schedule Phase. Start with information — the more accessible and customized instructions you can provide someone, the better their experience will be. This is true in any customer service situation, not just events. As you work with your lead sponsor in the Schedule Phase, develop the resources that make it easier for people to schedule their participation.

"Making it easier" could take the form of sharing registration tips through various media outlets. These tips should cover all types of stakeholders and focus on improving their journey. The addition of online chat or telephone customer service support might enhance the scheduling experience. For an event that wants to cater to VIP stakeholders, you could provide a concierge service that manages the scheduling process on behalf of the stakeholder.

You and your sponsor can collaborate to create tutorials, online videos, and social media bulletins, all designed to inform, educate, and support your purchasers. None of these is going to require a massive investment. All of them are going to generate substantial goodwill and provide a unique touch point for your sponsor to connect with their key stakeholders.

Imagine the benefits for your sponsor. Consider that your sponsor may be seeking social media growth, wishes to grow their database, or is looking for people with whom to seed a new product. The simple act of requesting consent, an opt-in when consumers are taking advantage of the scheduling information or help services will generate a significant amount of very valuable leads and hand raisers of which your sponsor is searching.

If your sponsor has partnered with your property to borrow your equity and position themselves as service oriented, they have an ideal platform for communicating their story of being helpful. Facilitation of a smoother scheduling process will reinforce that story. The likelihood your sponsor will share their positive experiences with their friends and associates increases as the sponsor enables the improvement of the scheduling experience, helps smooth the registration process, explains the access levels for your event tickets, and improves the understanding of how to donate. The sponsor, who is telling a story of a premium service provider, will benefit greatly from their concierge service for influencers, VIPs, or most loyal customers.

If money was no object

If your sponsor really wants to make a big impact on stakeholders during the Schedule Phase, then their commitment to increase their resources will enable you to do so. Coupled with your sponsor's resources, you will need to ensure that you have the internal alignment to make significant changes, and the lead time to do so in a flawless manner. Assuming that all the boxes are ticked, you can now create something bespoke for your sponsor.

Making it happen

Let us begin with online ticket sales, registration, and invitation providers. First, these providers add value given their reach, technology infrastructure, and cost effectiveness. That said, you should compare whether it would make more sense to build your own infrastructure (probably through a vendor), find a new solution provider or tools that allow for more customization, or pay your current provider for experience improvements. The benefits of gaining control are significant for both you and your sponsor.

If you can control the scheduling experience, you can make it part of your brand experience. It can reflect your value proposition with perfect clarity and communicate your partner's affiliation. You can directly add branding, communication, and activation elements all the while ensuring that the process reflects your desired protocols and preserves your property's integrity. Additionally, you will now have direct access to your stakeholders, and the opportunity to communicate with them throughout the remaining phases of the Activation Cycle.

What can you do when your ticketing mechanism is out of your control, regardless of how much funding you have? Perhaps your property is part of a league, series, tour, or some other franchise that requires you to be a part of a single, centralized ticketing system. The good news is that those systems are generally quite consumer friendly by virtue of the number of stakeholders and transactions they support. The better news is that there are still plenty of opportunities for you and your sponsor to build a significant impact.

You can apply some of the thinking behind the ideas presented earlier, and with your added resources, ensure that your systems are more robust and integrated. You can ensure that your hotlines or support resources are available 24 hours a day; this could be provided live or through automated bots or other tech services. You could layer on more hands-on service experiences, such as establishing a physical presence in your host venue, a local mall, or another nearby facility during the registration/scheduling period. If your event is being staged in a convention center, it may be possible to rent a ticket window and have it branded. You could then staff that window with a member of your team or a contractor from the ticketing organization; they could be cobranded with your sponsor partner. If you have a small event, this sort of live service kiosk can be an excellent opportunity to deploy volunteers, especially those who may be unable to help on event day or those who want to participate on event day.

Remember that whenever consumers make a purchase, large or small, they seek immediate reinforcement to reassure themselves that they made a smart decision. This holds true for your stakeholders. One of the best methods for ensuring that they feel comfortable is to issue a Thank You message as quickly as possible; whether it is in the form of an email reply, a post card, a video message, or a gift, it will have an impact. When working with your ticket/registration provider, develop a method that will allow you to connect with stakeholders as they are scheduling their participation. Deliver a welcome message and integrate it into your sponsor's story, helping to ensure they are satisfied with their commitment. The range of options is driven by your budget, infrastructure, and the assets you have available. If you have the opportunity to go beyond the written thank you or phone call, look to enhancements that add value such as providing a code that unlocks a digital site, an invitation to join a group social network group, or a combination of the two. This message will set up the next phase, the Anticipation Phase. This could be the first element of the Anticipation Phase if it is not essential for the lead partner who is fulfilling the Schedule Phase.

Typically, the Schedule Phase of the property is the emotional low point in the Activation Cycle. Money has been expended, time has been committed, as has been a commitment to exercising, training, or preparing, but like anything in life the individual or organization that helps to eliminate a negative is the organization that will garner the most prolonged loyalty from consumers. Take advantage of this emotional window and offer it up as a credible activation point for your sponsor.

I cannot think of a sponsor that would not be interested in helping the majority of your stakeholders.

Anticipate

Properties and sponsors do not pay enough attention to the Anticipation Phase. Maybe it is because they do not realize that it exists, but it certainly does. Anticipation is the window of time between when the stakeholder schedules their involvement and the moment when they begin their involvement.

Let us be clear: this is not the window between purchasing a ticket and attending the event. Anticipation begins before this window opens. For example, when you go to a movie, you often schedule to do so days or at least hours before you purchase a ticket, even if you buy your tickets online. This is anticipation, and it begins with your initial commitment.

The Anticipation Phase is the window of time between the moment when you book your holiday until the moment you get on the plane, or perhaps just before that, when you pass through security and head for a drink. It is that time in between spent packing, planning, researching, sharing with friends and colleagues, and telling yourself there are only so many more sleeps before you get to go away. That is the Anticipation Phase. Itis over once you board the plane.

The Anticipation Phase is full of excitement, and mostly full of positive emotions though not always. It is an excellent window for you as a marketer of the property and for your sponsor as an activator of the property to make some really exciting connections with key stakeholders.

Try to think of all the things your stakeholders do from the time they decide to participate in your event until the day they show up on the site, at your venue, turn on your broadcast, or sign in online. Are they training? Are they fundraising? Are they shopping for new clothes? Are they following other stops on the tour? Are they downloading the music of your performers? Are they shopping for new swag to support your team? Are they booking accommodations? Are they inviting friends to join them? Just what are they doing?

Asking these questions is important because as you do so, you will quickly realize that the answers represent a plethora of activation opportunities you can serve up to the lead sponsor(s) of the Anticipation Phase. Activations executed in this phase will have a multiplier effect, as they will not only please your stakeholders but also serve as recruiting efforts. This window gives you an opportunity to demonstrate that you are committed to your stakeholders, and have them join you in getting more people to attend your event, raising more fans, raising more funds, and generating more publicity.

Anticipation on a poster

Returning to the local event with the inventory of five posters. The first poster announced that the event was coming, which got people excited. The second poster, representing the Schedule Phase, might have told people where to buy tickets or how to buy them. The third poster, representing the Anticipation Phase, might have announced the headline act, or encouraged attendees to bring a friend, or asked community members to support the fundraising efforts of the registered stakeholders.

Let us not forget that the poster has a metaphorical element. The messaging could be delivered on a bus shelter ad, in a press release, on a website or event tickets, or in a print ad. The medium is irrelevant. It might seem impossible that only one sponsor can be the lead partner of this phase. They could in theory, because as a property you should strive to create substantial value in all five phases, but this is meant to be an extreme example. You could provide all your sponsors at a certain investment level with their own platform in each phase. The exact partnership structure for your property will be up to you.

What is not up to you is that you must look at the Anticipation Phase through the eyes of your stakeholders. What are they doing as they prepare to become involved with your property? How can you and your sponsor make this window in time even better for them? How can you ensure your sponsor gets the credit they deserve for their contribution to this phase?

The beauty of the poster's metaphor is that it allows you to test the value of your activation. If it's solid, then it doesn't need anything more impactful than a poster. Here are some thought starters your partners can use as engagement opportunities in the Anticipation Phase.

- Announce the headline act for a festival.
- Promote the time and location of sponsor-funded training runs for a marathon.
- Encourage registrants to bring a friend for half price.
- Reveal the secret location of the event
- Unveil the prizes for the event participants.
- Introduce new competitors or teams that will be featured at the event.
- Highlight additional celebrities who have recently confirmed their attendance.
- Communicate how to travel to the event.
- Promote social networks of people who are attending.
- Announce new attractions or rides at the carnival.
- Promote the fact that the first 1,000 attendees will receive a free food voucher from the sponsor.
- Provide updates on funds raised, tickets sold, number of people entered.

Activation triggers for anticipation

The Anticipation Phase is an extension of the Hear Phase, and it will significantly impact your marketing and revenue generation. It will begin as a scheduled period, though not necessarily triggered by stakeholders. In all cases, this phase is important.

If your event requires attendees/participants to have a certain level of fitness, a natural activation during the Anticipation Phase is training runs or combines. You may wish to organize these for free if they are subsidized by your partner or have the sponsor organize them at their cost. If these training programs are exceptional, you may wish to charge an additional amount, subsidized by your sponsor, or offer them exclusively to your sponsors' most loyal patrons.

For fundraising events, the Activation Phase of anticipation should focus on fundraising, especially peer-to-peer events, or programs that require your participants to connect with their personal and professional networks. A sponsorship activation engagement for this type of event could feature the distribution of physical or digital tools and assets that your participants can use. These tools could include templates, emails or social posts, video content, poster templates, or phone scripts, all with the objective of increasing funds raised. Other tools could include resources to execute a fundraising rally or an office event to help generate additional funds. Sophisticated programs could include incentives to inspire both your participants and/or their donors.

If your event is some sort of touring or travelling attraction that will feature performers or celebrities who are making appearances at other events, leverage these performances to promote your event's staging. Take advantage of their media channels and those of the leading events to drive content placements promoting your property. Invite your stakeholders and ticket buyers to follow your social feeds to receive your updates. All this content would be cobranded with the lead sponsor of this phase.

It is a good idea for you and your sponsor to create mechanisms for your stakeholders to share content with their social networks, friends, colleagues, and others. This will work especially well if you can create targeted content featuring your performers, who are sharing their anticipation of being involved in the event. If you're attending a music festival in a few weeks, you are likely to get excited when you hear from the headliner. The same can be said for athletes who are part of your property. If you are hosting competitors or teams that are competing in events in other markets, share the details with your social followers and stakeholders.

If your event or property is some sort of conference or symposium, your Anticipation Phase partner can play a role in travel planning, advanced learning, or pre-conference networking. Your lead sponsor can demonstrate their expertise or ability to connect by facilitating one of these activities. Given the high cost of attending a corporate conference, your sponsor's contribution will be seen as even more valuable, in turn helping them build a powerful connection with your attendees.

The net of the Anticipation Phase is that it is an often overlooked window of time for you to market to your most loyal stakeholders, creating impactful opportunities for sponsors. In addition to reaching ticket buyers and participants, Anticipation is an excellent window for reaching a sponsor's internal stakeholders. The same level of excitement exists within their organization as it does amongst your participants. Work with your sponsor to create internal staff challenges, pep events, and business challenges.

The same holds for B2B stakeholders, such as members of the media and social commentators. If your sponsor has prioritized earned media coverage, the Anticipation Phase is an excellent window for cultivating and nurturing these media relationships. Engage media outlets and individuals as you have your B2C stakeholders. Perhaps your sponsor can afford to take the media to attend performances by your talent. On a more cost-effective basis, you could conduct a virtual Q&A with that talent while they are in other markets. If your event is a fitness property, create a media challenge enabled by your lead sponsor. Business events have the advantage of sharing content and research that media relishes. One critical factor to remember about today's media is that they are all resource-challenged. If your sponsor can fund the dissemination of news and intelligence to the media, then you are both likely to be pleased with the results.

Experience

I define the Experience Phase as the moment when a stakeholder starts to connect with the property, whether it is an event, a broadcast, or an opened attraction. It begins with any travel your stakeholder undertakes to attend the event. How does your sponsor help facilitate that travel? Make it easier, less costly, or more comfortable? It can be as simple as providing transit and parking instructions. It could be as interesting as special buses, ride sharing, or luggage delivery to a campsite. What about stakeholders with families, including young, old, or access-challenged members? How does your lead Experience sponsor engage at this occasion?

Typically, most stakeholder engagement occurs during the Experience Phase. When planning this phase of the Activation Cycle, keep yourself in the head of your stakeholders and follow their journey — not your sponsors' — through your property to uncover the best activation opportunities.

Some, such as advocacy groups or educational properties, believe it can be difficult to identify the Experience Phase. It usually begins with the stakeholder's first interaction with the property, which should not be confused with first commitment made during

Anticipation. From that point on, the property is live. The most compelling part of creating and using a tool like the Activation Cycle is that you can ultimately determine when each phase begins or ends.

It is easy to imagine when a property goes live for a sports contest, the four sweltering days of a music festival, or the excitement of a school spelling bee, but "going live" can be applied to when an organization advocates for change, when a family utilizes a social service, or when an influencer shares her breakfast with thousands of social followers.

During the live window, participants and stakeholders alike are having their most in-depth experience with the property. That is why this has been the window where sponsors have leveraged their rights to the fullest and implemented the most comprehensive engagement programs. In some cases, this is all the sponsor believes they are paying for, to maximize engagement opportunities at that moment in time, to connect with their consumers when they are having their most enriching experience. Their excitement and joy are very intense. Their sense of accomplishment is peaking. Their emotions are at their strongest. They are, hopefully, satisfied with their commitment of time and money.

It makes good marketing sense to connect with your stakeholders when their emotions are so positive, to leverage the concentration of people and availability of property infrastructure, which quite often are the main reasons a company or organization has bought the sponsorship. The key parts of the purchase, or the assets, are the engagement opportunities the sponsorship facilitates. However, this often leads the sponsor to believe that they do not need to invest additional dollars to engage their stakeholders. They may be satisfied with their affiliation with the property and the opportunity to use the assets described in the agreement to tell their story.

They may believe that being onsite delivers what they were looking for, to borrow equity, but in sometimes the equity transfer may have been a low priority, and the sponsor's objective may have been to connect with as many people as possible. In this case, their entire ROI and evaluation will be based on intercepts during the live window.

In this case, our five-poster model works very well. Poster number four would feature our lead sponsor for this phase. If this were a music festival, our sponsor may own the main stage, and poster number four would promote its talent lineup. If the event was a community open house, the same poster may provide a map of the various historic homes open to a visit. If the event were a science fair, poster four could list booth locations. The lead Experience Phase sponsor is borrowing the equity of the property's main attraction and building their connection through signage and whatever additional options they have been given, such as PA announcements, sampling rights, or video content, but most of your sponsors will want an increase of deeper engagement more than a sign and some sampling can offer. More than one sponsor will want to showcase their brand during the Experience Phase, which is why journeying through the Activation Cycle as a stakeholder is so valuable. It will unlock several engagement opportunities for your sponsor.

Every property has its challenges instructing the public and guiding people to their tables, tents, rooms, and seats, but these challenges, along with food and beverages, restrooms, change rooms, and access to services are amenities that a sponsor can improve.

During the Experience Phase, your stakeholders are experiencing moments of glory. Their arrival. Changing into their uniform. Donning their team colours. Having their faces painted. Meeting up with their supporters. Receiving their conference guidebook. Their warm-up. Watching and cheering. Completing their course. Completing their swim.

You should identify each and every one of these triumphant moments, which can become the primary engagement moment for your sponsor. Create photo opportunities, cheer stations, gear stations, hosts, and guideposts that are all sponsor branded. Remember that sponsors who activate during the Experience Phase want to focus on what they bring to the property, not to get in the way of the consumer's moment.

The essential point of this is to remember that it is the Experience Phase. Your sponsors want engagement opportunities that have richer value than a sign or one-way sampling exercise. Your payback is far greater than having a sponsor who is thrilled with their ROI. An improved Experience Phase directly impacts your stakeholder satisfaction by leading to increased spending, more sharing, and deeper loyalty.

Share

The final phase of the Activation Cycle is to Share. This is where your stakeholders and participants share their experience or involvement with your property with their friends and social networks. Call it word-of-mouth or social sharing. Hopefully, you will be able to call it goodwill. A good old fashioned photo album qualifies as sharing — it can be a powerful marketing tool.

Sharing is an exciting opportunity for your sponsors, providing them with an extended engagement window. It allows them to target stakeholders who not only attended or watched the event, but those who have absorbed media coverage or have a passing interest. They are the beneficiaries of a built-in multiplier effect due to the significant involvement of your many stakeholders. It is not just you, the property, serving as a mouthpiece for what occurred. Reach is extended and credibility is reinforced.

Sharing has different dimensions, whether it is with a one-time property, an ongoing property, or a regularly scheduled property. Each provides nuances and variations your sponsor can exploit. Today, photo albums have been replaced by instant and live sharing. You need to work diligently with your partner to ensure that the sharing opportunities succeed.

Let us turn to our fifth and final poster of our example. You may wonder what sort of poster would make sense in this phase. Since the event is an annual one, your fifth poster may feature some memories or images of the most recent event with a callout noting that early bird tickets or reservations for next year's event are now available. If your event was a fundraising run, you are well aware of what happens at the end of the event. The cups need to be swept up, the barricades removed, the portable toilets trucked away, and most importantly, the money needs to be counted. Once counted, the amount needs to be announced and celebrated. Your fifth poster could be shipped to the companies who raised the most money or placed around town to thank the community. Your fifth poster could open the door to a new activation of some sort, perhaps a photo contest, a chance to nominate the volunteer of the year, or a request for suggestions for the next event.

Technology allows great opportunities for stakeholder sharing, so your creative skills will be given a stern test when developing sponsor engagements for this phase. Most stakeholders have so much editing power in the palm of their hand they do not really need you or your sponsor.

Still, you have assets that should be used. Stakeholders are already sharing content from your property, but they crave even more customized and specialized elements. Deploy your creative resources to create photos, videos, posters, augmented reality, and other elements. Tap into your celebrities, performers, influencers, and experts to contribute to this content. Provide your sponsor with an exclusive platform for distributing this content to your stakeholders.

The event may be finished, but the celebrations do not have to end. Create a reunion for your most avid stakeholders. A volunteer recognition event. An unveiling of the new purchases that used the funds raised. You could produce a documentary, a web series, or podcasts about your property. If your event was a major milestone in the community, a legacy project that celebrates hosting the event could be unveiled — a mural, a piece of artwork, or a statue funded by a key partner set to become an enduring legacy. What about providing your sponsor with a chance to issue a follow-up report based on post-event surveys of your stakeholders? Perhaps your sponsor wants to distribute a premium souvenir or keepsake to your most avid stakeholders.

The list goes on and on. Putting yourself in the shoes of your stakeholders and thinking about what they would like from your property will generate countless more ideas you can suggest to your partner.

BENEFITS OF THE ACTIVATION CYCLE

One of the amazing advantages of using or creating a tool like the Activation Cycle is that it allows you to reframe your sponsor categories. Instead of selling Gold-Silver-Bronze (GSB) packages, you could individually package each phase of the Activation Cycle and offer it to a different partner. This is currently done when a sports team sells off a Game Night, or a Stage or Pregame show, but it is rarely done in a sophisticated and integrated way. I recognize that it is not realistic to have only one sponsor own the Experience Phase, but you could have a lead, or you could give each partner a leading role in one phase and a complementary role in another phase.

In many cases, deciding whether to be the lead or a complimentary sponsor is not a sponsor's priority. Far too often, the right to be the lead or a complimentary sponsor is the primary benefit in a sponsorship proposal. Focusing on this results in "brandvertising" as it relates to consumers and corporate schmoozing or hosting as it relates to trade customers. This should not be the case.

Beyond ego satisfaction, there is no reason to be a sponsor for the simple benefit of hosting. Very few properties can exclude non-sponsors from hosting their events — the core business model of many properties includes facilitating hosting to a wider customer base than their sponsors alone. Even charities actively seek corporate teams, because of their enhanced ability to fundraise compared to that of an individual.

ENGAGEMENT BEYOND ACTIVATION

While activation is the most used mechanism for stakeholder engagement, certain sophisticated properties provide integrated engagement opportunities where activation is just one of the many weapons in the arsenal.

Integrated engagement opportunities are of great value to a sponsor given their ability to be seamlessly and naturally included in the property's programming. On the other hand, a lack of control over the content of an integrated opportunity can be challenging. As sponsorship marketing evolves, I anticipate properties will offer sponsors even more connected and compelling integrated engagement opportunities — and at least some control over content.

To be clear, in-game giveaways such as t-shirt tosses or on-air sponsored segments are not integrated engagement. Integrated engagement is highly programmatic. The event curators have scheduled it to become part of the entertainment, competition, or event ambience. This applies whether the property is event based or mission based. Mission-based properties are those that typically operate on a year-round basis to advance a cause or provide services. They can be described as social enterprises.

Content Integration

The opportunity for content integration is one of the most valuable for a sponsor, but it should not be confused with social media or marketing content. True content integration happens when a property utilizes the assets of a sponsor in their programming. One of the oldest examples occurs when a sports event utilizes sponsored talent like a performer or host in their ceremonies. Advanced content integration features the use of a sponsor's intellectual property, such as research data, opinion papers, or consumer advice in the property's programming. This is a sensitive and nuanced mechanism, and both parties need to be vigilant when applying it for maximum effect.

Technology Integration

The longest-standing example of technology integration can be seen in auto racing, where all the competing teams may be required to use the technology (engines, tires, chassis, etc.) of a main series sponsor. In this example, the sponsor is recognized not just for their financial support, but more importantly for the performance of their technology.

There is a critical difference between technology integration and product integration: technology integration refers to the use of the sponsor's technology to create specific equipment or infrastructure for the property, but the technology is not available to the retail public in the same format. An advanced example of technology integration is found in the not-for-profit sector. In many disease-based causes, sponsors who are health care innovators are involved in the advancement of research or treatment assistance.

Product Integration

The easiest and most recognized example of product integration is the sports drink category, where companies such as Gatorade provide rehydration drinks on the sidelines of games. Other examples would be uniform, shoe, and ball sponsors in team and individual sports. Another very common use of product integration is found in extreme adventure challenges, where the product is supporting the success, or even ensuring the survival, of the participants. Product integration is a simple way for fundraisers, food events, and festivals to showcase food and beverage sponsors. It can be useful for automobile sponsors providing shuttles, clothing sponsors providing wardrobe, or furniture sponsors providing seating or decor.

Marketing Integration

The utilization of marketing integration is quite similar to the way it is used in the Activation Cycle. Such opportunities become integrated when they focus on using the sponsor's assets to promote the property rather than on the sponsor's involvement. A simple example is the use of a sponsor's digital assets to deliver advertising. Other common examples are placing program enrolment materials in a sponsor's retail location, painting messages on sponsors' trucks, or tagging television commercials with ticket purchase promos.

Partner Integration

An argument could be made that partner integration could be an activation tactic. There is definitely significant overlap, though I have identified it as a separate type of integrated engagement because it should be driven by you, the managers of the property.

Partner integration typically works in two ways. The first occurs when two or more sponsors of a property collaborate on an activation. These partners often have complementary needs. For example, one may have retail locations while the other may have media inventory. Typically, these sponsors would collaborate on contests, participant rewards, or in-store displays. In the eye of the consumer, and especially given the multiple supporters, it may appear that the sponsor is delivering these programs.

The second way partner integration usually works is when the sponsor of a property utilizes their pass-through rights, their right to share some of the benefits of partnering with a property with their business partners. This is usually an asset provided with retail sponsors who then liquidate their sponsorship investment by selling benefits to their vendors who do not keep company with the sponsor's other partners. In reverse, a brand may have the right to carry along a retail partner in their promotional activation.

BRAD SIMS

I don't know how many of you reading this attended Bono's 40th party, but Brad Sims can say he was there. Perhaps if you meet him in real life, you can ask him how that came about, and while you are at it, perhaps you should quiz him on why he has pulled a tarp on and off a baseball field over one thousand times. Focusing on Brad's career mile-stones, it should be understood what it took for him to become one of the first people in the National Basketball Association (NBA) to carry the title of Chief Revenue Officer. What you will find is man with a relentless focus on achieving results who works for all parties in a sponsorship deal: the sponsor, the property, the team, the league, and the media partners. Like a point guard ensuring every scorer on the team is happy, Brad spreads the points around while helping his team come out on top.

Tell us about your current role with the Cleveland Cavaliers and the path you took to get there.

I am the Senior Vice President, Chief Revenue Officer for the Cleveland Cavaliers and Quicken Loan Arena and all other proper-ties we own. My role is to oversee all areas of revenue generation including corporate sponsorships. I manage a team of about 100 people and have been in this role for almost five years. Previously, I worked with the NBA league office in New York, which supports NBA and NBA G-League. The G-League originally had five primary teams, one being Cleveland, which ultimately led to my current role. I have spent my entire career on the sport side, starting in minor league baseball, went to the Orioles, then Philadelphia, with the Flyers and 76ers.

What is your viewpoint on sponsorship and its importance in the marketing communications mix?

Sponsorship can play a major role. If executed properly, it can act as a major vehicle for brands. In today's world, that execution needs to be done authentically. You can no longer just sell adver-tisements like radio spots or web banners; marketers are moving away from traditional means. Sponsors' needs have changed, and they are expecting a lot more. Part of this movement is due to the change in the way people consume sports. Live sports are the only

"DVR Proof" programming that exists; this can allow for high impact sponsorship.

What was the motivation or story behind Cavs Australia Day?
The Cavs organization is always looking to do something different, and they saw growing their brand internationally as a big opportunity. Manchester United can be used as a great example or case study, as from a business standpoint, their brand has had a ton of success from all over the globe.

The Cavs did a lot of research and actually determined the Manchester market was very similar to the Cleveland market regarding size, industry, etc. The Cavs took this information, and the insight that they had multiple international players on their team that they could leverage, including two Australians (Irving and Dellavedova). I had a connection with the Property Consulting Group, who had experience working with a number of leagues in Australia. I was then introduced to someone at Sanitarium, who happened to be travelling through the U.S. During a layover we grabbed lunch, we brainstormed some ideas and determined that there was an opportunity to tell an authentic story if it was done correctly. The Cavaliers happened to have a 7:00 p.m. game the night before Australia Day. That time is actually 9:00 a.m. in Australia, so it worked perfectly.

How did you determine Sanitarium Health & Wellbeing Company and its UP&GO brand had the same values as the Cavaliers? Can you expand on the importance that aligning on values plays in the world of sponsorship?
There would not have been a deal if there was not the alignment of company values on both sides. That includes the values of the people involved. There were a lot of hurdles and challenges in getting an international deal done. A lot of companies would

have walked away from such a complicated deal, so it would not have happened if both sides were not fully onboard from the start.

Sanitarium saw the value in what the Cavs were presenting, the value of something new, and were willing to stick it out. Both sides feel the deal was done together and both sides contributed equally. As a result, both sides wanted to see it come to life, which is very important when making sponsorship deals.

How successful was the partnership with UP&GO?
Firstly, it was imperative to measure anything and everything the Cavs could. We wanted to be able to show we could generate results, and that this kind of deal could work. We were trying to use this as a test case that would show that a partner could achieve their objectives even if they are targeting fans anywhere in the world.

Targeting Australians through social media and digital was a critical piece, as was ensuring that the NBA would broadcast the game live in Australia. We thought it was very successful, given that Australia Day is their national holiday, and the biggest event every year at this time is the Australian Open. Cavs Australia Day outperformed the Australian Open and went viral, taking over the sports scene that day. It could be compared to having the Super Bowl on the 4th of July in the U.S.

Describe the power of using sponsorship to help establish your brand globally.
Using sponsorship to establish and grow your brand globally is hugely important. For the Cavs, we wanted to partner with a large brand in Australia, one that gave the Cavs credibility. The idea was to become "Australia's Team." Being able to partner

with a similar type of company in their own respective country helps. For example, Sanitarium does not have superior brand recognition in only one country. Sanitarium was a great fit for the Cavs in Australia. Finding countries where there already is a following and being genuine to the brands/people through sponsorship is important.

At the time of this interview, Brad was the Senior Vice President, Chief Revenue Officer at Cleveland Cavaliers. Prior to this, Brad worked for almost four years as the Vice President of Team Development for the NBA. Before working in the basketball industry, Brad worked for Opening Day Partners, a company that owns and operates independent baseball teams in the U.S., where he was the Vice President.

KIM MCCONNIE

Kim is a big believer in people who speak their mind and add value, but she is also not a fan of people who ramble. So, if you get an opportunity to meet Kim, have a point of view and make it succinct.

Cutting to the chase is probably a career survival technique for someone like Kim. She has risen from being a one-time pizza delivery driver to her position as the head of Sports Marketing for Pepsi. When you go from delivering pizza during the Super Bowl to orchestrating the sponsorship of the halftime show, you need to not waste energy worrying about things out of your control.

Her passion and experience come through in her work, her belief in her brands, and the unique partnerships she has forged. An avid runner, cooking enthusiast (when time permits), and admirer of Billy Jean King, Kim is not just predicting the future of sponsorship, she is contributing to it. Her picture of the future sees tomorrow's athlete as their own brand, producer, and media channel. I can only imagine how that paradigm shift will impact what sponsors want then.

What is your current role with Pepsi?

I am the Senior Director, Sports Marketing for PepsiCo U.S. This involves leading the strategy and development of sports marketing plans for PepsiCo Beverages, North America. I am involved with creating plans for some of the biggest events in the U.S., including All Star programs, Super Bowl Halftime show, etc.

What is your viewpoint on how properties should approach sponsorship?

I believe that cold calling or cold emailing is a general waste of time, especially with a brand as large as Pepsi. The best way to approach sponsorship is to network at relevant events and build these relationships. These relationships are what lead to partnerships down the road. You need to find a way to meet your prospective clients at an event. I cannot recall the last time cold calling led to a sponsorship deal. The human side of sponsorship is very important, as making it personal can help make deals happen. People will buy into ideas that they help build or create. When both sides build a deal together, it can lead to better sponsorship fulfillment, as both sides want to see the idea comes to life.

How did the NBA G-League happen? What went into this process?

We went with an organic strategy where both sides worked together. There was not any discussion of price at the time. We had a workshop to build a plan together. It was important to know cultural fit and exactly what both sides brought to the table, not just the sponsor. We went into the meeting well prepared and knowing how they could push boundaries, what they could and could not execute. This type of preparation creates a stronger deal for both sides.

What is the most important dialogue that you can have with a potential partner? How do you prepare for this?
Building sponsorship and activation ideas together is definitely the most important. This allows for engagement on both sides and helps gauge interest in whether they will get a "No" or not on a specific ask. It is important to know what you are looking for going into a deal or meeting. This will help eliminate a lot of the back and forth. Preparation in knowing exactly what you want going into a deal eliminates jumping into partnerships, and sees these deals turn into something what had not been expected. Coaching and developing your team with this approach is also very important.

What can properties do better when seeking sponsorship?
Properties can be open to building ideas together. Properties currently are not driving the process of working together. This is what brands want. Being able to show you are capable of sponsorship fulfilment and servicing can go a long way. Skip the "big proposal" and instead sit down and have a workshop together.

At the time of this interview, Kim was the Senior Director of Sports Marketing for PepsiCo in New York. Kim started off working for PepsiCo in 2004 in Thailand as the Marketing Director of Foods for Asia Pacific. Before making the move to work in New York, Kim worked in Australia for PepsiCo, this time as the Marketing Director for Beverages for Australia and New Zealand.

Chapter 6

TO SEE PROOF — DON'T BE AFRAID
OF THE TRUTH

IT SHALL SET YOU FREE

Sponsors want proof. They want proof before they partner with you that you will be a good fit, that your property is going to have a positive impact on their business, and that you are going to have a positive impact on society.

Sponsors want to sell partnering with your property to their internal stakeholders. They want to help you sell, and they do not want to get fired if your property does not perform — they want to help you do your job.

Sponsors are not asking for data, facts, insights, results, key indicators, or feedback for the good of their health or to be a nuisance. They are asking because they have been entrusted with investing the company's money wisely and generating a return. They should not have to ask. Your property should overwhelm your sponsors with facts. From the moment you first connected to explore the opportunity, through every moment that the property is live, your job is to make sure that you are a storehouse of information. The last thing in the world a property should be afraid of is the truth.

The more a property understands itself, the better the sponsor partnerships it will have. The property will better manage upfront expectations. It will be able to take better advantage of its uniqueness when selling. It will have a more confident understanding of the deliverables it can promise. There will be fewer surprises when the property is transparent. There will be greater trust between you and your sponsors.

In sponsorship, the truth is in the numbers, and the numbers are your friend.

I suspect most properties are afraid of the truth because they either do not understand their own metrics or they have not taken the time to source them. In the first instance, smaller properties may perceive that the only metric sponsors want is a mass audience. Reach is important, but mass advertising can often outreach a sponsorship. Properties do not understand that sponsors want affiliation, avidity, and access. A property may be fearful because it has not invested in the resources to understand themselves. They do not know their own data, and they fear that weak data will scare sponsors away. That is completely unacceptable.

What is more unacceptable is the property that will not invest to understand themselves, blames poor sales or low renewal rates on a whole host of other factors, but they have only themselves to blame. Even the smallest property can provide a comprehensive profile of itself. Even the smallest property can provide evaluation reports. Regardless of size, any property can commit to fulfilling their partner's needs. The truth comes in two shapes and sizes:

- The information a sponsor needs to value your property prior to partnering.
- The information a sponsor needs to evaluate your property during the partnership.

Delivering what sponsors want begins with a simple act: commitment. You need to convince your property to commit to fact-based selling, fact-based evaluation, and fact-based self-assessment. If they do, an unbelievable competitive advantage awaits, because they will be one of the few properties delivering what your sponsors want.

VALUATION

There is a joke in the sponsorship world that nobody ever got fired for recommending their company sponsor the New York Yankees, their local children's hospital, the Dallas Cowboys, a U2 Tour, or any mega property.

When a sponsor evaluates your property, they want to understand its potential to build their business and their career. If your prospect's boss has their heart set on sponsoring the local food and wine festival, and your prospect wants to partner with you, you will have a lot of proving to do.

To determine if they should partner with you, the sponsor prospect conducts a valuation. This is essentially a property analysis, part of the sponsor's due diligence to assess the potential of a partnership. Once the sponsorship has ended, the sponsor conducts an evaluation. This assesses outcomes from the partnership, such as Return on Investment or Return on Objectives.

Being subject to a valuation by a prospect should be viewed as a good thing. It means someone is interested in you, someone interested enough to invest the time and resources to understand you better. Think of how frustrated you were by all those unanswered calls and emails when soliciting partners. Rejoice when someone wants to ask you questions and understand you better. The worst-case scenario is that you get to know yourself even better and amass more data for future prospects.

No matter how difficult and invasive the process, you can make it better with the right attitude. You need to approach the valuation with your prospect in a collegial way. They are now on your side. The two of you are now co-conspirators. You are collaborating to sell your property to the rest of her organization. It is a sales dream come true: you have a champion inside the company. Your job now is to equip, educate, and excite them to sell you to leadership.

However, you do not have good, actionable information about your property, and you do not know exactly what information your prospect wants. Is it possible to ask the sponsor what information she wants? Does it make your property look unprepared if you cannot offer the answers on a platter? Will the prospect tell you what information she needs? I would hope so, but if not, there are ways around these obstacles.

- Pitch your property to other people in the same business category who are perhaps not as attractive as partners. They will ask you enough questions so that without realizing it, they are educating you about the business and your property. As you answer their questions, you will begin amassing the data your primary prospect wants.
- Ask the people your prospect is already working with or people currently working with your competitors. Pick the brains of their ad agencies, their retail customers, their other suppliers, the media who cover their category, people who have worked in the sector, etc.

Work with your prospect to understand what data they need to convince their board, boss, or bosses, or sales team. Framing your

questions to gain an understanding of what others want will provide them their desired outcomes. Every sponsor wants to get
promoted, and you are going to help them do just that with this
great partnership.

SELF-ASSESSMENT

A comprehensive and rigorous self-assessment will enable you to
feel prepared when a sponsor prospect asks for information to
conduct their valuation. Most properties do not excel in this area.
To improve, you need to become your own harshest critic. I firmly
believe your standards should always be higher than others.

As an agency leader, I believe that I should always have higher
standards than any of our clients, even our best and smartest. If
our team presents something to a client that receives high
praise, but I still feel it fell short of being perfect, it is my role to
push the team further. That extends to all leaders in my organization, right down to entry-level people and even interns. We
cannot rest on the fact that the client said it was good. It needs
to be great. If the client said it was great, it needs to be amazing.
If the client said it was amazing, I want it to be amazing and
unexpected. You should push your property in the same way.
My message is not proprietary or unique. It is a universal truth
of any business.

Look at your property's latest proposal or your standard sponsorship sales deck. Every property out there likes to boast that they
will customize their proposal for the sponsor. News flash: that
doesn't make you special. If you want to gain an edge, take a harsh
look at the information you provide prospects. If you want to boast
about customization, impress me by presenting targeted valuation
information about the sponsor's category.

We did just that for one of our consulting clients, a large amateur sports body. Together, we identified five key business categories that we felt were most likely to produce significant sponsorship income. We then dug into those categories to understand the key industry drivers, consumer personas, and business needs. That groundwork yielded the information we needed to develop five — yes five — partnership introduction decks. Each was customized to showcase the strengths of each key category as it related to that business and that business alone.

Valuation Formatting

You cannot tell me your property does not have five key categories you would like to fill or ways to advance the current state of your partnership. The format of your assessment will be a personal choice, but you will be more efficient if you lay the groundwork to produce the same types of data that your sponsors will want for evaluations. Once you have identified these metrics, you should determine how they will be filtered and enhanced for different business categories. (See below for types of metrics).

You may already have a structure that can be adopted for this exercise. If your organization has a strategic or operating plan that includes metrics, it would be advisable to define the metrics and explain why they were adopted. It will reduce the need for translation and misinterpretation in your organization. It is very likely that there will be a high correlation between these organizational metrics and your performance management systems, such as compensation and personnel reviews. Such consistency may boost motivation, an additional benefit. Basing your metrics on existing systems like those for performance management will be welcomed by the leaders who have already endorsed them.

Ultimately, your sponsors will want you to provide metrics for three important areas: performance, efficiency, and behaviour. These together should form the foundation of your valuation metrics. For a brand-driven sponsorship evaluation, a substantial amount of this data will come from your partner's sources. Obviously, the more a property can provide, the better.

Performance metrics involve general attendance, fan/follower studies, specific metrics such as sponsor intercepts or social media views, media coverage, and food & beverage revenue. Efficiency metrics encompass cost per person engaged/intercepted, time per visit, increase in consumer favourability, and earned media ROI. Behavioural metrics can be onsite purchases, test drives, offer redemption, interest and affinity studies, sales inquiries.

These metrics are going to be based on your organization's history. If you have information that allows for a justifiable forecast, you should include that as well. If your event is planning to increase its budget for headline musical talent and you have planned for an increase in ticket sales, you should share these factors. You need to showcase your property as dynamically and honestly as possible.

You might be thinking that some of these sample metrics cannot apply to a prospective sponsor given they have not been involved with the property to date. That is somewhat true, but it is not the obstacle you may imagine it to be. You can use averages, numbers, and case studies to demonstrate your ability to deliver for your sponsors, as well as for specific business categories. Your prospect will covet similar or like category data. This is your opportunity to customize at a strategic level, which is significantly more powerful than customization at a tactical or activation level.

INVALUABLE NUMBERS

The biggest problem with the information in most sponsorship proposals lies in the way we were taught to count. Most proposals focus on what I call headline data — the number of people that attended, the amount of money that was raised, the number of souvenirs that were sold, and the age of the attendees.

Those numbers communicate nothing of value; at worst, they mask the truth. Sponsorship is not about reach, impressions, attendance or raw numbers, but about emotional impact, behaviour change, and engagement. Sponsorship metrics must reflect this to unlock the secrets to the value within your property.

You can easily establish an exciting competitive advantage by providing your sponsorship prospects with compelling, insightful data. Your prospects should be pleasantly surprised after being accustomed to being underwhelmed by the usual generic information, and your credibility will be established at the outset. This will benefit you substantially throughout the sales and negotiation processes.

What will your sponsor want to know? Let's begin with attendance. For this example, let us assume many proposals tell the reader that 52% of your attendees are female, and remarkably, the other 48% are male, or that daily attendance is 17,000 people. Who cares? I do not. Your sponsors will not. Your prospects do not.

Your sponsors want to know everything about the people who attend your event. Sponsors and prospects want to know about your fans, your participants, your volunteers. They want to understand what motivates them, what excites them, and what inspires them. They want to understand how they shop, make decisions, and socialize. Most importantly, they want to understand how they interact with your property. Some of this information can be secured through surveys, some of it through observation, some of it through emerging technologies, and some of it can be gleaned from stakeholders' interviews.

You should review marketplace information. I will guarantee you that somewhere in the world, somebody has written a research report about a property or event just like yours. There are probably multiple reports; utilize these to provide industry benchmarks and market standards. They do not have to be exact or perfect, but it is essential that you read, summarize, and translate them for your sponsors.

You should strive to get data from similar and even competing properties. Start by initiating the most powerful process in business. Ask your competitors, ask properties like yours, ask properties like yours. What do they have they are willing to share, and what do they want in return? Maybe asking your competitors is a bad idea but asking other sources about them is not. Similar properties in other markets may be interested in collaborating with you to get better data. Perhaps you pool resources to hire one research company or consultants who can conduct the analysis cost effectively by tapping into multiple properties. While not all the data will be specific to you, the research will still be invaluable, as its findings will sufficiently demonstrate the value of your property based on the category of the property.

I must admit that I am a bit of a hypocrite when it comes to research. I am a firm believer in utilizing data and facts when it comes to valuing (calculating/determining the value of) sponsorship opportunities and evaluating results. However, I am violently opposed to using research to measure the potential of an idea or concept. This is an important distinction. Data are really useful in helping you understand which cause, partnership, and property appeals to different population segments, but I do not believe relying on data is the best way to test ideas.

I am equally adamant about measurement. Every single program, event, game, fundraiser or activation needs to be measured. There is no excuse for not doing so, but I believe creativity, insight, experience, and instinct for an idea should not be overruled by a focus group or an online test.

As sponsorship marketing evolves, you will find strategic and enlightened partners who want to collaborate and build partnerships with you more and more. Those partners will be willing to work with you on the valuation. They have access to resources, budgets, and tools to conduct a thorough valuation of your property. Cooperate by allowing them to access your databases, stakeholders, and partners. In exchange, secure the right to utilize the data for any purpose you require, including pursuing additional sponsors and reporting to your current partners.

VALUE OF EQUITY

One of your hardest tasks will be quantifying and substantiating the value of your equity. How much should a company pay to use your logo? How much should you charge them to be affiliated with you? What is the rights fee when no other benefits are provided?

I cannot overstate the importance of these questions. For me it is the crux of everything I believe in sponsorship. There is nothing more important than the power of the property and its ability to impact the sponsor's brand; it is more important than reach and audiences. I believe that sponsorship must be about the power to move people. If it cannot inspire, motivate, or resonate with a certain cohort, I really do not care about a property that can reach many people.

Malls sell sponsorships. Lots of them, but that is their use of the word, not mine. I think they sell consumer intercepts. Any sponsorship proposal for a mall promotes its reach, traffic, expenditures, demographics, etc., which is all fantastic, but a mall does not have equity — unless it is very unique — that a brand seeks to borrow. Do not believe me? Try placing the mall's logo on a poster that reads "XYZ is the Official Sponsor of the Local Mall." Hopefully that seems as ridiculous to you as it does to me. If the mall occupied a rare and majestic niche, then yes, it could have some equity.

Compare that to a property that has very little traffic, very little exposure, very little reach, but incredible importance in society. Perhaps it is an organization that is very close to curing a major disease. My poster proclaiming its pride to be supporting the "Close to a Cure Lab" would have untold impact. This sponsorship would be all about the "Borrowing of Equity". This property would definitely move consumers and definitely possesses significant equity.

Which of your metrics provides a valuation of your equity? How do you propose and justify a number to a prospect? This is the hardest part of sponsorship valuation.

Some experts advise classifying assets according to tangible and intangible; they support their premise by saying that the latter relate to equity, but it is probably not as simple as drawing a dividing line. Others compare the requested fees of various properties in similar market situations. Many properties have created arbitrary amounts based on a combination of what they hope to get and what the market has demonstrated it will pay. This is not necessarily wrong — any business or asset is as valuable as the amount you can sell it for.

A small property is never going to have the resources to conduct a sophisticated brand valuation. We use various models at our agency to provide estimates and validate them, but that take times and money.

The simplest approach may be to think of your data as a proxy for your equity. The longer your property has existed, the more prestige it has built. The more funds per person it raises, the more loyalty it commands. The more media it generates, the more impact it has. These numbers contribute to the equity of a property, though they do not help my argument for lesser known vital properties, which is where you need to talk with consumers in your community. You need to understand what they think local companies should support. You need to understand their emotional drivers. You need to get acquainted with the expectations they have for businesses.

By conducting research or asking a local partner to undertake researching, you can build a case for the strength of your equity compared to other properties. You can utilize this research in your pitches and presentations, incorporate the findings throughout your marketing and communications calendar, and educate local donors and supporters.

There is no exact science for measuring equity. There are many models that purport to do so — some of them are quite good — but at this stage, you do not need to overcomplicate the issue. Focus on demonstrating the value and impact of your property to ensure that you secure the support you deserve.

EVALUATION

Not every property provides results, even some of the biggest, most expensive properties.

This does not mean that these properties are not providing reports to their brands. Most are, but are they providing proof? Are they providing tangible results? The best approach is this: do not be afraid of the truth. Sponsors want to see two types of proof: the first is societal proof, the second is business proof.

Societal proof is a demonstration that their investment in your organization allowed you to further your mission. This ties directly back to the origins of sponsorship where the principle reason for a company to help an organization is that the activity could not occur without their support. To respond, your organization should demonstrate the impact it had on society. I know this sounds basic, but shockingly, it is not done. When it is done, it is not in terms of impact. A music festival that may talk about how many attendees it had, but what about the impact on the artists, local music programs, the economy, or the access it provided to economically challenged groups? The sponsor wants to be able to tell her boss that because of your investment, athletes won medals, students were able to try new experiments, and citizens were able to see works of art they would otherwise never have encountered.

With business proof, your sponsor wants to know if the sponsorship worked. Again, this would seem apparent to any newcomer to the industry, but I have sat in on enough major property reporting presentations and read enough reports to know that their main emotion is guilt. Sponsorship reporting is not practiced with the rigour or integrity that it deserves. Did the sponsorship achieve the goals the partners agreed on at the outset? Did brand consideration increase? Did new channels of distribution open up? Did we reach our target market through the program? Whatever you do, do not be afraid of the truth.

The most important consideration in providing proof is to develop your plan for doing so before the sponsorship program begins. You must develop your proof plan before the relationship goes live. Figuring out what you want to evaluate midway through the program or after will result in an incomplete deliverable — it will ensure you will have unhappy partners. By following the same process with all sponsorship relationships, you will build a well-oiled machine that, over time, will make reporting easier, if not enjoyable. Addressing societal and business proof together will lead you to create a capture plan, the process for collecting the results, and to provide the details and data your sponsor will be thrilled to put to use.

The five imperatives of a proof plan are to: identify key metrics, determine report timing, enlist data sources, establish collection timing, and build a report structure. Remember that timing is critical, so the plan needs to be developed before the sponsorship or related activations go live. The approach does not prevent changes or adjustments from being made, but the creation of the proof plan in advance is the single most critical factor in your attempts to be successful.

1. Identify Key Metrics

I love the expression "What gets measured gets done." It directly feeds into the importance of establishing your measurements up front before the partnership goes live. Did the team win? Did the charity reach their goals? How many new accounts did the salesperson open?

In sponsorship, a tremendous amount of measures can be tracked and reported. Doing so in a professional and objective manner will provide the property with the information it needs to grow their partnerships, achieve high renewal rates, and secure new partners, and a partnership needs to be measured by more than gut feel. While I recognize that data will never completely eliminate the need for opinion, they are still a powerful elixir. Therefore, set your measurements up front.

My approach is to create different categories of measurement: performance, efficiency, and behaviour. You may want more or fewer, but I am one of those people that is stuck, I mean really stuck, on the Power of 3. It is a good idea to create categories of metrics to manage your reporting efforts; accordingly, well-defined categories will help you focus your analysis and audit activities. You could consider categorizing your metrics based on your deliverables, your sponsor's deliverables, partner deliverables, etc. Another way to categorize your metrics could be onsite versus offsite or use the Activation Cycle and build five categories that align perfectly with the five phases.

Categories are like dresser drawers. If you want to find your t-shirts, you are best to look in the t-shirt drawer. Evaluation can be intimidating and confusing, and it can tax your resources. However, if you build a structured approach, the benefits of categorization will be immense. I guarantee it.

Performance metrics

What we mean by performance metrics may seem obvious, and it should be. How many people visited the sponsor's booth or social feeds? How many people attended? How many people watched? How much revenue was generated? How much money was raised? However, we know from the valuation discussion that your sponsors want to go deeper. What performance metrics will convince your sponsor that your property is the best fit for them for a long,

long time? The answer should be obvious: sponsors want to dive deep into your business results.

A deep dive is required because sponsors want more than just gobs of generic information. They want performance metrics that clearly indicate the interactions of their target stakeholders with your property. Record attendance matters to you, but it does not mean much to a sponsor if none of their target consumers visited the property. Amazing social media results may excite your communications team, but they may be less meaningful to your sponsor who was solely focused on interactions with their content. Onsite sales are meaningless if they did not bear sales for the sponsor's just launched new product.

The importance of performance metrics lies in the fact that every data point represents something your organization should want to know. Hopefully, it is information you were already collecting, though I suspect not. Now that your sponsors see the value, you will benefit from its collection and analysis. If you are a property that is having problems convincing your board to invest in measurement tools and business tracking, you now have a dream ally: your sponsors. Make it clear to your board, or your boss, that your partners absolutely expect to have this information, and the only smart choice is to accept their demands. I hope you do not have to resort to such internal coercion, but it is 1,000% true.

Coveted performance metrics

- Attendee profile based on number of years attending an event
- Donor profile based on number of charities supported
- Season ticket holders versus single-game purchasers
- Visitors' attendance at individual onsite attractions
- Total unique visitors/attendees/fans to the event/team/venue compared to total visitors

- Daily/hourly attendance. Can be correlated to weather. Map attendance by temperature
- Average time spent onsite per visitor
- Number of people who donated per participant. Number of people each participant approached for fundraising

Efficiency metrics

What was the cost per person engaged? The value of efficiency metrics can be hotly debated if all parties are not clear on their meaning and use. If your property is an event and your sponsor has a booth, does your sponsor want high traffic but quick visits, or intense, longer visits which would mean less traffic? Are you measuring efficiency by cost per intercept or by cost per consumer engagement minute? Which is more important to your sponsor?

Efficiency metrics measure the cost per unit, click or action of any key metric you and the sponsor have identified. These metrics allow for a better comparative analysis of the different properties a sponsor may support. They allow you to compare results across your sponsor portfolio, and efficiency metrics create a common denominator for evaluating the sponsorship's performance in different markets, during different days or seasons, or on different dimensions of the sponsorship. These metrics are excellent inputs for your sponsor to consider when adjusting their engagement and activation plans.

Coveted efficiency metrics

- Cost per dollar raised
- Fixed cost (i.e. the sponsorship fee) per consumer engagement minute
- Total cost (fee plus activation costs) per consumer engagement minute
- Unaided/aided awareness of the sponsorship

- Cost per new followers secured
- Cost per earned media mention/reach achieved

Behavioural metrics

Behavioural metrics provide the greatest risk and the greatest reward for your property. The risk must be managed upfront, when establishing the sponsorship. Did people transact with our organization as a result of the partnership? If you feel your property can generate leads for your sponsor, but you do not feel comfortable committing to sales, you need to be clear about which results should be used in the evaluation. Your event may be able to drive people to the car dealership (a lead), but will you be accountable if the car does not appeal to those prospects? Sales are the ultimate behavioural metric, but you can generate a long list of other actions to measure.

Coveted behavioural metrics

- Increase in consumers who express interest in trying or buying
- Improvement in sponsor favourability scores
- Increased awareness and comprehension of the sponsor
- Number of offer (coupon, incentive, prize) redemptions
- Number of purchases made one week/four weeks/three months following the program
- Number of new social followers by channel
- Number of content downloads
- Number of demos registered
- Number of test drives taken
- Number of trial subscriptions placed
- Opt-ins for further communications

The objective of this exercise is not to have an endless list of metrics you cannot possibly remember; a comprehensive list that identifies and tracks actionable information will serve you much better. Metrics are like antiques — they get better over time. The more intervals for collecting and comparing data, the better the information becomes. In essence, the last round of metrics gathering increases the usefulness of all previous collections.

Another benefit of establishing these metrics up front before the partnership is formalized, or at least the activation is built, is that it initiates a constant dialogue about resource allocation. If improving relevance is the most important measure for a sponsor, the partners should constantly focus their energies on actions that will move that specific needle. An even bigger benefit is that clearly defined metrics will tell you and your entire organization what your sponsors deem to be their priorities.

2. Determine Report Timing

In a sponsorship marketing relationship, it is sound strategy to plan for more reporting windows than less. The first driver in establishing a reporting calendar is the duration of the partnership. It is the extent to which it is live for the public — is it live, almost live, or just warming up? The next driver is the frequency of the activity. If the partnership is a one-off event, you will have less frequent reporting than a global music tour or a season-long sport. However, if your one-off event has multiple weeks of registration or fundraising or ticket sales campaigns leading up to it, you should be reporting frequently during those periods.

Another component of report timing is the depth of reporting. If you think of the final report as the most complete submission, it is easy to understand that more frequent reports will scale appropriately, with a mid-term report being one-third to one-half of a final report, and flash or weekly reports closer to snapshots.

More reporting is better than less. An easy comparison would be something akin to a performance review. It is well recognized that providing employees with feedback only once a year generally leads to negative outcomes, which is why sponsors should be given the opportunity to provide feedback on an ongoing basis. Given that this is a partnership, it is wiser to be engaged with your sponsors along the way. If something is going better than expected, how do you jointly take more advantage of that circumstance? If things are going poorly, how do you enlist your sponsor to be an ally in solving the problem? At the very least, you are giving them the opportunity to develop contingency plans, manage expectations with internal stakeholders, and time to embrace the situation rather than being shocked. Remember, sponsorship marketing is a people business.

Report timing

This is a process that is best served by agreeing with your partners early on about when exactly reports will be delivered and how detailed they will be. This is not a function of how much time or resources you have, but a function of the duration of your partnership. You need to consider any needs your sponsor may have, such as their internal reporting windows or frequency of status meetings.

A large, one-off event that occurs on a single day may appear to lend itself to one comprehensive final report delivered within a few weeks of the event, or definitely no later than two months after if research or business results needed to be tallied. This makes sense until you assess the Activation Cycle for the property. Even one-day events can have long lead-up times for registration, training, recruitment, fundraising, or marketing. Think of major concerts in your community with go-on-sale dates over a year out, or an annual fundraising run that launches recruitment 180 days out. Perhaps it is a weekend sporting event that travels around the country.

The property is live from the date that event is awarded to the community. Therefore, for events such as this one, you need to consider periodic reports, which update the sponsors on key performance metrics for your property and more specifically, on their activation, if it has launched. For an event that involves registration and fundraising, I would advise weekly or perhaps bi-weekly reports. You could lengthen this to a monthly report for an event with less activity during the Anticipation Phase. Depending on the activation intensity, you may want to track a few efficiency metrics at this point.

If your property is a tour or a sport with a defined season, you then need to incorporate mid-term reports along with your weekly or bi-weekly reports. The mid-term reports are going to be deeper and provide more of an opportunity to assess if any corrective action needs to be taken. The mid-term report will provide a look at efficiency metrics and potentially some behavioural metrics. Your regular/weekly performance metrics reports will provide more details, as you will have other comparative metrics to utilize. Therefore, you may be providing more frequent analysis of both past and upcoming events in the calendar.

Properties that do not have events or milestones should develop a reporting schedule with their sponsor. It should meet the sponsor's expectations and be realistic and be capable of being fulfilled. Regardless of how long the property remains live, I would suggest a monthly report. If your partners do not want monthly reports, you could suggest quarterly reports for a program that runs for an entire year. Such a property should include all three types of metrics in their period reports. Regardless of how long the property remains live, it must deliver a comprehensive, final report that goes far beyond sharing a photo album or highlight reel.

Report depth

The worst report ever written is the report written for the sake of writing a report. I do not ask my team to provide reports to me just because I want to sit behind a desk and look important. I like regular reports because I believe it is the best way for people to self-manage and because being provided regular information allows me to understand how best I can help them succeed. Unfortunately, the use of reports as a cover your ass (CYA) strategy in the business world has jaded many people.

You should approach your strategy around reporting depth with enthusiasm. What information can you provide to your sponsor that will help them, their staff, and their agency partners? What information can you collect that will help your colleagues do their jobs better? If you start from here, you will confidently build a plan of what should be shared when.

Final reports should be written with the knowledge that this is your first renewal discussion or one for long-term partnerships. It is your first attempt to extend the contract. Reports should include every-thing, especially a critical assessment of future activities.

Mid-term reports should focus on flagging issues, good or bad. The reports provide your last chance to course correct before it is too late. On the positive side, they provide an opportunity to recom-mend increased investment that will help the partnership succeed.

Flash/Weekly reports highlight what your sponsor believes are the three most important elements of the partnership. If they have not been able to experience the partnership in person yet, bring it to life for them through testimonials/imagery/content from stake-holders. There is no more accurate label for this report than "a one-pager."

Report delivery

Bad news is always better delivered in person. The delivery of good news is much more fun in person.

A client once scolded me because my agency's lead on their business always wanted to do conference calls, even though they were only a 15-minute drive away. They were right, and I was shocked, because I have always preached that discussing business face-to-face is best. Email, conference calls, and live meeting technologies obviously help expedite the flow of information, but they do nothing for relationship building. Nothing.

Guess what I am going to recommend for your report delivery?

You should try to deliver bad news in person, unless it is an emergency situation, in which case you need to immediately activate your crisis management protocol. Bad news is always best explained live. When establishing your reporting frequency with your sponsor, you should establish how you will deliver the report. If you are providing a weekly report, it is not always going to be realistic to have a live meeting, but you should offer that option to your sponsor, or at minimum, schedule a call or video conference. It is more important that you establish a structure and delivery date. I love live meetings, but not at the expense of providing vital information a sponsor may need. For example, if they have a weekly one-to-one with their boss or sales manager on Wednesdays, they probably want your weekly report by Monday at noon, so they have time to confirm the information and incorporate the data into their regular report.

Let's work backwards

Final reports must be delivered live, even if it means getting on planes or trains. If your senior officials cannot make it, do not have them call in. Suggest they do a one-to-one with senior sponsor executives later. Mid-Term Reports must be delivered live as well.

Weekly/Monthly/Periodic reports should be delivered on time. Perhaps you deliver some of them live, but all of them must be accompanied by an offer for some sort of discussion. A weekly, standing 30-minute call noted in your calendars can be a true blessing. It will not be long before meeting regularly becomes muscle memory. It will be painless, strong, and a joyful exercise.

This is a people business. I am always surprised when getting a property to provide results feels like pulling teeth. I firmly believe that being asked a question demonstrates that the other party is interested and vested in your relationship. There is no question that some queries can be scary, intimidating, or simply confusing, but when it comes to reporting, you should both welcome questions and strive to get ahead of them. In other words, answer your sponsor's questions before they are asked. The more opportunities you have to share information and results with your partners, the better. The more interest and inquisitiveness they exhibit, the better off you will all be.

3. Enlist Data Sources

Your data gatherers will prove to be one of the most important partners in your sponsorship ecosystem. A sophisticated capture plan involves many participants who need to be briefed and whose activities need to coordinate throughout. The number and types of participants will be driven by the scale of the partnership. While it is important to establish what you want up front, it is important to determine who is involved and what role each participant will play.

Participants' sources can include some of the property's internal departments, including communications, ticket sales, fundraising, programming, and volunteer management. From the sponsor's side, participants should include marketing communications, market research, public relations, brand teams, sales, and social media specialists. Costs and resources required increase when external service providers are included, but their contribution to ROI cannot be underestimated.

Clients will often have their own external research suppliers whose expertise should be loaned to a smaller property, if the sponsor will allow. Larger properties need research vendors, social media analytics, validated crowd measurement, media measurement, and economic impact expertise. Each of these experts will help influence the overall capture plan.

Third party research

I believe unequivocally in working with third-party research partners who can provide unbiased measurement. They are essential for demonstrating to your sponsors that you are open to a candid assessment of your partnership programs.

Many small properties will use budget as an excuse for not partnering with a research provider. This is just an excuse; there is a partner for every size and shape of property but convincing your leadership team of the value of research will likely be a challenge. Your sponsors can be a great ally in getting leadership on your side. Get them to vote with their wallets and their voices. Besides sharing sponsors' requests for data with your bosses, you could ask them to pay an incremental fee to cover the cost of a research tool. If your sponsors refuse, perhaps you could ask them to share their research with you.

There are large and small research practitioners in every corner of the market. In some cases, you may need to find a start-up or a firm that has not worked in your market. Freelance consultants can often pull a team together to tackle your needs. Ask your marketing agency or radio partner if they have research resources. I am not a big fan of outsourcing research to a group of students, but many college professors operate consultancies that can tackle work; if they are managing students, then that is more than acceptable.

If I were running a not-for-profit, I would pitch my research company on being a sponsor or partial sponsor, with some sort of built-in model for them to generate revenue from add-ons or by working directly with your partners.

Agency partners

You need to use your agency and media partners to support your evaluation. Each agency, supplier or media partner you work with has their own tools and approaches for collecting data. There is a bias, of course, in their involvement, as they want their work or campaign to succeed, but there is a safeguard in that they too need to be credible, as many of your sponsors may be their clients or advertisers.

Sit with your PR, digital, social, and licensing partners to understand what information they have. Each of them should be tasked with educating your team on their expertise. You will find that a farmer's field of data is now available to you. Push to understand how you can ensure that your partners can provide both general and specific data to your key sponsors. A sponsor is impressed by your earned media impressions, but they are more interested in their mentions and brand attribution.

You should ask your agencies to include managing the research partner in their scope of work. Perhaps your agency has better volume rates with them due to other work they refer. There is a potential cost saving, given they will have more experience in managing research partners, which will reduce your time commitment.

Do not forget that local entrepreneurs often run work with your local agency and media partners. Perhaps the idea of a new division specializing in research will intrigue them; you can be their shiny first client.

Online tools

There are so many online tools appearing daily that I am loathe to suggest any single one for fear that it may have disappeared by the time you read this. Luckily, you are doing business in an era where new tools appear daily, especially those for understanding people, but you can say that *unfortunately* for you, you are doing business in an era where new tools appear daily, especially those for understanding people. You need to decide which of these new ways works for you and focus on them.

There are online tools for conducting surveys, following people's shopping patterns, mapping their whereabouts, targeting their behaviour, and measuring their emotions, activities, and interests. Task number one is to find the tool that provides the insights you want, given your metrics plan, then you need to validate its utility for current users and litmus test its credibility with your sponsors. This last point is vital. If your sponsor doesn't trust the tool, they won't trust the information. Ultimately, they will stop trusting you.

Another approach to using online tools is to leverage those that were not designed for research. This can be really helpful when you are informing the valuation stage. You can learn a lot about your audience reach and impact by working with online media salespeople to profile your attendees for a potential ad campaign.

Informing the publisher about your target attendee group will yield a trove of data about who they are and what they like. In simple terms, when you are buying online ads, ask for robust info about your audience. For evaluation purposes, you can use this info to map changes over time.

The last and most important online tool is the one you own. Every property should have some sort of digital "ticket" that all your stakeholders must use to register to be included in your program. This may be an app or a microsite, or one activated by a wearable. It could be a temporary badge, wristband, or ID. It does not matter. You need to create a digital footprint and fingerprints of all your stakeholders. These tools will allow you to map, track, probe, and monitor their every interaction with your property. You can create virtual wallets, passports, training regimes, event instructions, property content, all of which are inputs into an unbelievable information treasure chest.

Onsite tools

Online tools with onsite tools are two sides of the same coin. The technology that now allows you to register/sell/recruit participants and follow their journey through intelligent tickets and sophisticated online registration handlers is ground-breaking.

Onsite at your event, the deployment of beacons, hot spots, check-ins, video tracking, electronic gating, and location based tracking all provide you with amazing feedback for your partners. They will inform internal discussions about what works and what does not at your property. There is nothing stopping you from jumping on these tools immediately. The upfront cost is immediately neutralized by increased funds raised, souvenirs sold, and beverages consumed. You can charge your participants for the convenience of having a virtual wallet. Your sponsors can invest as a sure-fire way to draw attention and trigger engagement with their activation programs. There is virtually nothing stopping you.

Coalition approach

I made the comment earlier that not enlisting research partners due to their cost is just an excuse. You probably reacted by thinking, "Try telling that to my boss!" Point taken. Every idea in this section is designed to help you get over the cost hump.

If you have some money for research, but not enough to get the attention of a research firm, find partners with whom you can pool funds. Those partners could be similar events in nearby markets or competitive properties in your market. This latter idea may seem heretical, but it can work very well with the right guidelines in place. By pooling your funds, you are sharing the upfront costs and burden of launching the research. You may not get the depth of custom data you had hoped for, but the opportunity to compare your property to others is well worth the effort.

You may end up in a situation where no data are shared, but your resource commitment alone is enough for the research company to take you on. In that case, perhaps you can agree that your data can be compared generically to other like properties with whom your researcher is working. Sponsors love benchmarks, especially when they are shopping for properties. Make it easier for them to compare yours to others.

There is an art to ensuring that you have the right partners for data collection. Their credibility in the marketplace will have a direct impact on your credibility. They must be experts in sponsorship and experientially focused to benefit you and your partners, and they need to buy into measuring what matters. The investment in research and data gathering is well worth the reduction in sponsor churn, increase in rights fees, and the activation spend that will result from the partners' enhanced understanding of the impact.

4. Establish Collection Timing

Your collection timing is linked directly to your report timing, though not exclusively; it should identify if and when you want to be sourcing results prior to forming the partnership, during the partnership period, or after. You need to determine how often you will collect this information. At every performance, game, or event? On a weekly, monthly, or annual basis? One and done? The frequency of collection timing is driven by the duration of the live partnership window. How long is the partnership active in the eyes of the public? The longer the duration, the more frequent the activities, the more collection windows that are required.

You need to build a collection timetable with each of your data sources and secure alignment with your sponsor. Your research specialists will provide expert input regarding the appropriate windows for talking to stakeholders. In a similar manner, your agency partners will know best when to utilize their tools to gather marketing channel results. The best action you can take is to create and publish a calendar that is clear to all partners and shows when they need to gather and share their information.

While your collection timetable is somewhat driven by your reporting calendar, the two are not identical. You need to determine what information is being collected for the more frequent flash or periodic reports and identify what is being utilized in the mid-term or final reports. You need to be clear about which report you are seeking to populate to ensure clarity in planning collection timing.

The most important lesson in collection timing is to repeat my mantra, "Plan ahead." Leaving out windows for collecting data is like cramming for a final exam. You may pass or you may even do well, but your depth of understanding will not compare to one gained by the person who kept up with their studies and assignments throughout the course period.

5. Build Report Structure

Benjamin Franklin once apologized for the length of a letter, saying "I have already made this paper too long, for which I must crave pardon, not having now time to make it shorter." Great reports are not necessarily the longest documents in the world. They are the documents that provide the right information in the most insightful and succinct manner possible. However, displaying brevity while maintaining accuracy requires time and hard work.

Imagine that your property runs over several weeks with multiple milestones or events. This could be a music tour, a ballet season, a baseball season, a weekly farmer's market, or any other property with multiple hits of programming. You have committed to providing your sponsors with weekly reports, two mid-term reports, and a final report. Your sponsor is pleased but asks you to describe the different reports so they understand what they are receiving. You should not only document what will be included in the reports, but how they will be delivered to the sponsor. Remember that your sponsor contact is invariably not the final audience for this information, so understanding the delivery format is critical — especially if they want to extract content when building their own internal reports. Understanding your sponsor's reporting requirements will determine the report's format.

If your sponsor has requirements that go beyond the use of common software, you should not be shy about asking to be compensated for additional reporting work. It would be unfair for your sponsor to require everything to be delivered in a file format that a graphic design studio would prepare.

Weekly/Periodic report structure

In reality, it is the opposite, with your client often requesting a low-tech version of your submissions. The weekly/periodic report will focus on performance metrics. A key on efficiency metrics may be included or easy to access behavioural metrics, but these reports could easily be labeled performance updates. A weekly report can be one page and considered perfect. Focus on the five key results from the most recent event, media push, or activity. You should compare those results to your period goals. You could provide a running or year-to-date tally of these results.

The results should be the bulk of the report, and it should feature some pictures or samples of media postings or other images. Visuals cannot be understated, especially if the activity was not witnessed by the sponsor. Think carefully about the photos you select so they show the story specific to that event. It may be a location shot, a particularly striking group of fans, or a perspective on the other programs nearby, but it should reinforce the narrative you are helping to shape.

The report should include concise commentary on extraordinary circumstances, such as inclement weather, increased competition, or a local holiday that may have presented a challenge or an opportunity. This information should be tracked for the mid-term and final reports, which will use the data to analyze the performance by event.

Mid-term report structure

A mid-term report provides a window for identifying emerging opportunities or to course-correct any issues within the partnership.

Focus on a thorough analysis of the performance metrics with a quick dive into efficiency metrics. This report, which will be several pages long, needs to give you and your partners a clear picture of what is and is not working. You need to ensure that the report contains only critical data with no generic or meaningless information.

An easy way to make this report accessible is to take a chronological approach. A week-by-week review of what has been achieved, leading to a summary of results, followed by a look at all upcoming events will make for a logical reading journey. The report would have the following sections:

- **Report Purpose:** Why it was developed and what actions should be considered after its review.
- **Weekly Review:** A summary, week by week, of the results achieved to date.
- **Mid-Term Results:** A tally of the results achieved, introduction of critical efficiency metrics.
- **Look Forward:** A preview of the schedule, stakeholder engagements, and leading performance indicators.
- **Action Step:** A list of any major action steps that should be taken to maximize the partnership for the balance of the schedule.

The mid-term report's utility is dependent on its timing and its content. The structure of the report is very much an action plan, not a storybook.

Final report structure

The final report needs to be both comprehensive and comprehendible. Structure it to reflect your various categories of metrics so that it is consistent with the entire data collection and reporting steps taken to date. Add some analysis, evaluation, and recommendations for the future to ensure that it's a robust report.

I have written a few hundred final reports, ranging from sponsorships of a few thousand dollars to multimillion dollar, multinational programs. There is no right way to write a final report, but there are plenty of wrong ways. One of the biggest errors a report writer can make is to speak to the audience as if they were not involved in the project. Most of the final report recipients were probably deeply involved, or they were in a position of authority behind the scenes. Therefore, when a report writer drafts their document, they invariably take the summer vacation approach. Lots of pictures, a boatload of quips, and no substance. Here is a simple structure to follow:

- **Executive Summary:** Tell the audience what they are going to hear and the document's purpose.
- **Performance Metrics:** Final measures, with a significant analysis outlining how the numbers were achieved.
- **Efficiency Metrics:** Final results, with clear comparison between objectives and other benchmarks.
- **Behavioural Metrics:** Year-to-date business results achieved for the sponsor with analysis.
- **What Worked:** What went well.
- **What Didn't Work:** What did not go so well.
- **What We Should Stop Doing:** Clear recommendations on partnership components should be deleted.
- **What Should We Start Doing:** Strategic recommendations for the next phase of the partnership.
- **Conclusion:** Mirror your executive summary, but now populate it with highlights.
- **Appendix:** You need to ensure the report is reasonable in length, so build a section to store everything that is not essential, but that may need to be referenced.

Companions for your choices about structure are your choices about delivery. Your weekly reports are most likely to be electronically delivered to your sponsors. Nevertheless, you should attempt to connect with them live as many times as is feasible. Whether that is in person or on some sort of call will be driven by their significance, geography, and access.

Both of your mid-term and final reports should be delivered in person. If geography is a barrier, then an online, live presentation should be arranged. Technology is a valuable delivery tool for all levels of reporting, but it should not be a crutch to avoid an in-person discussion.

YOERI GEERITS

You can see the benefit of holding a Masters degree in Finance when working in the sponsorship business if you have ever sat down with Yoeri. The Belgium native's early stint in the derivatives industry fostered a career long affinity for helping clients achieve their commercial objectives utilizing sport and entertainment strategies, but to call this globetrotting Flemish native a numbers geek would be inappropriate. He has worked in Asia, Europe, and North America on properties ranging from F1 to Government to Museums with incomparable passion, an approach he takes to his personal life whether it be climbing a mountain in the Rockies or completing a cycling challenge in the mountains of San Francisco.

What is your perspective on sponsorship and its importance within the marketing mix?
It is very important, and the importance is only going to increase. There is more competition for consumers, and sponsorship allows for that connection with your audience. It is great to connect with sports fan. It forces consumers to see brand integration, which is powerful.

How can brands leverage sponsorship to build a strategy?
The biggest thing is the brand's lack of understanding of what they want to achieve and how they want to achieve these things. Basically, not understanding their objectives and their own audience. They may have a decent idea, but they should have a much

better understanding of target consumers, including their habits, how they consume media, etc. Brands need to understand all these things to fully leverage sponsorship. Another part is understanding sponsorship platforms or rights holder's platforms that allow the brand to speak to their audience. Once they understand, they should spend USD$50K with another USD$50K dedicated to activating that sponsorship. This could allow brands to see the value in sponsorship. At IMG, for Formula 1 Racing we made sure to have three budgets, one for sponsorship fees, one for activation, and another for media, which allows for total integration, and of course, there was a separate budget for measurement.

How does sponsorship change globally, from one country to another?
When at IMG, we did research into the ten biggest platforms in the world for sports. Very few platforms can connect with fans globally. Formula 1 doesn't work well in Canada for example. We looked at cycling, soccer, etc. Found that there is no platform that worked in every continent. Soccer is very complicated with all the different federations, leagues, platforms, etc. Even comparing Canada to the U.S.A., they are very different. In Canada, all major cities have a couple pro teams, and there are two big broadcasters.

Every country has a unique footprint based on sports they have, industry, etc. Canada, for example, is natural resource driven, which impacts how brands activate. In Calgary, brands don't want to activate, they just want to be associated with the Calgary Flames, because it's "cool." Canada is lagging on the activation piece, there is not enough innovation, but lots of room for growth compared to Europe where there is a ton of competition already.

Comparing Canada again, there are 20 or 21 pro teams across, whereas in Australia, which is considered a similar country to Canada, there are 95 professional teams. Much more competition in Australia for sponsorship, they need to activate more and more. Maple Leaf Sport Entertainment in Canada does not have to activate if they do not want to, brands still come.

What never changes about sponsorship?
The fact that it buys an emotional connection to fans whether it is through sports, entertainment, etc. and this is a very unique attribute to sponsorship.

How important is measurement when it comes to sponsorship? Do you think measurement is given enough attention?
Measurement is critical in sponsorship, if you cannot measure then you cannot account for it. You are not able to define why or why it is not working without measurement. I find it baffling that there is a lack of measurement and market research. Brands, rights holders, etc. all over think measurement. IMG has been successful because they did the work, put the measurement plan in place for Formula 1. They measured before, mid, and at the end of the season to determine if perceptions, etc. were changing.

Measurement is only going to increase in importance because there is becoming more accountability. Scotiabank for example, fighting for more dollars, trying to tap into traditional media dollars. More competition for marketing dollars, therefore more importance to prove results through measurement and research. More competition for rights holders (properties), which creates more need to prove results, therefore, better measurement.

What is the future of sponsorship?
In an ideal world, sponsorship will increase in importance, but it is difficult to say what will be around in five years with the rapid increase in technology. Sponsorship will become more sophisticated and fragmented. What needs to happen is how sponsorships

are managed by brands, sponsorship needs to be integrated and leveraged by all communication groups.

On the property side, they will need to become more sophisticated with their offerings. I only see positive things happening with sponsorship in the future. The brands are still underestimating. This has to do with the old school model. An example would be how media budgets are owned by media agencies, so they have an vested interest in keeping the budget in traditional platforms. This will take time to change but believe it will.

Any final remarks?
In Canada specifically, there is a dominance of traditional sports (NHL, MLB, NBA). There is so much great content available (cycling events, winter sports). All these sponsorship platforms are out there with great, high quality content. I am hoping that streams and technology allows the smaller properties to become more visible. Networks are lazy and only care about products they have vested interest in, like Rogers and showcasing baseball.

In Belgium, there is an obligation from the national broadcaster to provide high quality content for all relevant sports (this goes way beyond soccer and cycling). They focus on what is relevant for those less visible sports. This creates additional sponsorship opportunities and platforms.

At the time of this interview, Yoeri was the Senior Vice President of Neilson Sports Canada and the Senior Vice President at Repucom Canada. Yoeri started off his career working for ING, where over 13 years in several different countries, he held positions such as Program Manager of ING Globerunners and Head of Sponsorship. After leaving ING, he founded 3 different companies; XTERRA, YAVYA and ThreesixtyInc before eventually finding himself in his current positions.

ZAILEEN JANMOHAMED

Zaileen has been a client-side marketer, an agency consultant, and a property rights holder. She's a woman who has seen and observed from each and every vantage point the sponsorship marketing industry has to offer. Along the way, she has made her mark in the enthusiastic and dogged pursuit of understanding a fundamental truth, and what she believes that you and every organization should understand is simple: does your sponsorship work for your business?

To succeed in her quest, she has endlessly invested in building models and tools that support the objective valuation, evaluation, and justification of sponsorship programs. Her passion for this topic is only exceeded by her capability. Her Evaluation Model is proprietary to her: she is sharing it with you to be learnt, used, borrowed, tweaked, adapted, adopted, and embraced. In short, she has done this for you.

How crucial is it to understand the business objectives/values of a given property before investing sponsorship dollars?
The time of sponsorship for the sake of sponsorship is behind us. Early on in my career, I remember circumstances by which a property was able to sell a sponsorship just because the person at the brand "liked soccer," or "was a former college soccer player," or "has kids who play soccer." Now, more than 10 years later, and as I support brands in their sponsorship decisions, all my work goes into determining, analyzing, and communicating how a particular partnership can help drive business objectives. At the end of the day, chances are good that the ultimate business objective will be bottom-line growth and increased revenue. This can be achieved via sponsorship through increased sales, increased awareness, or an increase in brand perception. The tough but very necessary piece of sponsorship optimization is linking your sponsorship objectives to these underlying business objectives.

How important is internal justification when making sponsorship decisions?

The sponsorship market today calls for elevated investment levels that, most often, will require senior level approvals. Internal alignment is not only necessary as it relates to approvals and sign-off. If you are leading the sponsorship charge for your company, senior alignment internally allows for buy-in, enhanced activation and transparency across the organization. This alignment facilitates support through the negotiation and asset activation stages of a sponsorship lifecycle. Within many industries and companies, marketing, and therefore sponsorship, budgets are decreasing and/or under tremendous scrutiny. Why invest in a sponsorship when you can invest in a new product offering or a direct marketing effort tied to conversion? In order to openly educate and justify why a particular sponsorship works, internal alignment across a quantifiable and objective-based business case is essential.

Do you think measurement is given enough attention when it comes to sponsorship decisions?

Not yet, but it is getting better and changing exponentially every day. I do believe most companies now understand that measurement is important, if not required, when the large expenditures that sponsorship requires are made. However, sponsorships are inherently tough to measure. There are many (perceived) intangible benefits, and it can be very difficult at times to tie these benefits and results to business growth and revenue.

How can businesses improve on measurement practices?

This will sound funny, but the first thing is to not be afraid of the question. Because this is tough to do; it is easy to walk or shy away from really getting into the metrics that link sponsorship to business objectives. The second thing is the other extreme — do not list too many metrics for success. If you try to build a sponsorship that is focused on too many metrics, you will not be successful. Finally, business objectives frequently change as businesses and industries adapt to changing consumer needs and advances in technology. Because of this, measurement practices and metrics should change. I try to revisit sponsorship metrics at least annually to ensure that they are still linked to changing business objectives.

In addition to measurement practices, what else do businesses need to consider when evaluating sponsorship?
A few things. If your company has a sponsorship portfolio greater than one, it is just as important to look at the entire portfolio as it is to look at a particular property to measure success. You need both a portfolio and a property scorecard or analysis to really understand if sponsorships are working for your business.

Start with your consumer in mind when evaluating a potential sponsorship property. Who are you trying to target? What are their passion points? Where do they spend their time? Get as many insights on your target as possible and then determine what type of sponsorship (if any) will allow you to align and engage with that target.

Once you determine the right property, it becomes as important to determine how much the sponsorship is worth and the value of the assets to you and your company. The sponsorship industry is like the housing market; prices are set based on supply and demand. Do your homework to figure out what the "going market rate" is.

At the time of this interview, Zaileen was the Senior Vice President of Client Services at GMR Marketing. Prior to this position, Zaileen worked for Visa as the Senior Director of Global Brands, Product and Sponsorship Marketing and the Head of Olympic Management. Prior to her time at Visa, Zaileen was at the same place she is today, GMR Marketing, but as an Account Director.

Chapter 7

TO GET PROMOTED ... NOT FIRED

GETTING YOUR SPONSOR PROMOTED

Your job is to help your sponsor do their job better.

That is the sum total of your job description. It is the sole focus of this chapter, although the title may have led you to believe otherwise. What follows is not a discussion about your efforts to promote and publicize your sponsors' brands, although that is one objective of sponsorship marketing. The focus of this chapter is sponsor servicing, how you work with the individuals who represent the companies that sponsor your property.

The heart and soul of sponsorship servicing is relationship building.

You will earn favour if you help the person at the desk across from you get promoted, regardless of your business. In the sponsorship industry, your impact on the potential outcome of a partnership makes that statement even more relevant. Given the nature of the sponsorship marketing industry and the amount of judgment involved, your partners will be concerned whether you and your property can deliver for them. This would not necessarily apply to a large, well-established property, although they should be given the higher investment required. The higher the spend, the higher the risk, but dealing with small, midsize, or new properties causes significant concern and uncertainty. The first concern of your sponsor contact is: will I get fired for spending my company's money with you?

Your sponsor contacts are besieged by concerns from every possible angle. Did you realize this? Have you ever thought about the relationship from their point of view? Do you take time to sympathize?

What could possibly be concerning them, you ask? Don't they have a cushy job with a big budget, dedicated staff, and even a stable of agencies to do the work they don't want to handle? Looks pretty good from your side of the desk, doesn't it? Look again.

Is your property going to be the strategic fit you as you pitched it? What guarantees do they have you will succeed? How does your contact know you will attract the volunteers, ticket buyers, participants, fundraisers, fans, media attention, musical talent, or performing artists you have promised?

The property may end up being a strong fit for their brand, but will it generate the business results that management seeks? Will consumers or customers engage with the activation program? What happens if the partnership doesn't drive business results even if the property is successful?

Your sponsor contact is also concerned about you. Are you trustworthy, reliable, and ethical? Are you and the property easy to work with? Will you be timely and thorough when communicating? Will you act on behalf of my company to provide us with added value? Will you ensure that all my customers, VIPs, and partners are treated professionally? Your property could be the perfect fit and deliver outstanding results, but if your sponsor's best customer did not get their ticket delivery, that success will be overshadowed.

Here I recommend a servicing protocol for you as a property representative, selling and managing sponsorships to a company's sponsorship manager. Everything you do as a property representative should be done with the mindset that you are helping your sponsor — it is the foundation on which I have built my career, no matter my role, and while I may be biased, it should be your foundation.

OVERPAID FOR OVER-DELIVERING

Early in my career, I received an assignment from a large festival. My task was to help the festival determine how to deal with industry convergence in a certain category. As technology was evolving, this category was becoming cluttered, and the defining lines of competition were becoming less clear. My client, the festival property, wanted to ensure they secured the right types of category partners in the future. They hired me to assess the landscape, wanted to ensure they maximized revenue and activation, and that they did not box themselves into a corner while the sector continued to evolve. When I was hired, we negotiated a base fee for the consulting, and a success fee if we exceeded the revenue target for the category.

Off I went, meeting with as many companies in the industry as possible and drafting as best I could a picture of the future. Before too long, my client and I were excited about the opportunity a revised category structure could provide, as well as the potential partners who appeared very interested. Given our confidence, we decided to reverse engineer the selling process and not issue sales proposals to the interested partners. Instead, we decided that they would pitch us. We drafted a robust outline of the opportunity informed by my research, along with a clear picture of the evolution of the festival and how it would impact the category. We then issued the package, along with submission guidelines, in the form of a Request for Proposal (RFP).

This approach received a wide variety of responses. We were merging three categories, and one of the largest incumbents was displeased with us — they had been displeased all along. One of their issues was that I, the consultant, was from out of town. The incumbent and the festival were in the same city. However, none of their competitors were, so they were angry and concerned. They argued that they were not being given fair right to renew, although their clause had been fully exercised. In this case, I was helping my client do their job and became the scapegoat for the incumbent's complaints, shielding my client from comments made by their board. The smaller incumbents and the prospects that wanted the property welcomed the RFP process. There were a few reasons for this. First, I believed most sponsors thought they could write a better proposal document than the property, so this gave them the chance to do so. Secondly, it demonstrated openness in finding a new partner, as the prospects thought the aforementioned incumbent had a hometown advantage. Thirdly, it allowed the prospects to negotiate on the true value they saw in the property, instead of getting into a high-low bidding game.

The grump incumbent bid the most, but in rights fees only. Two other companies blew them away in terms of activation commitment, and more importantly, with their overall enthusiasm for working with the festival property. This includes one of the prospect's intentions to position the festival as their flagship property for the region. Naturally, this message had a major impact on the property's leadership. Without much finessing around the offers, we ultimately selected one of the prospects and rejected the incumbent's offer. The latter, of course, lost their temper again and issued all sorts of complaints, most of which were directed at me. Such is the life of the consultant.

When I completed my assignment, I travelled to the festival's offices for a final debrief and to pick up my cheque. I felt a bit awkward heading into this meeting — the final offer we accepted, while not quite as large as the incumbent's, was very substantial. So substantial that my success fee was larger than it could have been in my wildest dreams. This was at a very early time in the history of my young company, and while I coveted the money, I felt a bit conflicted about my windfall. Remember, it was based entirely on exceeding a projection for the category, one with which we were all aligned, but we had beaten the target by 250%!

Should I accept the payment or suggest a reduced amount?

The minute my client's boss appeared to deliver my cheque, I demurred slightly and mumbled about it being excessive. He stopped me in my tracks, as if he had expected my rebuttal. He told me that my work was going to ensure his entire team achieved their target for the year and had thus triggered their bonus, a convincing point. My involvement had allowed them to deflect the emotional criticism of the local incumbent, which was vital for my client and his board. They were going to live in the community with the incumbent, and their lives might intersect, so I became the blame magnet. Finally, he advised me that the work I had done was informing other similar exercises they were undertaking.

The story ends on a good note. I got my clients promoted. I helped them achieve their business targets. I protected them from grief. In the end and in their eyes, the money they paid me was well spent.

IT'S A PEOPLE BUSINESS

Most people in business want to do a good job. Most of them want to advance their careers. Most people have ambitions. A person working for a sponsorship property needs to understand that after all the due diligence, fact finding, and valuation, the person on the sponsor side is going to look at you and your organization and ask a simple question. Will I get fired if I work with you? If we want it to be more positive, will I get promoted if I work with you?

Remember, this is a people business, and the person across the desk from you is not a building, a brick, a brand, or a business. They are human. Read the name on the email. Listen to the voice on the phone. Look into the eyes looking into yours.

This person is your sponsor, your partner, and your champion. It is your job to help them do their job better. It is the job of your entire organization and everybody involved, paid or unpaid, to help them and all their associates improve at their jobs. It is a central underpinning of all services businesses, and it is fundamentally crucial to succeeding in sponsorship marketing, I suspect a great deal more than most people realize.

It is too late to turn your attention to building a strong relationship when renewal time rolls around. It needs to be established at the outset. When servicing and fulfillment issues arise, they introduce unnecessary pain and tension into the relationship. Servicing issues often cloud the entire dynamic of your partnership, cracking the lens through which all aspects of the sponsorship become viewed with disdain. It is an old truism in the advertising agency world that clients often fire agencies and attribute the dismissal to creative differences, but a closer examination of the situation often reveals that the root cause of friction was client servicing.

The What Sponsors' Want (WSW) model encourages properties to make getting promoted a core part of their value proposition. The model should paint a robust picture of how working together will look like right from the initial meeting. The property will identify the process to be deployed, the resources that will be allocated, and the tools that will be provided. This is the picture that will be painted in the proposal phase. It will be your secret weapon, your competitive advantage, and your ultimate tiebreaker when you are compared to other properties. It will help you sell more business. If you keep your end of the bargain, it will help you sell more renewals, but it cannot just be you; success requires that your organization must live it as well.

If they do not, you are going to hear it from your sponsors. I hear it, see it, and work in it every day. You would be surprised at what happens when common sense should have eliminated such trials, especially when you consider how hard it is to secure a sponsor. Perhaps it is like dating: all the effort is put into the chase, but the relationship gets ignored.

How else to explain some of the actions to which properties subject their sponsors? Would you subject someone you love to these things? Probably not, but perhaps you just haven't noticed the rift forming. Perhaps you work in an environment where the revenue pressure is overwhelming. Regardless, these things are happening.

It is the big stuff and the small stuff. Recently, I was giving the new president of one of our clients a tour through the activation zone being staged by a large sports property they sponsor. The president had been briefed on the sponsor and the amount of traffic projected during their sales pitch. Needless to say, the numbers were light, and candidly, I was trying to hide my anxiety. I was pissed off at the property for not doing the marketing job they had promised. The new president made it clear he knew by asking me what methodology the property used to conduct traffic counts. I was convinced he was going to challenge them when it came time to evaluate the relationship.

Too many properties overstate their numbers. It is a game that is played right from the outset. Inflated marketing plans and media numbers. Unsubstantiated followers. Loose attendance numbers, especially for un-ticketed events; suspect consumer engagement. I understand the need to sell and the challenge of competing with other properties, but when the slippery slope of loose numbers starts at the beginning, you will not be able to stop yourself or the downslide.

Too many properties do not deliver what they promise. We recently spent a significant amount of a client's money on an insert for a publication. Research, creative development, writing, design, photography, and more. We consumed client budget, agency time, and our client's time. Everyone felt great about the work and the final approved product. Even the property. Unfortunately, they did not bother to advise us that they had decided not to proceed with the publication. We were informed that they had cancelled the initiative only after we had continuously harassed them over what we thought were missed publication dates. How is that possible? How do you allow your partners to waste their resources? Perhaps it was disorganization on their part, potentially an honest mistake. More likely fear, knowing we would be upset. Hopefully it was not a total lack of respect, though it is hard not to go there given the circumstances.

Some properties have an amazing ability to minimalize their obligations to a partner, especially in the coveted area of exclusivity. I have seen charity partners add new programming to their events, such as a VIP dinner the week of their major fundraising event and sell entitlement to the former to a company that directly competes with the lead sponsor of the latter. Simply put, the fundraising weekend is titled by the "Blue Bank", and the charity partners with the "Red Bank" on the dinner. To make matters worse, this charity did not seek the approval of their existing partner, nor did they even bother to inform them. How did their partner uncover they had been betrayed? When they received a competitively branded invitation to buy a table for the event.

In another similar but less egregious example, we worked with an ethnic festival on a local sponsorship for an automotive client. The festivals were part of a national network of festivals, and at the last minute they sold a national deal to one of our competitors. We had done our due diligence previously to ensure the category had not been sold, but we had not been flagged on this 11th-hour change. Once again, my client and our agency discovered the conflict when we saw the invitation. The invitations this time were sent to our client's regional dealers, to be passed along to their best customers. The good news is that these were for a complementary and exclusive event. The bad news is that the national competitor had purchased the rights to all these events and their branding was prominent on the materials. Thankfully, the local festival understood our dilemma and helped us reproduce generic invitations. The better news was that none of my client's dealers had used the original materials.

Neither of these examples is meant to portray the property as being malicious. People get busy. Many properties don't have adequate resources. Often, they staff critical positions with junior people who do not have the expertise or savvy to understand what will constitute an issue or concern in the eyes of their sponsor. We often see this in marketing initiatives.

I am not sure why, but many properties have a significant issue understanding the marketing dynamics of their sponsors. To me it would be as simple as asking. I have often seen our clients sit back and exhibit major angst when they discover that their properties have developed a marketing or public relations plan without their input. Imagine your sponsor contact's frustration when they must inform their boss that a major property partner is doing a social campaign or a customer outreach in the next week, and that you only just found out about it. It makes your sponsor rep look incompetent, not on top of their work, or us out of the loop. I am going to assume this is not how you intended to portray them, but that is what happened.

Most properties have far less marketing reach, resources, or savvy than their sponsors. While this may not be true for the top 1% of properties, it is bang on for the core 99%. In addition to capability, your sponsor has a desire and strong will to be engaged, as their involvement will only benefit the partnership and related engagement programs, but it does not seem to happen. I remember doing a strategy audit for a large cycling event and interviewing their contact at their title sponsor. She was beside herself over the issue of social media. It was a big priority for her brand, and she wanted to leverage her channels to promote the event and her company's entitlement. Yet two years in a row, the property unveiled its own social plan with no time for input or collaboration with sponsor. They executed an online media buy without input. The sponsor was certain her company's rates — due to buying power — would have allowed the property to deploy an even broader campaign. It was beyond her to understand why the property behaved in this way, despite assurances after the first instance that it would be corrected.

Marketing, media, and communications can be a messy sponsor-property dynamic, as each wants to build their own following, brand, traffic counts, and loyalty. As data, purchase behaviour, and insights become more significant inputs to marketing, these conflicts will only amplify. The information will become more valuable. The insights more useful. The opportunities more actionable.

STOP SELLING, START HELPING

In order to get your client promoted, you need to stop selling and start helping. You need to move from a transactional relationship to a consultative relationship. The sponsor should begin to view you as a trusted advisor and true partner. A source of information and support for business issues beyond the pages of the sponsorship agreement. Think of the fundamental shift this will create in your approach and that of your organizations. The best sponsorship properties have impenetrable relationships with their contacts. That should be a tantalizing prospect for you.

In any personal or professional situation, the best way to help someone is to understand their pain. If you do not know their pain, you do not know the person. Do you know your sponsor's pain points? Do you know your sponsor? I often ask properties who attend workshops I conduct how much they know about their sponsors. I will repeatedly remind you that I am referring to the person, not the business. Think of them like a client.

The word "pain" is a catchall for a person's hot buttons, triggers, drivers, peeves, and aspirations all rolled into one complicated, messy ball scientifically known as a human being. If you do not like the word "pain", that is okay too. It is more important that you embrace the notion of getting to know your client on an entirely new level. One of my earliest mentors wisely advised me that the best way to solve a difficult client was to get on a plane. He was so right. Travelling shows the true person, and spending time on an intense level, in a very small space, is the most enduring way to get know somebody. I know it is not feasible to travel with all your sponsors but imagine how great it would be if you could connect with one a year.

Whether it is travelling together, a long lunch, going for a hike, or just seeing each other on a regular basis, you should seek to learn as much as you can about your sponsor. Do you know how they are evaluated in their company? What sort of performance evaluations are conducted? Do you understand how they earn bonuses, or what it takes to earn a promotion? Do you understand how the company makes money, how decisions get made, and what the dynamics of the internal relationships are like?

I can tell you that in the single biggest business loss of my career, I failed to understand all of this and more. The situation was one where we started a sponsorship program for a large company with one group of people, only to see a new team get hired who would ultimately have control over sponsorship. This team was led by a smart and ambitious individual who intimidated me. There was also some friction between the group who originally hired me and his new group.

In the end, I lost the business, and then spent years sulking as I saw it grow into one of the largest sponsorship accounts in Canada, but

I have no one to blame but myself. I suspect that if I had spent time to understand the new power brokers, especially the gentlemen on top, and understood what they were trying to achieve, what makes them tick, and how they wanted to approach things, I would have fared much better. Instead, I was probably perceived as a perfectionist and a person who was only interested in the dollars from the business, as opposed to getting them promoted.

Hopefully, you can avoid the calamity that befell me by keeping the human aspect of the relationship in mind. I didn't follow my own advice. Shame on me. I cannot say it was my only screw up in my career, but I can say with confidence it was my worst.

HANDBOOK FOR SUCCESS

I want to share with you some thoughts on how to make this sermon of mine more actionable. It is all very well to pontificate about transitioning from being focused on sales to a loftier platform, as a trusted helper. Attend any industry conference or read any industry blog and you will practically choke on the propaganda. The easy part is to talk about it. The good news is that it really is not that hard to act upon. At least in my opinion.

I hope I am being consistent in sharing with you my ideas on certain topics as a means to spurring the development of your own ideas. You can adopt any of mine that you wish, but they are mere suggestions and by no means perfect. Success for me would see you embrace the spirit of and philosophy I have tried to share and create your own approaches that will help you fulfill your sponsor's wants.

The protocols you develop will be a competitive advantage when talking to new sponsors, and an even stronger benefit when dealing with your current partners. Over time, they will so strongly impact your renewal rates that your prospecting efforts will be less intensive and will help you educate the people in your organization about your corporate founders' expectations. To be successful, you should consider creating processes in the following areas.

Relationship Framework

I believe the first partnership to form is the hardest. The shift in the dynamic from the courting phase to the marriage phase is akin to seeing someone cry for the first time. You step back and realize, "Hey, there is a real person over there." Organizations are like people; each of them has their own way of doing things. The most important aspect of helping your sponsors to get promoted is to discover how their organization operates. Who needs to be involved in what decisions? What is important to different people? Where does the real power lie? From that understanding you can develop a relationship framework for working with your partners and create a harmonious path to success. Being meticulous and developing a relationship framework, often called an account plan for all your major partners, may seem laborious, but the long-term benefits will be substantial. The most basic goal of the plan should be to clarify the approval process. Who is the authority that binds the sponsor? Is it your contact, or their boss, or their agency?

There are probably different approval leads for different elements of the relationship, even when your sponsor maintains that everything goes through them. Even in a small company, the person approving an online video is probably not the same individual authorizing a day off for employees to volunteer at your event site. Like government, you need to understand how machinery works in your sponsor's bureaucracy. It will help you determine the composition and timing of requests that you make. It will help you understand when to pressure your sponsor contact and when to back off, what tools you need to provide, and it will help you explain to your own team why certain things are happening or not happening with your sponsors.

When developing the relationship framework, you should help your sponsor understand the inner workings of your organization. Illuminate the chain of command and approval loci you must navigate internally to service the partnership. This education will help your sponsor better understand why certain initiatives can be implemented and others may face tough scrutiny. If all of this sounds like over-communicating, that is exactly what it is. The framework provides clarity around how the two organizations will interact during the partnership. The risk of not sharing these insights is that it leads people to make assumptions. Unfortunately, people almost always assume the worst.

Fulfillment Plans

I suspect the concept of planning has generated more clichés than one-word warrants, but I have always loved the expression "plan the work, work the plan." I might add "process makes perfect," because really, a plan is a formalization, clarification, and written articulation of your processes. A plan communicates to its readers what will happen, when it will happen, where it will happen, and who will make it happen. I think it is important to add "Why." That added context is such a powerful tool in communication. I often find when I forget the why, everything else I discuss is lost. Without the context of purpose, the listener is not sure how my words are benefitting them, and they tune out. This is surprising given that one of my earliest clients was a tough as nails former engineer who had been transferred into marketing. She was scary smart, and just scary at times, and brought her engineering perspective to every single one of our meetings. No matter how clearly I presented concepts or ideas, she would not let me finish until I answered when, where, why, what, and how. It did not take long for me to reinvent my presentation style and lead with the why.

That is what your sponsors want to know, a clear and specific roadmap of how the partnership assets will be created and deployed. They want a fulfillment plan. This plan should be the document they can socialize throughout their organization to inform everyone who needs or wants to know. The plan should provide not just a schedule of events, but a marketing calendar, a planning calendar, and approvals calendar. The plan should include all the other elements shared in this chapter, including the communication protocol, support tools, meeting schedules, and reporting plan. Building the fulfillment plan should be initiated and completed by you, but you should involve your sponsor contact as part of establishing the relationship framework, at least for your major partners. For smaller partners, you should create a standardized template that is populated with their specific assets. You do not need to customize the plan for lower level investments, but everyone who is categorized as a sponsor should receive a plan. To be explicitly clear, I do not consider a company donating water for a run a sponsor, unless we are talking about a donation value nearing or exceeding six figures. A really useful fulfillment plan will monitor and be updated throughout the contract term. Think of it as a checklist with each deliverable waiting to be crossed off as they are fulfilled. It may sound simple, but I could point to a bunch of six figure partnerships in our office right now where our team has to chase the property to provide us with the deliverables they have committed to our clients or their sponsors.

Communications Protocol

I am a tremendously big fan of standing meetings. Maybe it is my coaching background or perhaps it is due to my wandering mind, but either way I find that a consistent weekly, bi-weekly, monthly, or annual meeting is a powerful tool. The same for report timing; a robust communication protocol should clarify the timing, purpose, and participants in meetings, reports, and communications. This protocol should be categorized to differentiate between ongoing activities, planning activities, and abnormal activities such as a crisis or a world event.

Let us start with the simplest of decisions. In your framework, you have identified who approves collateral materials or activation budgets. Ensure that your communication protocol reflects this approval process, so it is clear to all exactly who needs to be included in an approval chain. In your discussions to confirm tools, you will plan what types of reports should be provided and when. Your communication protocol should establish to whom those reports are distributed and how. It needs to be clarified who receives a live briefing of the report and who receives a digital version.

It may sound overly prescriptive, but meeting protocols need to be established. Some meetings are operational or status-oriented, featuring ongoing updates to keep all parties informed. Others are focus meetings to discuss a specific topic. Still others can be reporting meetings. Defining the principles of purpose, timing, agenda, attendees, and outcomes will produce better meetings and reduce inefficiencies. When implementing these protocols, remember that they are guidelines.

Circumstances and situations will always throw plans somewhat off track, but if a firm communications protocol backbone has been established, the disruption will be significantly less. For that reason, I cannot stress enough that you should have contingency plans in your protocols. There should be a contingency plan for when opportunity arises, such as an extended playoff run in sports, and a contingency plan when a crisis arises, such as an injury to a volunteer at a fundraising event. I have had people protest, arrested, assaulted, and die at my events. We were able to survive some pretty horrible circumstances only because we had planned for each situation. I have had events and activations where more people than planned showed up, musical stars performed impromptu, or there was unexpected media coverage. The proactive discussions held by all parties may not have predicted what opportunity would arise, but they did prepare everyone on how to think and react when it did.

Support Tools

When I first started activating major sponsorships, few documents were more impressive than the binder that multinational sports organizations would publish for their sponsors. These binders included approval forms for creative, logo/brand design guidelines, premium ordering forms, critical ticket ordering dates, contact lists, and on. Today, your organization has all the technology it needs to create a digital binder or toolbox that can make your sponsor's life easy. These tools will reduce your resource requirements and should reduce the time spent on administration.

Support tools enable the partnership to be administered as efficiently as possible. To develop your potential list of tools, your team should workshop every inquiry you receive from your sponsors and assess what can be affordably addressed. If you think of the end product like a toolbox or chapter, you will see the beauty in categorizing the tools. So will your sponsors when they access the end product. As you workshop the questions, think about how deep you can go on resources. For something as seemingly simple as event signage, you should do more than just share dimensions. Provide best creative examples for readability, identify the time of year or day the signage would be used, and if lighting is a factor. Similarly, with the weather, wind, etc. Provide shipping and packaging advice. Provide your sponsors with three preferred vendors who know your property well and will produce excellent materials for your sponsors.

It may seem that I am dwelling on a simple detail, but when your sponsor's boss arrives on site and their branding is poorly presented, you will not have fulfilled your professional mission to get them promoted. That is before you include the negative impact of low participant recall on your partnership's performance. From signage to reports to media clips, you need to create tools that allow your sponsors to easily utilize every component of the partnership. Remember that many companies have the money to sponsor your property, but that the bigger issue is the time and commitment of their people.

Added Value

As you embrace the shift from seller to helper, you are really becoming a consultant. This means that you should position yourself as not just the representative for your property, but as an expert in your industry who will be able to advise your sponsor in a consultative manner on topics such as trends, best practices, government policy, and key stakeholders. Your relationship with your sponsor will transform from seller-buyer to consultant-client.

There are numerous initiatives that you can embrace to make this come to life. One that we found exceptionally useful was the curation of sector news to form a weekly or monthly newsletter that can be distributed across multiple stakeholders. This can be easily executed by having a coordinator or intern scan for articles related to your industry that will be shared as a list of links and previews.

The newsletter will serve to educate your sponsor even further on the power of what your organization does without appearing self-serving. It will make briefing and ideation much stronger. The next level would see you start generating your own content through position papers, blogs, or other content pieces. The focus of these elements is educational, and definitely never meant to be another form of direct sales. While this will take more time and effort, it will position you as a thought leader in the sector.

Notice how I have not suggested that added value is more tickets or something of that sort? You are meant to be delivering benefits that are not explicitly stated in the contract that both delight the sponsor and enhance your position as a helper.

Another deep and invaluable reservoir is your direct intellectual property. Whether that is research you have conducted, expertise within your organization, or access to information, your sponsors would benefit from sharing it. While many properties offer sponsors' research as it relates to their visibility with the property or superficial data regarding future purchase behaviour, there is an opportunity to go much deeper. As you are conducting your research — whether it is first or third party — work with your sponsors to understand what learnings they may be seeking from your stakeholders, and whether they are related to the partnership or a broader context.

DIARMAID MURPHY

Diarmaid's first proper job was as an Account Executive in a PR company, Slattery PR, now Teneo PSG. She has been one of the lucky ones that has always worked in sport and on great brands like Guinness, Heineken, FedEx, Adidas and many more.

Named after a captured couple in mythical romantic Irish history, Diarmaid & Grainne, she coaches her kid's sports teams in Gaelic Football (Ireland's most popular sport) and rugby. She plays tennis, and golf is probably her favourite thing to do.

Tell us about your role with GAA & Croke Park.
My title is the Commercial and Sponsorship Manager, GAA & Croke Park.

I run the commercial programme of sponsors, stadium suppliers and licensing with the GAA in Croke Park. Croke Park is the 3rd biggest stadium in Europe, while the GAA has two main sports, Hurling and Gaelic Football.

If you want branding in Croke Park, you go through GAA, and I help manage these partnerships, both senior sponsors (six total), and technical sponsors (technology, statistics, score) such as Hawkeye technology (scoring and timing technology).

As a reference for us Canadians, what is "hurling" and "Gaelic football," and how big of a sport are they in Ireland?
Ireland is one of few countries where football (soccer) and hurling are two of the biggest sports. The Gaelic Games have always existed but in 1884, games were given rules, tags, etc. Hurling is very much a part of Irish Culture; it is more widely played compared to most countries. There is a museum in Croke Park that is linked to the Irish education system.

Hurling is a very skillful game played at breakneck speed, the only protection is a helmet, which was only made mandatory in 2010. Gaelic football is the largest team sport in Ireland.

What makes the Gaelic Games unique is that in August/September, they could sell out the Stadium two times over for Hurling and four times over for Gaelic Football, but the athletes do not get paid. They train, compete on the weekend and return to their jobs. The main reasoning behind no pay is tradition and the community links of the GAA; it is a community-based association. The league does not allow transfers, so there is no transfer market. Players are required to play in the county they were born. The current process works so there has been no need to change. Amateur state of the game although this is sometimes debated but does not look like it will change anytime soon.

Over 80% of GAA surplus goes back into the clubs and counties around the country. This is a major reason it is so attractive to sponsors, because they know exactly where their money is going. It really represents community.

How important is sponsorship revenue for sport properties?
Very, very important, as in double digits in terms of a percentage of GAA revenue. The importance of the sponsorship program goes above and beyond the money and fees invested. It also brings a tremendous degree of marketing expertise and brand know-how of the associations and games. In an age of ever-growing social media, sponsors also add many more promotional tentacles then what would be achievable by the association on its own. This is almost as important as the money invested.

Sponsorship brings awareness through digital. AIB Bank is a good example or case study. The bank was looking to rehabilitate their image following one of the countries deepest recessions and they have chosen the GAA as a platform to do that.

They brought a hockey player from Canada to play hurling and then brought Irish player (Lee Chin) to Canada to play hockey. The idea is to capture "What if Gretzky played hurling?" The kind of chat you would have in a bar with friends.

The financial side is obviously important, but mostly it is the promotional value sponsorship can bring. When you get a world-famous sponsoring brand, there is a brand equity transfer that not only goes from brand to sponsor but also sponsor to brand.

What advice do you have for a property seeking to acquire partners?
First bit of advice, the property should have a very clear view of itself. When you are selling a sponsorship, you are selling an audience. Need to know who and what your audience is and how are they consuming what you are selling. How do they consume your sport? All demographic (gender, region, etc.) info. Same with participants.

Secondly, if you do not have a structure of how and what you are selling, then you need figure this out. Is it a multi-sponsor model? Is it a title sponsor model? 100 sponsors?

When you are sitting in front of potential sponsors, they will want to know this — are they one of one, or one of 100 other sponsors? Always have the ability to be flexible to adjust to the situation. You need to be willing to compromise on your structure.

Lastly, what do you stand for, what is the vision and values of your organization? The higher up you go in a company, they will be more interested in vision, direction what you stand for, compared to tickets in the rights package. Have a clear vision.

Once partners have been acquired, how do you work to retain them?
It is a consultative sell, not a transactional sell — it is not buying a can of Coca-Cola. Sponsorship is consultative in nature. It could take anywhere from three months to three years to get a sponsor

on board. You need to be very patient. Just because you are not right for the brand that is in front of you today, does not mean that the brand will not be back in front of you in a different scenario. Having your head around the concept of selling is important.

At a minimum, deliver the schedule of rights that were agreed upon. If you can win the trust of that brand, you are better positioned to marry two brands and strike upon creativity that could benefit both. You need to know your sponsor intimately, but this could take a long time.

What is success for your partner?

As a company, part of the Return on Investment (ROI) for the sponsor is what they have set for themselves. You should know if you have a better chance of delivering on it. When you are retaining partners, you need an agency-type mindset: stay close to your clients, keep them informed with all relevant updates, not just bad news, and good news as well. For example, structural changes can have profound effect on deliverables for a sponsor. If you have a marketing director, and you know they have five objectives, you could deliver upon one of those objectives, and they will want to renew you. Important to have that agency mindset. What is going on, what is going to happen before it happens? Every day is a good day to renew. You do not want to be picking up the phone two years into a three-year deal.

Would you agree that sponsorship is very much a people business? Explain.

Agree with that entirely, although I do not like the cliché of "a people business." It is absolutely about relationships; the foundation stone of relationships is communication.

When focusing on communication, it is always important to consider what form of communication should be used. There are times when email is the right or wrong form, and sometimes face-to-face meeting is required. For me, it is very important to establish lines of communication with sponsors and partners in relation to their wider business. Ultimately, always trying to add value to the relationship. Finding out a sponsor's objectives, then delivering on those objectives.

Yes, it is relationship business; it is about being able to manage multiple relationships. You are balancing and managing multiple relationships which can quickly lead to politics. You must manage this very carefully.

What advice do you have for your younger self?
Don't jump to judgement, spend some more time listening and learning, and read more, much more.

Any mentorship advice?
Yes, find yourself two mentors early, and remember that people love to be asked for their advice. Try to make your passion into your job.

At the time of this interview, Diarmaid was the Commercial and Sponsorship Manager at GAA & Croke Park in Ireland. Prior to this Diarmaid worked for 13 years for the European Rugby Cup as both the Communications Manager and the Commercial Manager. Diarmaid started off working as Account Manager for Slattery Communications Limited for four years.

PATRICK O'BRIEN

How did Patrick get from tiny Westville, Nova Scotia (population 3,500) to work at the Greatest Outdoor Show on Earth? My answer would be passion, but not just the mainstream enthusiastic to a fault form of passion. No, Patrick possesses a unique blend of passion for his job, his team, and his sponsors. Patrick is authentic. It oozes out of his every pore and into everything he does.

It is rare to find him without his trademark cowboy hat on his head and even more odd to ever see him without a smile on his face. He is dedicated to the industry, working with the Sponsorship Marketing Council of Canada, attending numerous industry events, and routinely speaking when asked. He is as comfortable leading a team as he is in being part of a team.

Describe your role and responsibilities with the Calgary Stampede.
As the Sponsorship Manager of the Calgary Stampede, my role and responsibilities include but are not limited to securing corporate sponsorship using promotional and marketing endeavours that will deliver measurable benefits to sponsors.

- Development and implementation of strategies that drive increased sponsorship revenue for the Stampede's diverse programming.
- Negotiate and execute sponsorship agreements between Calgary Stampede and its sponsors/partners.
- Responsible for the profitability of pricing strategies, marketing plans, sales materials and sales execution.
- Liaise with internal departments and volunteer committees to facilitate multilevel promotions and cross-marketing efforts between the Stampede and its sponsors.
- Execute a perquisite program that delivers a consistent set of benefits to all levels of sponsors — based on investment.
- Responsible for managing and leading the sponsorship team
- Currently 10 full time employees, including myself.

How long have you been working with the Calgary Stampede?
It was 11 years on March 1, 2017.

What is Calgary Stampede's sponsorship fulfillment philosophy?
To answer this question, you should first know our mission statement that the sponsorship team created in October 2011: generate

revenue by connecting sponsors/partners with Calgary Stampede programs to create value/ROI through exceptional experiences.

The organization realized years ago that we cannot be "good" at what we do — we need to be "Great, Amazing, and Outstanding" for our guests and sponsors to truly appreciate what we have to offer. This includes the fulfillment of our mutually agreed on sponsorships. Our sponsors are excited to work with us and to meet their marketing and sponsorship objectives. The corporations who do not work with us typically will not stay long-term, as they will not see the value we can bring to a brand.

What is your best advice for properties when it comes to sponsor fulfillment?

As I mentioned above, you need to work collaboratively with the right influencers within the brands/agencies who "get it," and see how they need to push the properties as much as we push the brands. Both are represented together in the sponsorship and building the relationship at all levels of management (middle to executive) is crucial to have a long-term, successful sponsorship. I say this a lot to brands who want to know more about the Calgary Stampede — it is an investment and like any investment you will not see as much ROI in year one or two or three, but long-term growth will come in time. The property needs to be committed to exceed expectations consistently, be transparent with the brand and grow your business together.

What is the expectation of brands when it comes to sponsorship fulfillment? Are these expectations changing?

Depending on the industry, the expectations of brands for sponsorship fulfillment differ dramatically. For example, if you are in the consumable goods industry, then simply "meeting expectations" by the property would be considered a failure. Brands want the properties to exceed expectations, they want new and unique opportunities to be presented to them, ideally with no incremental investment.

Properties should be very open to this and expect constant change, especially if the opportunity can be created with a low-cost, high-value proposition and as a win/win for the partnership. Why would the property provide incremental opportunities for the brand when there are no advantages to the event/sports team? Being good partners? Don't want to lose the business? If it is a small ask, e.g., additional access to a VIP area or additional parking for the event, then the property should be accommodating and provide it. If it is a larger ask, then the property needs to leverage their relationship and show the brand the value of the access (market driven) and explain the additional cost. Any educated brand will know when they are asking for too many incremental benefits and needs to be aware, they should not be exceeding their limits of the property.

As "partners," the brands and properties need to be on the same page with what they agreed on in being partners and how they can grow together with new opportunities.

Another industry to discuss would be Oil and Gas. As a brand who is investing in a property, they are not as concerned about their brand exposure and showcasing it to the audience; rather, they need access to experiences and ticketed events (hosting). Exceeding expectations with this industry is extremely important. As a property that is looking to maintain this business, you need to be proactive with these brands and present incremental benefits to them to assist in building relationships and the unique value proposition associated with sponsoring your organization. Engage their constant need for employee retention with offerings for the staff; include a hosting credit for their executive to use at your VIP experiences for their board or how to recognize senior management at your event with unique experiences. All will provide the ROI selling you need to either close or maintain a strong relationship with your client.

Do you think there is a gap between what the property and brand think is "sufficient" when it comes to sponsorship fulfillment?
As a property or a brand, you should never settle for "sufficient," and always continue to look for new ways to grow and exceed your objectives and goals. Currently, I believe there are properties that only provide what is expected of them and do not think of the longer-term opportunity (revenue) the brand can bring to their business. To help close the gap between "sufficient" and "exceeding expectations," the property needs to work with the brand on a consultative basis — ask questions, understand your brand's objectives and come back to them with ideas that will grow their ROI.

The most successful sponsorships include an openness to grow and work together annually. You need to collaborate with your colleagues internally to help you bring this new sponsorship to life. As a sponsorship professional you can build relationships, but eventually you will need to provide the right proposal to the client. Your colleagues and team will help you — they will even come up with amazing ideas and problem solvers for you to include in your next meeting.

Engagement with your internal departments is crucial and will allow for stronger program fulfillment, convincing your client (sponsor) to come back every year, or even better, create a multi-year strategy with you as a true partner.

At the time of this interview, Patrick was the Sponsorship Manager for the Calgary Stampede. Patrick has worked for the Calgary Stampede for the past 10 years, starting off working as the Sponsor Account Manager. Prior to this, Patrick worked at Alpine Canada as the Manger of Partner Services and Race Events.

Chapter 8

BUILDING A STRATEGY — PLANNING FOR SUCCESS

WHAT IS STRATEGY?

A model is just a model until you find a way to operationalize it. Once you have mastered the model and feel absolutely comfortable that you understand what sponsors want, you will need to put it into action. To do so, we will build a strategy for your property to design, build, market, and deliver a new value proposition, which will be built entirely around your orientation to meeting sponsors' and potential sponsors' needs.

Let us clarify the use of the word "strategy": it is a great word, but it is also a curse. Everybody in business wants to be strategic. They think the strategy guy has the fun job, the most respect, and the biggest paycheck.

Well, there is no question that strategy is vitally important, but to be clear, it is just the beginning. I like to think of the strategy as the big brother of a plan. A great strategy identifies what you want to achieve and how you are going to achieve it. It is a roadmap of plans and actions to be taken. Let us not get too caught up in glory of the word and develop a strategy you can easily implement to guide your property to success.

Now that you understand what sponsors want, how do you build a robust strategy that will enable you to deploy your newfound learnings? What is the first step — which by the way is always the hardest step in any project — towards developing a comprehensive, easy to understand approach?

I am a big believer in the use of repetition to make planning more manageable, and when you follow the same process over and over, you can eliminate the confusion over what to do when, and focus on what needs to be done. It is building muscle memory that allows you to bypass the confusing aspects of the project, and move right into the most important, meaty parts.

THE T180 PROCESS

Most of the organizations we work with are in some sort of pain. Quite often, severe pain. They are either in need of something new, facing declining revenues, or have realized that they are missing out on substantial opportunities. Therefore, it made more sense for me to position the process as a turnaround, a complete 180° about face from where the organization is currently headed. A complete reversal of fortune. To work with our clients and help them develop a strategy that can incorporate all the learnings in this chapter, we created a process focused on a turnaround, and we call it the T180.

The T180 is a seven-step approach broken into distinct, consecutive phases, each designed to use the information gathered at every stage along the way. Over the years, we have found that the T180 is easily adaptable and applicable to a wide variety of sponsorship stations and environments. We have deployed this process with major properties, domestic properties, international properties, grassroots organizations, cultural events, advocacy groups, professional sports, amateur sports, and music festivals.

If you follow the process, the T180 will provide sound, data-based valuations along with vital insights that will populate a successful strategy for your organization. The process is adaptable to your specific situation and circumstances. I cannot stress enough that the models I have presented are just models. Your mandate is to take the key learnings and adapt them to fit your organization's needs. Over time, as you stress test and implement your model, necessary adjustments for your situation will become apparent. This, in effect, means your model will self-correct and become stronger as its refined over time.

The process unfolds chronologically; though you can work on some of the elements simultaneously, I do not recommend it. I believe that each step and its related questions not only fulfill that phase's intention, but also help inform the questions that will arise in the next phase. In short order, proceed step-by-step in order to ensure that as you advance, there will be opportunities to identify new questions that arise and figure out their answers. However, you should always keep the outcome you are pursuing in mind so that you do not lose course.

PHASE I – OUTCOME ALIGNMENT

I am a big believer in beginning with the end in mind. This is a paraphrase of a critical line from the great management authority, Stephen Covey. If you do not truly understand where you are going, how will you know when you get there? Don't underestimate the importance of this first phase or write it off as administrative work.

This first phase is the license your organization gives you to go ahead and tackle this turnaround. You need to align yourself with your organization on the process, so that when the work is done, you don't run into coworkers who do not have an interest in making the required change. This is crucial in any change management exercise, even more so in one where you are going to identify where people in the organization have failed. If you do not align yourself, then you will not make the process work.

The first task in securing alignment is to discuss what role sponsorship is going to play or has played in your marketing, your customer experience, and your revenue mix. Is sponsorship an important source of direct revenue for your organization? Is sponsorship a marketing priority? Does your organization benefit most from the sponsor's corporate dollars or from their employees' participation in your event and the fundraising dollars they attract? Similarly, does your corporate partnership drive revenue from a rights fee or ticket sales, or does it profit from hospitality sales, food and beverage per caps?

Some properties pursue sponsors who are more marketing partners than corporate funders. This can be a shrewd strategy, because their marketing clout may generate much more revenue from participant transactions (e.g. concert tickets) for which you could ever convince the sponsor to pay. A corporation with a large consumer base that can generate lots of funding will usually be a more important partner than one with a small employee base.

Other properties view sponsorship as a valuable cobranding strategy. Aligning with a highly popular sports apparel brand would bring obvious cachet and brand halo to a new sporting event. So too would an energy drink in gaming or a technology company. This almost seems like reverse sponsorship in a way. Quite literally, who is borrowing who's equity?

Let us say that you have not aligned on the role that sponsorship will play in your organization. This is a highly acceptable approach — but only as long it is clear to all involved that the role sponsorship currently plays will be subject to objective scrutiny.

What other key parameters need to be agreed on in this phase? It is important to remember that these are your marching orders for the project. I am not saying you cannot adjust them after you begin, of course you can, but sweating them out rigorously at this point will help ensure that you fulfill your important mandates.

After the discussion of roles, you may want to look at other key aspects. What is our offering to corporate partners? Do we have the right assets? Are the assets priced properly? Are we structured to deliver on what our sponsors want? Is our value proposition for these partners well-articulated?

It will be an unavoidable outcome, but this exercise will lead you to understand your resource deployment. Are there appropriate resources in the corporate partnership group to deliver the new strategy? This needs to be evaluated considering the number of people, their expertise, and depth of experience, but this is a much broader discussion, one that extends beyond the corporate development team. Sponsorship marketing cuts a wide swath across your organization. The people who are impacted and impact sponsorship must be included in this exercise. They must be aligned with the potential outcome that may reveal that retooling the resource pool is a priority.

Three questions, and the answers to them, are the foundation of this exercise:

- What role does sponsorship play in our organization?
- What is our sponsorship value proposition?
- What resourcing do we require to deliver on a new strategy?

The other key aspect of the Alignment phase is formal project planning. It includes the development of teams, development of timelines, and development of resource allocations.

Teams

Identify who needs to be involved and in what ways using an approach such as a simplified RASCI Matrix. Identify who will be tasked with doing the work, reporting on the work, and who will be asked to approve the work. A final consideration is to decide who will be tasked with implementing the work when it is completed.

In general, I would expect that these people would have been part of the process, at least from an input standpoint if not in varying degrees to the doing and approvals processes as well. At this point, you should determine if external resources are needed, such as consultants, agencies, or researchers. Additional external participants should include current sponsors, lapsed sponsors, and potential sponsors. Their voices must be heard throughout the process. I recommend that you cast an even wider net for external stakeholders, who will be asked to participate at some point on a limited basis; this group should include volunteers, event participants, talent, competitors, and suppliers. I do not believe in consulting these individuals for the clichéd purpose of "securing buy-in," I believe in consulting these individuals because they can be a source of invaluable knowledge for the team conducting the project. A lapsed sponsor, or a mildly disgruntled current sponsor, will provide more truths about your business that your boss ever will.

Build a simple document that identifies everyone's role and involvement ahead of time to provide clarity. We have found it beneficial to create different types of working and advisory groups to streamline when people are involved and not over tax them. You can have certain people on certain tasks and not others, given that they all have ongoing duties in your organization. During the alignment phase, socialize this document and ensure that it is well understood. Do not forget to refer to it later in the process and make any necessary adjustments.

Timeline

Develop a timeline with which your organization can live and execute. This will require a keen understanding of when it is best to implement a new sponsorship strategy, given the business cycle of your property. Understandably, this process cannot be completed during your peak sales period, but it is something that cannot be left until there is a total lull for the evident reason that there rarely is a lull. I recommend that you undertake this exercise at least six months before your next sales cycle and in some cases, up to 18 months before. The time range may be broad, but it is a function of your organization's complexity. Even a smaller local property will want to take three months — at a minimum — to conduct this exercise. Larger national properties need to start earlier because of the number of stakeholders that would be involved in developing and implementing the new strategy. Stakeholders can range from venue partners and broadcast outlets to agency suppliers.

Once you have established your deadline for this project, which is based on the desired launch date of the new approach, you can then get unto the finite details of the schedule. The easiest way to build a schedule is to map out your milestones. When will your property be going live to the public? When is your annual general meeting? When do sponsorship sales start? What is the timing of key contract renewals? Is your organization, or your department, about to get new leadership? When is your next board meeting? Each of these milestones will provide the tent poles for your scheduling process.

Overlay the amount of time you think that each step will take. This can be done in a few ways, and I would not suggest that any one is easier than another. Preparing a schedule is a function of experience. To start, I would suggest polling each of the key people involved and asking for their estimate of time. Then, double their estimate and lay out a consecutive/concurrent schedule. Each phase is consecutive, but you should allow for a 25% overlap across phases. For example, if Phase III is to last four weeks, start it during the last week of Phase II. Doubling the individual's estimates will allow for some slack due to unforeseen circumstances, and the overlapping will ensure that if one phase does get off track, you could push to start the next phase, even if it means proceeding with less than complete information.

A timeline is only good if you use it. Appoint someone on the team to be its owner; every week, they need to review the status, update progress, and publish it to all key individuals. Utilize a set of indicators that can pinpoint where issues exist and require attention. This can be as easy as grading each task in the phase with a red/yellow/ green indicator. If the task is sliding towards an urgent status, the pace of internal escalation needs to be increased. If you want to be dramatic, add a black or skull and crossbones indicator to the mix. If I were your boss, I would want to understand when an issue is about to be tagged with a skull and crossbones icon, so share with all involved.

Budget

Set a budget that includes the Full-time Equivalent (FTE) cost of all internal people involved — the feed for any external consultants or agencies, travel costs, out of pockets, investments in research reports, social listening, or other tools. Establish an internal docket, project number, job jacket, or billing code for the project. It is important that you report your return over the next one to three years. Establishing a budget provides a clean way to manage your resource pool. Advising internal peers that they have a certain allotment of hours is an example of effective management communication. The budgeting of time provides clear direction on how much involvement you want from certain people. It is a concrete measure for managing behaviour and, ultimately, outcomes.

You will need to adjust the budgeting process based on whether your team is doing it internally or if you are using external consultants. You can often receive more objective feedback by using external consultants who have completed this process many, many times. However, I do recognize that we consultants cost money. If your organization does not have the funds to invest, this model and industry resources can guide you through the exercise.

The final task is to get alignment on the project's final deliverable. If I could dream, every project we undertake would begin by drafting the final report. Every sponsorship you sell should begin with a draft of what the post-Evaluation will include. The benefit? You now know exactly what information you need to source and prepare. If you share the prospective draft with key decision-makers, have them brought in early. Most importantly, you have made a commitment. You are now mandated to deliver what you promised. It's your personal accountability statement.

With your peers, discuss whether the deliverable will be a standalone report — and the only item in the report — or if it will be information included in a larger strategic plan. Will there be an onboarding process complete with internal training sessions for sharing the new approach with key stakeholders? Your Implementation Plan will provide you with the opportunity to dig into this in detail, but the best time to consider it is at the beginning.

PHASE II – INTERNAL ASSESSMENT

If you think you understood how your organization works, think again. The Internal Assessment phase needs to be conducted with the rigor of a tax audit, the intimacy of a therapist, and the objectivity of a court official. You need to find a way to lose your biases and assumptions about your enterprise. This is an easier task for an external consultant, but even then, the internal members of the team need to be ready for a very thorough exploration.

The Internal Assessment is about discovery. Where are the pain points in the organization? Where do the opportunities lie? What is working? What is not working? What do our partners think of us? What about our volunteers? Our participants? Our regional offices? Our lapsed partners? Our suppliers? Our international affiliates?

The Internal Assessment should uncover facts. What are our business results? How have we done with sponsorship for the past five years? What about other forms of revenue, whether they be fundraising, licensing, or hospitality? This is an opportunity to examine the books. Has your property tracked the performance of its sales team, and identified how many prospects have been pursued compared to those that have been secured? Are there records that will allow you to examine the financial investment made for every sponsorship dollar secured? In similar fashion, once those sponsors are secured, what is the expected return for servicing and fulfilling them? In summary, you need to analyze the profitability of your sponsorship business.

Next, you need to develop a profile, an understanding of your sponsorship portfolio. You should uncover and assess key criteria such as the length of time your various sponsors have been affiliated with you, their level of engagement with the property, the extent of activation they conduct, and the involvement of their stakeholders with your property. Try to correlate the success metrics of your property over time with your sponsorship portfolio. Success metrics are results such as ticket sales for a music festival, fundraising dollars for a charity run, and wins for a sports team. Another interesting exercise is to map the categories from which your sponsorship partners have come. It will be worthwhile to include this comparison in the external assessment.

You should conduct a thorough examination of your sales success. Your organization should track the size, value, and engagement levels in your pipeline; understanding the success rate for pitches, renewals, etc. can be invaluable. As you develop your strategy, your resource plan will become a critical component. Understanding how many pitches are required for your organization to achieve its revenue goal will help drive some of that resource planning. It will impact your go-to-market strategy and related components such as your B2B marketing plan to attract sponsors.

Overall, you need to assess your property to provide the metrics that will enable you to correlate your property to your sponsorship success. This assessment should cover three strategic elements: financial results, property performance, and fan engagement.

Financial Results

In order to properly understand the business success of your current sponsorship program, it is important to conduct a five-year review of your revenue from an overall enterprise standpoint with details for each revenue stream. Break down sponsorship, donations, capital gifts, advertising, hospitality, citrate sales, licensing sales, media rights, etc. You should try to create a P&L for sponsorship as if it were a standalone business. You need to include the direct costs and the indirect costs — such as the full-time people employed on the partnership teams, and the amount of time a person from another department may have spent on fulfilling sponsorship respectively.

Property Performance

You need a set of metrics that are objective indicators of how success-ful the property has been. The performance metrics often have a strong correlation to financial results. We want to understand their specific impact on sponsorship, as well as on other aspects of the busi-ness. For a sports team property, measuring performance is easy: wins, losses, playoff success, individual player success, etc. Do not forget to include other important analytics such as coaching turnover, uniform changes, player scandals, and more. If your property is a charity, look at metrics like funds raised, breakthrough in treatments, and awards won. For festivals or community events, you could analyze ticket sales, weather, headline act appearances, or celebrity appearances.

Fan Engagement

A direct correlation to the health and equity of your property is the level of engagement demonstrated by your fans and other stake-holders. The list of metrics here can be endless as you strive to paint a picture of fan avidity. In the case of a charity, you should track your supporters by as many meaningful metrics as you can access, including participation in events, funds they raise, funds they donate, volunteer hours, amount of advocacy, campaign engagement, and social media following. A music festival would want to understand its fans based on duration of stay, acts watched, travel distance, size of attending group, word of mouth, social engagement, and overall satisfaction from the event. You can easily imagine developing a similar fan profile for a sports property, gam-ing event, or a series of theatrical performances.

You may have difficulty determining where a metric should live in some cases. That is okay, as long as you are capturing the metric and using it in your analysis. The final decision on where it resides is less important than the importance of actually having the data.

The flipside of the factual phase of your internal assessment is a collection of robust input from internal stakeholders. Your first task is to clearly understand what sort of feedback you want, and from whom you want it. In addition, you need to know how to collect this feedback.

I have worked on projects where we have focused our internal reviews on a dozen key officials, projects where surveys were conducted with thousands of volunteers from across the country. The ideal approach to this activity is a blended approach. You need to have a significant number of people providing input, and you need to source these people from all perspectives. I would suggest that you develop your plan for each group with consistency of intent but with variety in terms of process. While you want to discover the information that your plan identified, you do no know what you do not know. Therefore, build flexibility into your process to ensure that open discovery can occur, and so that when it does occur, you will be able to adjust your next round of conversations accordingly.

You should remember that the process of discovery is like developing an athletic skill. It is important to conduct a proper warm-up before you begin training; you should use a coach or a teammate to provide feedback. Walk through your first few attempts before you go full speed. Play an exhibition game or two before launching into a full-fledged, competitive situation.

I strongly suggest that you do not start your internal assessment with the most important individuals or groups. Early in this phase, you will have a clear understanding of who will be the most influential groups in the process. They could be people you need to influence, the individuals who will authorize change, or perhaps the group that holds the keys to the most valuable insights and data. You should see any of these groups after you have seen the first group.

Start with a group that appears to be the most eager to participate. Perhaps it is the group that most wants change or the group that is most neglected. It does not matter. What matters is that you practice and collect their feedback. These early conversations will provide insights that will help you understand what you will be up against when you meet with the more challenging groups. Perhaps your project will not have naysayers, but I highly doubt it. Even in situations where every constituent is on board for change, they will be promoting their own version of change.

Another benefit of plotting the order of your discovery sessions strategically is the impact of being able to bring forward some of your early findings. If you know that the board believes they are funding sufficient levels of sponsorship management staff, any feedback from sponsors that servicing levels are substandard would be powerful. It will definitely change the answers to your questions about resources and willingness to invest more in the sponsorship area.

A Game Plan

To fuel your internal assessment, let's put together an effective game plan to conduct discussions with a wide variety of stakeholders. These stakeholders will range in their centrality to the current sponsorship operation and in their level of engagement with the property. Build a process that allows you to generate the greatest amount of useful information while remaining realistic about managing the project resources from time and investment standpoints. Below is an outline of a plan with the stakeholders loosely ranked in order of importance.

Board of directors

This group is most important in not-for-profit and publicly traded organizations. You should conduct one-to-one interviews with the chairperson, directors on the revenue or marketing subcommittees, and one or two rising stars if possible. These interviews should be conducted at the directors' places of work, with a senior level individual from your department present, or by a senior external consultant. You should provide a background summary of the project and the questions you want to ask approximately a week ahead of time. You should limit yourself to six or eight questions and avoid constructions that accept yes/no answers.

Ask questions that encourage the board member to provide their opinion and position on the topic. Your objective with board members is to understand their overall vision for the property, their support and understanding of the role of sponsorship, their willingness to support foundational changes to help sponsorship succeed, and their personal opinions regarding best-in-class sponsorship marketing outside of your organization.

C-level executives

The best way to determine who to interview on the leadership team is to make it simple and interview them all. This approach makes sense, as every department in your organization plays a critical role in delivering the overall product along with sponsor benefits. Your project could die quickly if the leadership team is asked to approve your recommendations, and all facets of your enterprise have not been properly considered.

These meetings should be conducted by the persons in charge of developing the strategy. Assuming the leadership team understands the project, you may be able to skip the summary, but you will still need to send your questions in advance. Tailor these questions with a narrower focus and ensure they are tweaked in a relevant manner for each department head. Approach these meetings as purely information gathering sessions, not as an opportunity to pitch your position. Your objective with the C-Level executives is to understand the strategic priority of the sponsor function in the ongoing operation of the enterprise. You are attempting to understand areas of frustration, extract new ideas, and discover unmet opportunities that perhaps have never been exposed to the development team.

Department staff

You should assemble a broad, diverse list of staff from various levels across the organization. Divide these interviews among various members of your project team, so you can cast a wide net and get lots of input. These sessions can be held in a group format to manage resources and reduce the time you must spend. Offer participants an opportunity to provide their written input to you as well. It is important that these discussions stay positive and remain a true discovery exercise. There is nothing wrong with hearing about the pitfalls, but it would be unfortunate not to extract more beneficial learnings. A simple approach to any discussion with frontline personnel is to ask four open-ended questions:

- Presently, what is working well?
- What is not working well?
- What should we keep doing?
- What should we start doing?

Volunteers

Your approach to volunteers is somewhat like the approach to staff. You should have direct face-to-face conversations with key volunteers, committee chairpersons, and long-standing contributors. If access is a problem, you can use a telephone or online discussions. In many circumstances, you will have too many volunteers with which to meet; you can segment this group to determine who you wish to interview, and those you wish to survey. Deploy a simple online survey to gain insights into the property and get even closer to your consumers.

Customers, fans, and attendees

You have passionate stakeholder groups who want to be heard from, and this project is an opportunity to collect feedback from them. A survey of social posts, including a video from your organization's leadership, can be a powerful tool for listening to the sentiments of your most engaged audience. Use this audience to find out what your fans want from your sponsors. You should scour all research ever conducted by your organization or third parties to learn more about your customers. Most properties track their fans to understand support and/or sponsor avidity but treat those reports as only the beginning. Look across your enterprise for more. If your entity went through a branding or positioning exercise, research from this exercise will no doubt be available. Canvas your sponsors and ask if any of them have done research they are willing to share. Many will have. Check external sources, such as local universities or research companies, to see if they have written a case study about your property. Market research firms will often have done omnibus studies that may include your property. Another excellent source are governmental and public organizations. Request access to economic impact studies, tourism reports, industry reports, or societal studies. You will be amazed at what you will find.

Participants

Your participants, competitors, and talent are the face of your property. In some cases, getting their input may be impossible. In other cases, they can be a vital part of the equation. For example, you may get to understand their needs better, which could result in your pursuit of new sponsorship categories. You may learn that they want to help promote your sponsors, which has an obvious beneficial impact on your value proposition. You may come to understand their frustrations around making sponsor appearances, providing you with the input you need to pursue changes to procedures. You should connect with your participants through the proper internal channels, but the conversations need to be confidential to staff (i.e. coaches, booking managers), who can impact the participants' involvement with your property.

Sponsors

There are specific segments of this group that you should attempt to include: current sponsors, lapsed sponsors, and key prospects.

The last group will be the hardest to secure, because they will just view this as a veiled attempt for you to conduct a pitch meeting. However, each of the three will provide the most important internal feedback in the Internal Assessment. You are going to hear directly from your current sponsors what they want. They need to understand the purpose of the project before you ask to interview them. They need to receive senior-level communications from your team and ensure that they have an opportunity to discuss the process. You need to position the project as one that will greatly benefit the sponsor, not as an exercise that is going to result in higher fees, less assets, or a more cluttered property. At the same time, you should be open about the fact that you are investigating the property's value proposition. Approach your most important sponsors in a manner that mirrors your board approach. Convenience, communication, and clarity are vital. You should have an outside person who interviews or surveys your sponsors. I have found that the best approach is to agree that your sponsors' comments will be reported verbatim, but that there will be no attribution.

You would be very successful if you were able to convince some lapsed sponsors to participate. Adjust your questions to under-stand why the sponsor left, what was lacking in the value proposi-tion, and what changes would be required to motivate them to return or refer the property to a colleague. Position your appeal to these sponsors as their desire to contribute. Make it clear that your property is seeking to be best in class, and that their input can help support that development.

Depending on your property, the complexity of collecting sponsor input may be overwhelming. You may need to develop a collection plan to ensure that all your sponsors have at least an opportunity to answer a survey, especially if your event is a festival or fair with dozens of tradeshow-style vendors, who consider themselves sponsors. Any survey that goes to more than ten respondents should have quantitative or multiple choice style answers that make the results easy to review and understand.

You should take a more personal approach to gathering feedback from lapsed sponsors and sponsor prospects. These individuals will be more receptive to a one-on-one interview than if they are asked to complete a survey. Their particular type of feedback will be more conducive to a discussion, as it will include nuances and sub-tleties that will only be apparent in conversation. Lastly, these indi-viduals are doing your organization a favour, so making it easy for them to provide input and promising that their information will be utilized are very important.

I have found that it is never difficult to get passionate people to talk about something they love. This will make your Internal Assessment process easier, if you do not overcomplicate it. Make it easy to meet with your project team. Make the questions you ask straight-forward and understandable. Do not ask too much of people, and they will provide more than you need. Remember to be flexible. Some interview subjects will want to ramble off topic. Do not stop them, because they may be on a tangent that could significantly impact your strategy. Adjust your approach and methodology as you proceed to take advantage of what you are uncovering along the way. Thank people and ensure that you give them feedback when the project has been completed. There are few things as frustrating as being asked for input and not knowing if your comments were valuable. Let your participants know it was!

PHASE III – EXTERNAL ASSESSMENT

The primary purpose of the External Assessment is to remove the inherent bias that your organization has about itself. Unfortunately, it seems that at times the sponsorship industry is fueled by braggarts and claim-makers. You would be hard pressed to find someone who will not boast about their ticket sales, sponsorship revenue, or the impact of their property. For whatever reason, people are afraid of the truth. Perhaps it is the pressure to always be selling in this business.

The reality, however, is that not all properties are equal. There are great properties in terms of business metrics, and then there are the not so great properties. If your leadership team is falsely convinced that your enterprise has no faults, you need data to show them why change is necessary. Having candid feedback from your internal stakeholder groups will be an excellent start. Combining it with an external industry analysis will make it even more powerful.

In planning your external assessment, you should understand who you are competing against, both directly and indirectly, as well as best-in-class organizations you can learn from. You will look to these groups later in the process to help you determine your market value. To complete the total picture, add a look at the overall sponsorship industry for your trade market. In this stage, you will focus on understanding the strategic approaches of organizations in each group and the industry as a whole. Look for organizations that have been in similar situations as yours, such as declining revenue streams, and addressed it by launching a fundraising event, increasing public awareness, or hiring a new CEO or board. Any organization's recent history should parallel your own as closely as possible.

Direct Competitors

Start with examining your direct competitors. I am not referring to the teams you compete with during the season, rather, these are the organizations that you routinely go head-to-head with for sponsorship dollars. Typically, they would be organizations in a similar sector competing in a similar trading area. A simple example would be the local community youth baseball association competing head on with a local community youth soccer association. Both are going to approach the same local businesses for sponsorship. Both are going to make similar pitches about community involvement, youth participation, and employee volunteerism. They are direct competitors — so too are charity runs, competing art festivals, or competing trade shows. On a broader, national scale, the same approach would apply. A national disease-based charity competes against all other national, diseased-based charities. Your target sponsors, your value proposition, and your core offerings are all similar.

You do not want to cut corners when you are trying to understand your direct competitors. Begin by developing a list of the 12 to 15 organizations that you compete with for dollars. In some circumstances, this list may have only five or six organizations, say a major league sports franchise in a community that already has three, along with one major college. In this case, you should aim for a longer list. The benefit of a long list is that the first entities you remove from the direct competitor list should immediately cascade to the indirect competitor list. The same effect will occur when you shortlist your indirect competitor roster. You will be starting to populate your industry leaders list. All this to say that I want you to build a robust list of competitors.

Before proceeding, ensure you secure alignment from the project decision makers on the list. Have candid conversations with your development and marketing teams about who they see as their competitors. If your sales team is highly sophisticated and tracks the activities of their prospects that declined, perform a reality check by cross-referencing the properties those companies are supporting. Once your list is finalized, develop a capture plan to inform the process of information gathering. What data do you want on each competitor, and how do you plan to secure it?

Conduct your data gathering in a thorough, ethical manner. Be excited by the fact that by conducting this exercise, you are moving the organization ahead, without breaking any laws or moral contracts to secure information. While I am sure you would love to copy one of your competitor's latest major proposals, you have no need.

In building your capture plan, map out the information you would like to understand about each. Begin with the following major categories: property profile, stakeholder data, sponsorship assets, sponsor portfolio, and resources.

Property Profile

This should be a summary of every salient fact about the property that you use for a direct comparison to yours.

History: Age and duration of the property.

Market: What market do they pursue in terms of fans, followers, participants, volunteers?

Results: Compare their fandom to yours in terms of ticket sales, ticket revenue, fan engagement, social media engagement, online followers.

Media Coverage: Perform an audit of the earned media coverage the property receives in comparison to yours. Identify the TV, online, radio, and print coverage separately. Earned media is of a different (higher) value due to the fact it is provided at the discretion of journalists.

Media Partners: This should be captured separately from the earned media coverage, as it is either sold or purchased media. This channel is very important, as it is a direct addition to the assets that a property can offer a sponsor. In a sponsor's mind, this media is more valuable, because there usually is more opportunity for brand integration as well.

Stakeholder Data: Develop a profile of the people who attend, follow, and are involved in the property.

Asset Inventory

Compile an asset inventory of your competitors. This will provide a side-by-side comparison of what each of you has to offer a partner; this exercise should be conducted with the other groups in the external analysis discussion. When completed, it will provide a clear picture of what the market is expecting. It is important that you find simple ways to standardize the different types of assets when you develop these inventories. Too much standardization can be problematic. If one competitor sells game programs at their events and another distributes them for free, the two methods should be described differently, as the value of a paid product is worth more than a non-paid product.

Sponsor Portfolio

Understanding your competitors' sponsorship success is very important. This will probably be the first item on the agenda when your executives discuss the project. Every organization wants to know why their competitor has more sponsors, or why they have certain companies as sponsors that you do not have. Remember they may not be competitors in your mind, but they definitely are one if your sponsor or donor supports them. To provide clarity, and to level the assessment playing field, you should create a common framework for assessing each competitor's sponsors.

- Develop an equivalency chart to hold all a competitor's sponsors. I suggest that you build five tiers (title, major, minor, official, and promotional) to rank each sponsor consistently. Every competitor has their own labels for their sponsors, so creating this chart will make it easier to compare.
- Map each competitor on the chart. You can try to assess the sponsor's tenure. Include that on the chart as well.
- As you plot each sponsor, keep a tally of the business category they represent. Ultimately, we will want to identify the top categories that are spending with your competitors and understand your performance in these categories.
- Review the awards won by the property and their sponsors over the last five years.
- Search online articles, the websites of their sponsors, and annual reports to compile feedback on the property. While this will be overwhelmingly positive, it will provide excellent intelligence on what sponsors value from your competitors.

- Map out the strategic purpose of each property's top eight to 10 sponsors. Gain an understanding of what type of data their sponsors are leveraging and map it. List up to three key objectives for each partner. Use common language so you can rank and quantify the objectives. For example, use the term "recruitment" as a standard label to cover the similar objectives of: generate trial, build our consumer base, or attract new users.
- Who they are and how long they have been involved?

Resources

It is important to know your competitor's output considering the resources they apply to sponsorship. This will include an understanding of the amount allocated to internal personnel, the utilization of external suppliers, and other resources to which they have access. For each competitor, create a detailed organizational chart of their sponsorship team and a high-level snapshot of the complete entity, including outside suppliers. The information is readily available:

- Use online networks such as LinkedIn to search for current employees and their titles.
- Review the contact pages on the organization's website to find staff directories.
- Conduct online searches for articles, appointment notices, press releases, and other content for references to key stakeholders.
- Meet with your HR team or your recruitment firm to learn about the titles and market for personnel in your trading area.

Indirect Competitors

Indirect Competitors are organizations that are not in your sector or trading area, or both, but still compete for the same sponsorship dollars as you. The word "competitor" is deliberate — these entities are competing with you for money, but quite often, properties do not realize that is what is happening. A sports property can very easily be competing with a cultural property for support. This can be especially true with a sophisticated sponsor who first considers opportunities for a strategic fit with their business needs and then starts to examine sectorial opportunities.

The first challenge is to identify your indirect competitors. Perhaps your partnership team has been aware of them for some time. If so, then your job will be easy, but what if your partnership team does not understand this group? How do you figure out who you are battling against for dollars? Begin with the easiest stakeholders to access, your current partners.

Examining who your sponsors support will give you your first indication of who else is after the same money as you are. The easiest and least intrusive method to source could be your partners' websites given that most organizations like to promote their various relationships. Build your list from there, but if you can go further, you should take it. When meeting with your current sponsors, it would be a good idea to ask them who else they sponsor or ask them why they sponsor the organizations you have seen on their website. If your sponsors are willing to share who else they have considered, your list of direct and indirect competitors will fill up rapidly.

A similar questioning and examination of your lapsed sponsors and your top prospects will provide additional data. Identifying the organizations that replaced your property in the portfolio of a lapsed sponsor is indisputable proof they are your competitors. You may have people in senior management who do not believe in your theory about indirect competitors; however, following the money always provides irrefutable data.

While it is ideal to have a defensible rationale, there is a case to be made for sleuthing when it comes to building this list. Look at organizations in your area that have common mission statements. Any property that is promoting health is competing with all others who have the same societal mission. Any property that is promoting community is competing with all others who make the same claim. It does not matter if one is a youth group, another is a sports organization, or a third is a music festival. In the eyes of the sponsor, each of them can provide a similar equity affiliation, which they have identified to be essential to their marketing plans.

Best-in-Class Industry Leaders

An inherent benefit of taking the time to analyze your industry is the opportunity to learn from best-in-class industry participants. Consider this new, third group of organizations, and keep in mind that these organizations may be your direct competitors or your indirect competitors.

Determining who is best-in-class is clearly a subjective exercise, something we want to minimize while tackling the first task of building our list of properties to assess. In order to manage resource investment, you can take two different approaches: you can determine that the best approach is to look deeply at approximately six organizations and develop full profiles or even entire case studies, or you could identify up to 20 organizations that will each be highlighted for an aspect of their sponsorship approach that is best in class. This latter approach will provide a lengthy list of interesting ideas, though it will lack depth and context.

Ultimately, you need to pick the organizations that your project team feels are best in class, but there are a few ways to inform that decision with unbiased input.

- Identify the properties who are partnering with the companies or sectors that you most seek to add.
- Ask your current sponsors which properties they most admire.
- Review industry award winners. List those properties that appear to be successful either as direct entrants or via their sponsors, who will often enter their cases in marketing awards.
- Try to find organizations that have had enduring (three or more years) success versus those that have had the sort of sudden success that couldn't be replicated over time.

To understand that organization's sudden success, conduct executive interviews to understand their approach. If they will not share information, former employees or partners may be willing.

Industry Landscape

Your final task in the external assessment is to look at key indicators and trends in the industry. It is important that you go deeper than the blanket headlines or sweeping judgments that sometimes accompany industry reports. However, they are very useful in building your case with senior management and board members to demonstrate that your strategy is soundly aligned with changes in the sector. To meet their expectations, take a two-pronged approach to your industry assessment.

First, report and interpret the numbers that represent the overall industry. The interpretation part is more important than the reporting. Second, you should mine these reports for key insights that can fuel your thinking. Many authors of these reports will prepare industry articles or white papers to accompany their work; these white papers often reveal their more subjective assessment of what is happening across the landscape. You will find these perspectives will resonate powerfully with your peers and project sponsors. To begin, you should access the most relevant sector and industry reports, studies, and presentations. I would suggest that you look for the following:

- National and international sponsorship spending reports
- Consumer studies
- Industry revenue reports
- Economic impact reports
- Tourism reports
- Media tracking reports
- Online media trends
- Participation trends
- Volunteerism trends
- Donation and philanthropy reports
- Investment banking reports

Each of the above will fulfill a different purpose in developing your strategy. Some will provide an overall status and trend summary. Others will provide you with a more focused look on where change is happening. Some reports will provide insights and commentary that can help identify opportunities for you. You will find synthesizing your reports will be much more efficient if you begin with a specific objective. Your property may be new, so mine the reports for results related to newer properties, or similar case studies.

PHASE IV – BENCHMARKING ANALYSIS

There are many benefits to conducting a benchmarking analysis of your property. However, I will caution you that given the difficulty in finding data, it will not be a simple task. You will need to be creative, diligent, and resourceful to find the stockpile of data points to support the exercise. The payoff is more than worth the effort.

Benchmarking Analysis can be useful in many ways, and three of the most important are:

- Determining if your property is achieving its full sponsorship revenue potential;
- Establishing price points for your sponsorship offerings, and
- Positioning the value of your property in relation to others.

Data on the pricing of sponsorships is the most difficult data to obtain. When our agency conducts benchmarking, we utilize a proprietary database that we have spent years building with properties across every sector, but even that does not guarantee 100% accuracy. For your benchmarking, you may end up needing to use publicly available information, which is not the end of the world — any benchmarking is better than no benchmarking. Even non-financial benchmarking will help you validate how your property stacks up against others.

I would suggest that the more consistent you are with your benchmarking, the better your approach and results will become. Plan the time to enable you to conduct this exercise annually. If at some point you can afford to purchase external data or expertise to help set a foundation, an annual exercise will produce telling learnings. It will be somewhat daunting to conduct the benchmarking process I describe unless you have a stable research staff. I recommend you build a streamlined model.

An ideal benchmarking process is conducted with three separate groups, who you will recall from our External Analysis: direct competitors, indirect competitors, and best-in-class examples. We conduct the benchmarking with each group to understand the options presented to potential corporate partners. Like buying real estate, choosing a stock, or even selecting a graduate school program, the buyer is deciding based on multiple attributes. There is no straight-line pricing in sponsorship. A sponsorship buyer is not always comparing a sports property to a sports property. They are often comparing a sports property to a music property or a community festival.

The benefit of benchmarking best-in-class examples is to understand which attributes allow them to generate the sponsorship returns they do. This will help guide your organization's investment and improvement strategies. To maximize the learnings, ensure that you design your benchmarking so the attributes being measured are the most relevant to your property.

Benchmarking Process

Determine measurement outcome

First, you want to determine what you are trying to benchmark. Is it the total amount of sponsorship revenue that a property earns? Is it the price points for different levels of sponsorship? In the absence of being to access financial data, are you trying to rank the properties? Do you want to tier the properties or map them on an XY axis? While financials such as naming rights are often publicly disclosed, the dollars spent on sponsorships are more tightly held, but even a ranking of properties can be helpful for your strategic planning.

Collect data points

In order to create an undistorted and accurate picture, you need to collect at least eight to 12 different data points for each property. This will ensure that your benchmarking process is not overly skewed by one or two dominating characteristics. For example, the age of a property is often used as proxy for heritage or prestige, but an 80 year old property should not have 10 times more impact on your rankings than an eight year old property. Having multiple data points will even out the measurement. You need to ensure that your data points are a cross-section of attributes that are important to a sponsor, and reflect the equity value of your property. Too many data points focused on the same area is problematic. If all you measure is attendance, ticket sales, and visitors, you have three data points that essentially provide the same perspective. The following sample list of data points illustrates the type of information and its relevance to the What Sponsors' Want Model:

- **Age:** The age of a property can be a proxy for heritage or prestige.
- **Media Impressions:** How much earned media a property achieves in a year demonstrates its relevance.
- **Online Followers:** You want to measure the avidity of a property's followers, as it reflects a property's importance to consumers.
- **Volunteers/Volunteer hours:** A very strong indicator of importance to consumers and community.
- **Funds raised:** Demonstrates impact, proof. Good to measure funds raised by person.
- **Donors:** Measure donors and total donors pitched to get unique measures of properties reach.
- **Media Coverage:** Exposure provided by the property through all media channels.
- **Attendees/Ticket Sales:** Self-explanatory.
- **Participants:** You should measure not only sheer number, but how long they prepare or train for your event, and how involved they are.
- **Per Caps:** Revenue achieved from participants or attendees.
- **Number of Sponsors:** Demonstrates corporate interest, always good to classify this, so that every donor is not included.
- **Government Support:** Grant revenue and public funds also demonstrate a property's importance to regions or communities

- **Total revenue:** A measure of scale.
- **Economic Impact:** Another measure of scale.

Apply scoring method

Once you have gathered your data, you will want to rank the properties and compare their scores to their earning power. To rank the score, you need a way to add up the data points to produce a score, but the reality is that each data point will be of a different shape and size. Some will be financially based, others will be media impressions, some will be number of years, and others will be people counts. You need a scoring method to create a common measurement unit. You will want to examine if applying weighting may ensure that the priority data points for your property are having the appropriate impact on your evaluation. Referring to the years conducting measurements, you may feel this far less important than social media followers, so you may cut the age of a property metric in half by applying a 0.5 weighting to it.

An easy approach to creating a common denominator and solving the weighting-impact issue is to score and compare each attribute to the best-scoring property for the same attribute. If one property had 10,000 volunteers and that was the highest of any property, it would receive a score of 1.0. All other properties would receive proportional scores. The second best property may have 8,000 volunteers, thereby earning a score of 0.8. This simple method is an easy math exercise and eliminates wild swings caused by properties that have incredible numbers.

Once you have scored each property, compare their score to their revenue-generating ability (Table 1). If Property A achieved a score of 10 points and generated USD$1,000,000 in sponsorship, you could suggest they generate USD$100,000 per point. Now look

Table 1: Benchmarking Example

Organization	Total Revenue		Property Age		Current Sponsors		Google Search Hits		Social Media		Government Funding		Total Points	Total Ranking
	T	P	T	P	T	P	T	P	T	P	T	P	T	R
Property 1	$85,571,000	91	76	71	5	17	111,000	43	21,600	46	$43,714,000	100	368	2
Property 2	$12,300,000	13	107	100	16	53	259,000	100	21,159	45	$259,224	14	325	3
Property 3	$958,332	1	38	35	30	100	143,000	55	42,889	92	$268,333	1	294	5
Property 4	$10,194,955	11	104	97	25	83	134,000	52	23,600	50	$0	0	293	4
Property 5	$3,691,963	4	51	48	1	3	81,500	31	13,415	29	$147,679	0	115	7
Property 6	$94,168,273	100	52	49	20	67	113,000	44	46,822	100	$11,300,193	26	385	1
Your Property	**$7,435,793**	**8**	**22**	**21**	**1**	**3**	**205,000**	**79**	**7,280**	**16**	**$5,390,295**	**14**	**140**	**6**

at your property: you scored 12 points but only generated USD$600,000 in revenue. The bad news is you are doing only half the revenue per point; USD$50,000 versus USD$100,000. The good news is that, in theory, you could double your prices as you offer more value than Property A. If over time you could achieve this price increase, your total sponsorship revenue would rise from USD$600,000 to USD$1.2 millions.

PHASE V – DISTILL FINDINGS

At this point, you might be somewhat overwhelmed by the amount of insights and information you have collected. Now is the time for you to contemplate all of it and determine where you will go. What have you learned, and what can you use as you begin to develop your strategy? What are the most important findings? The bulk of your distillation effort should focus on articulating your equity.

I like to tell properties that all of them have a chest of gold. Some organizations keep it on display at their front desk, on their social channels, or in their public engagements. Others have it in a darkened back room, dusty under a tarp, or forgotten in a storage facility. Still other organizations do not know if they even have any gold. They are either convinced that they are worthless, or they have never made a substantial effort to discover their gold. Two of these groups are getting what they deserve — an underperforming sponsorship program that is subject to regular board criticism, ongoing staff frustration, and dissatisfied corporate partners.

For your property to maximize its potential, you must uncover your equity, articulate its value, and promote it to sponsors.

If I walked into your organization tomorrow, I would start tearing it apart to find your equity. I would want to read your annual reports, your latest strategic plan, your brand bible, research reports, and your operating plan. I would likely discover that half of you do not have such works of art. I would want to talk to everybody I could. Employees, participants, beneficiaries, sponsors, past sponsors, and sponsor prospects. I would talk to the media that covers you, the agencies that support you, and the consultants that have advised you. I would seek out your critics and your competitors. I would interview your board.

Once I had finished, I would want to sit with you and start sifting through all my findings. Together, we would start to understand your role in society in the eyes of your internal stakeholders, and how that aligns with the view of external stakeholders. We would categorize your offerings against the different types of equity I previously outlined. Objectively, we would assess where you are strong and where you are not as strong as you think you are.

Once we have distilled this information, we would start asking for the organization to support us. This can be a challenge for organizations that have spent significant time and resources on their mission, vision, and purpose statements. What we are doing should build off that, and unless they are poor quality (which they often are), we will have an entire other issue to deal with, but let us be optimistic and hope they are not. The value proposition or equity statement we are drafting is solely for B2B purposes.

- What is our value to a sponsor?
- Are we a Youth Sports Organization or a Partner in Health?

- Are we a Fall Fair or a Community Builder?
- Are we an Awards Show or an Inspiring Voice?
- Are we a Cultural Festival or a Celebration of Diversity?
- Are we a Music Tour or a Summer Escape?

Even from these simple headlines, you can understand that redefining who you are can dramatically change the impression of your property. Why write "sponsorship proposal" on the cover of your deck when you could invite a company to "Join Us in Building Our Community." That is what your equity is, and it is important enough to shout it out on the front cover.

You may now be convinced that equity is what a sponsor wants, yet you definitely still do not feel comfortable that it is something of value. You are much more comfortable articulating the tangible value of attendance figures, audience numbers, and hosting opportunities. Those facts will definitely play a role in pricing, but the dominant factor is the value of your property. How you demonstrate that value takes some work, but it's easily accomplished if you tackle it by building a list of all the attributes that make up your property.

Equity Attributes

If your organization cannot fulfill many of the items on this suggested list below, then it needs to assess its mandate immediately and start to pursue more important accomplishments. This sort of assessment is the ultimate test of doing versus achieving.

- Consumer research that demonstrates how much your fans love your property compared to other properties in the region.

- Your intellectual property, an often overlooked aspect of your equity.
- Your standing with government or regulatory bodies.
- Your heritage, how long have you been around.
- The amount people who donate to you compared to other charities, which demonstrates your value to the community.
- Your economic impact that demonstrates your commercial value to the area.
- Your subject matter expertise as demonstrated by the experts on your board/staff; publications you have issued, or media inquiries for your leadership team.
- Omnibus research that demonstrates the issues your property addresses are a prime concern for stakeholders.
- Demonstrated proof of societal impact through innovations, graduates produced, or athletes' accomplishments.
- Awards or honours bestowed on your organization or key individuals.

PHASE VI – STRATEGIC PLAN

A word on strategy. What is your high-level plan to achieve what needs to get done? We have an entire phase devoted to designing the plan, which is followed by the last phase, mapping out implementation.

My favourite strategy tool is the Objectives, Goals, Strategies, and Measures (OGSM) template. It is an amazing process first developed by Procter & Gamble, at least that is what I was told by an ex-P&G who shared it with me. We have utilized the tool for years in our agency, planning events, planning client side and property side sponsorship strategies. I love to tell clients that if they keep just one page of our work, keep the OGSM summary page. This one page encapsulates the entire plan.

OGSM DEVELOPMENT

Writing an OGSM is an iterative process. I strongly suggest you craft, edit, redraft, and get the one-page summary approved before you begin to produce all the supporting pages. Typically, when you develop a sponsorship strategy for a property, there are 20–40 pages of substantive content that follow the OGSM. Being able to present all that content in a simple format to your boss, board, or investors is a beautiful thing. I like to play with the puzzle pieces to ensure they make sense before I plough into the detail. If you cannot explain a strategy or goal in one sentence, then they are not sound. As I walk you through the OGSM sections, you should create a version that reflects how you currently see your organization's strategy.

Objectives

I come from the camp that believes objectives are qualitative and not bound by numbers or time. The best objectives are clear and motivating. They identify where your organization wishes to go. Sample objectives could be:

- Revitalize our sponsorship offering to become a prime revenue driver for the organization.
- Expand our market reach by expanding our geographic sponsor footprint.
- Improve our brand relevance by partnering with more contemporary sponsors
- Utilize sponsorship to improve our participant experience.

Sometimes I struggle writing objectives, because they can often sound like strategies. The best guideline to follow is to remember that the objective is what you want to achieve, and the strategy is how you are going to achieve it.

Goals

Your goals should be measurable, precise, and timely. I am a big believer in three objectives and three goals, but that does not mean that they need to match. For example, if your top objective is to improve sponsorship fulfillment, it does not mean your primary goal is to measure retention. Of course, that is okay if it is. Ensure that your goals do not overlap. If your first goal is to increase revenue by 50%, your second goal should not be to double the number of sponsors.

Strategies

This is the how you will achieve your objectives and goals. I recommend no less than four strategies and no more than seven, but if you have three solid strategies, I would not argue against it. More than seven is a recipe for failure. Develop your strategies chronologically. This is not to suggest you cannot work on more than one at a time, but later goals should not be completed before the earlier ones. Your strategies are the headline for your tactics, so they need to be titles, not tasks. An example would be a strategy recommending you launch a B2B marketing campaign to generate sponsor leads. Your tactics would then break out the major initiatives required to design and launch such a campaign.

Tactics

While tactics are not traditionally a part of the OGSM acronym, they are very important, representing the work you will actually be doing. You should have three tactics per strategy. They should be distinct and balanced, requiring approximately the same output of resources and effort. If one tactic is proving to

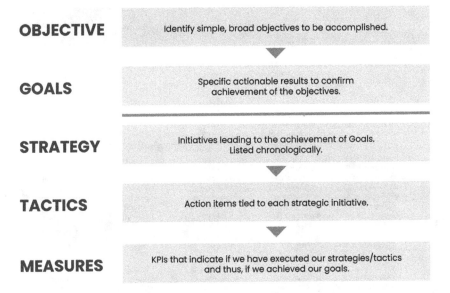

Figure 1:   OGSM One Page Summary Example

be cumbersome, determine if you can unbundle it into multiple tactics.

Measures

I like to develop the measures after the other sections of the OGSM are approved (Figure 1). You can indicate what those measures will be during the development process, but setting the exact targets takes time, especially when you will conceivably measure results that have never been tracked. Each strategy should have one to three key measures, but there is no pressing need for each strategy to have the same number of measures; relevance is more important. Some of your measures may directly reflect one of your goals, as achieving them needs to be embedded into your strategies (Figure 2).

SPONSORSHIP OGSM

OBJECTIVE
1. Create the Properties sponsorship value proposition to grow and sustain revenue
2. Clarify the Properties equity to maximize value for sponsors
3. Evolve the Property into a best-in-class sponsorship partner in the nation

GOALS
1. Achieve annual sponsorship revenue of at least $X,XXX by 20XX
2. Become a championed platform of at least one national corporation by 20XX
3. By 20XX, ensure at least 75% of Property's sponsors renew their partnership commitments

STRATEGIES

| 1. Embrace properties equity in heritage, environment, and healthy living | 2. Create a sponsorship approach with ownable elements to connect with the population | 3. Leverage key properties stakeholders in sponsorship acquisition and fulfillment | 4. Ensure an expert and systematic approach to sponsorship fulfillment | 5. Utilize the national celebration as a marquee moment |

TACTICS

| 1. Create and assess an inventory of existing sponsorable assets 2. Differentiate property sponsorship equity through a heritage platform 3. Establish activity- and equity- based sponsor segmentations | 1. Create a national retail program to increase in-market presence 2. Engage property users through new sponsorable events and programs 3. Create a sponsorship framework with defined opportunities and benefits | 1. Use public and private networks for outreach and facilitating connections 2. Secure media partnership assets to leverage in other sponsorships 3. Provide expertise and tools for partner organizations to supplement property funding | 1. Establish processes and templates for sponsor servicing 2. Make a commitment to best-in-class sponsorship activation 3. Create measures and tools for consistent sponsorship evaluation and reporting | 1. Create a celebration driven by event best practices and principles 2. Develop ownable activations to enhance the celebration 3. Leverage the momentum of the celebration and create a lasting legacy for property |

MEASURES

| 1. # of different property messages from both internal and external sources 2. # of sponsors secured per activity or equity type 3. Total revenue from new activity- and equity-based sponsorship opportunities | 1. Total revenue from retail partnerships 2. Total Canadians engaged in new events and programs 3. Total sponsors engages in new events and programs | 1. # of new corporate prospects attending networking events 2. Total new media opportunities created for sponsors 3. Total sponsorship revenue earned at local property level | 1. Efficiency / effectiveness in sponsorship execution 2. Adoption rate of processes and tools for measurements 3. Feedback from sponsors | 1. Participation rates in anniversary activities 2. % change in property usage during and after anniversary year 3. Sponsorship revenue from anniversary opportunities |

Figure 2: OGSM Example

PHASE VII – DEVELOP THE IMPLEMENTATION PLAN

Your final phase is to build a plan to get all this work done. With an approved OGSM in your pocket, you can now plan what needs to happen and when. While you are not doing the work yet, you do want to inform the person reading the proposal beforehand, so you can get approvals for needed resources.

The best implementation plans are realistic about what can be achieved. Both your available resources and the urgency of your situation will guide this. If your organization is facing a significant challenge in the area of sponsorship, you will need to tackle most of the changes identified in your OGSM almost immediately. Hopefully, you will be given the resources to do so.

I recommend that you start with an implementation timeline (Figure 3). It should cover off every element listed in the OGSM and include resource assignments, start dates, due dates, approval dates, etc. You should incorporate costs to provide a

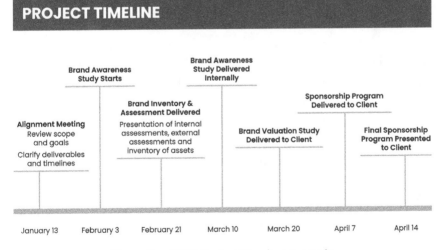

Figure 3: T180 Project Timeline Example

window into the financial impact of these changes if possible. If you have a strategy that requires increased staffing resources, a timeline for their hiring and corresponding financial impact is essential.

Human resource planning is a critical part of your implementation plan. You will not be able to change your strategic approach to any significant degree unless you repurpose your existing resources. In small organizations, the individual tasked with sponsorship sales often wears a programming or marketing hat; if their non-revenue-generating duties were removed, you could expect them to assume increased development duties. Pro sports teams often have over 100 individuals in business development; in such a case, a sophisticated plan involving personnel would be required. In many of my consulting experiences, we guide our clients on how to grow from a smaller to a midsize department. We like to plot the increased resource costs along with anticipated increased revenues. This provides guideposts for when investments should be made, and a metric for evaluating their success. In other cases, we have worked with our clients to secure new, external human resources, such as a sales agency. Here as well, investment must be tracked along with projected returns.

Beyond human resources, there are other investment considerations, which can include new resources, software, or other sales tools you should acquire — such as new sales materials, increased hosting, travel, or conference expenditures — and the development of new fulfillment tools, templates, and reporting mechanisms. The best time to request this support is when management is embracing this plan. Presumably, you have undertaken this exercise to solve problems and cure issues. Like your sponsor prospect, the existence of corporate pain often facilitates investment in new approaches.

THE WHAT SPONSORS' WANT (WSW) PROPOSAL DECK

I firmly believe that if you follow the WSW model, you can easily write a five-sentence, five-paragraph, or five-chapter proposal deck. Of course, that means you have first reimagined your value proposition, and secondly, secured internal commitment to fulfill it. If you have done those things, you can now put them into action. For many properties, the first outward sign that action has begun will be the appearance of sales materials.

You need to reimagine your sales materials. This is always a challenging topic for properties. What materials should they produce? How customized should they be? What will be best received by partners? In an era where corporate sponsors are habitually ignoring sales proposals, you need to think this through. Changing your sales materials is not enough — it needs to begin with the person who answers the phone, your boilerplate corporate descriptors, your sponsors page on your website. All actions and communications need to demonstrate the revitalized value proposition. Every touch point needs to be reoriented to put the sponsor first and your property second.

What are the sections of your new introduction deck? How does it read? How would I communicate what sponsors want in a deck?

Section 1 – Share the Gold

In this section, you should focus on the equity in your property and how it can benefit the sponsor. You need to look beyond just attendance numbers and media reach to communicate the brand value that your organization has achieved. Further, you need to demonstrate to the sponsor that stakeholders value you. By the end of this section, your prospect should want to bask in the spotlight alongside you.

Section 2 – Storytelling Platform

Because of your presented value, you are a great platform on which your sponsor can build their story. This is not about reach. This is about authenticity, legitimacy, and impact. That is what you can provide the sponsor. That is what they cannot achieve on their own.

Section 3 – Activate, Activate, Activate

How can you work with the sponsor to engage key stakeholders, customers, consumers, prospects, influencers, and decision makers? Prove that you have done it before. Talk about how you are creating for the future.

Section 4 – Prove It

Demonstrate the impact you can have on sponsor's business. Communicate the impact you have on society. Make a pledge that whatever you do together will get measured.

Section 5 – A Smart Decision

You are asking someone, a person, a breadwinner, to risk their corporate standing by investing in you. Demonstrate that you will be a great partner with which to work. Eliminate the risk. Stand out from other properties by your commitment to your sponsor.

Remember, this is just a model. Your WSW approach may have six parameters or four. You may focus your discussion on how your property services all the individuals who work for the sponsor. You may decide that borrowing equity and telling stories are the same thing or need to be flipped in order. All those decisions are right, because they are yours. Because you made them based on what was best for your sponsors. Because that is what you believe they want.

SEAN GOODALL

Sean Goodall is a hater of inefficiency, a fitness enthusiast, singer, a song-writer, and a part-time actor. All of these in addition to building a career in experiential marketing. He got his start in an ice cream shop that he managed before going to university. A worshipper of his grandfather, Sean lives by the words that "a day without laughter is a day lost." His quirky educational background — a major in Marketing, minor in Acting, and a sprinkle of French language and wine tasting — contribute to his passion for sponsorship marketing.

On top of his creative interests, Sean is a lover of all things finance, making him a coveted breed in our sector. A man committed to breakthrough work, as long as the results are delivered. His summary forecast for the sponsorship industry solidly reinforces that point. "As marketing channels become increasingly diluted, I predict brands will demand more tangible reporting and metrics, and properties will be forced to better define KPIs upfront. No longer will it be acceptable for properties to deliver post-program reporting months after the event, with a lack of detail."

Tell us about eSports and the growth of the industry over the past few years.

While many are surprised that video games can now sell out 40,000+ seat arenas, the writing has been on the wall for quite some time. Fox Sports wrote a great article about the history of eSports and competitive video game play. They are right to call out that competitive gaming really started back in 1958 with the introduction of "Tennis for Two." Since then, gaming habits have continued to evolve and almost every interactive game since has had multiplayer capabilities. Competition that expanded beyond a friend base began in the 1980s with game manufacturers such as Atari hosting national "high-score" tournaments that drew tens of thousands. From there, dial-up modems brought the comparison of high scores online. From there, online game play evolved to the point where in 2002, "Major League Gaming" was formed to promote video games as a sport. The first broadcast of gaming was in 2006 when the USA Network partnered with MLG to broadcast a Halo competition. The introduction of 'Live' gaming services whereby everyday players could compete against others from around the globe drove a global competitive market and from there, the current ecosystem of players, teams, tournaments, and live broadcasts has come to fruition.

Do you think this growth will continue? Why or why not?
Absolutely. In my opinion, eSports has been a long time coming for an industry that has been around for decades. Gaming has long been a pastime enjoyed in your parent's basement with friends, but the introduction of online gaming led to the emergence of pseudo-celebrities for each title, which ultimately led to competitive gaming. Technologies will undoubtedly continue to evolve and with the emergence of AR and VR, e-gaming will likely only get more realistic and more immersive, and become more of a spectacle for eSports enthusiasts, globally.

What kind of role does sponsorship currently play in eSports?
Sponsorship in eSports follows similar pattern to its role in traditional sports sponsorships. A brand can sponsor a player, a team, a league, or a tournament with rights varying from jersey sponsorships all the way to presenting sponsor status. According to Newzoo, a global leader in eSports reporting, brand investment in eSports will hit USD$517 million in 2017, up 41.3% from 2016. This is expected to more than double by 2020, with an expected spend of USD$1.5 billion. Brands are certainly taking notice of the opportunities within the online gaming community. North America represents 37% of this growth.

How can brands better leverage eSports?

I wrote an article a while back on this very question, and it is one, in my opinion, that continues to evolve. A year ago, my focus was on the following three considerations:

- **Aligning your brand with the experience:** finding commonalities between your marketing objectives and the fan experience.
- **Focus on the most relevant opportunities:** eSports has many different avenues for integration, many of which are less obvious — it is easy to spread far instead of focusing on a key opportunity that is right for the brand.
- **It is not right for every brand:** eSports has a range of appropriateness, so it certainly is not right for all brands.

Over the last year though, I would argue that while these three considerations are still relevant, additional channels have opened that can allow brands to test the waters before diving into a full-on sponsorship deal. The highly targeted and engaging social platform, Twitch, has brought the influencer game to the eSports community while more consumer-facing products such as VR shops that showcase e-Sports tournaments are expanding the scope beyond the traditional audience.

What makes eSports so appealing for potential sponsorship?
One key difference between eSports and traditional sports sponsorships (at least at this stage) is the audience. While sport sponsorships offer an extremely broad base of fans of varying demographics, eSports is still quite niche in the sense that there are few fans who are not gamers themselves. That said, with 65% of fans falling between the ages of 18 and 35 and almost all of them being avid fans, it offers brands a chance to speak with the coveted millennial demographic. If done right, it can make huge waves.

Where is eSports heading, and how will this impact marketers/ sponsorship in the future?

I would expect that in the coming years, brands will start to solidify their foothold in the eSports marketplace. Currently, especially in the Canadian marketplace, brands have dipped their toes in the water, but have yet to fully commit to long-term investing. Bell is probably the brand that has shown the most interest, but even then, it has limited its investment to Northern Arena, Canada's largest eSports tournament series. As the industry continues to grow and brands can validate the connection between them and the highly engaged market, more traditional multiyear contracts may come in to play.

At the time of this interview, Sean was an Account Manager at the T1 Agency. Sean started working at T1 in August 2016, prior to this Sean spent two years working for GMR Marketing in both Toronto and Vancouver. He is presently a Senior Manager at Scotiabank.

DON MAYO

Everyone in marketing needs to have their own Don Mayo. This is the person who calls out your ideas, who asks the endlessly annoying questions. Someone who shakes their head in a revealing sign of disgust when people tout their campaigns as the second coming. This guru is someone who looks at a global fundraising program and declares it dead three years before its burial. Before I got to know Don, I kept hearing about him from my competitors, my industry peers, and eventually my clients. Finally, I got to meet him and from that day on, I considered him my guru, as many others do.

Don is the managing partner of IMI International, a consultancy that spans four continents and has worked on tens of thousands of research projects in the sponsorship, advertising, digital, and promotional domains. His firm has worked on every sponsorship property possible, from the local county fair to FIFA World Cups. Their insight has helped drive hundreds of sponsorship decisions and changes to campaigns that result in improved optimization.

There is more than one guru in this industry. You need to find yours, but here is what mine wants you to know about sponsorship evaluation.

What are the five questions a researcher should always ask?
I think you should use a few open-ended questions including:

- First thoughts and feelings about the "XYZ event?"
- Please name all the brands, products, services that you know sponsor the "XYZ event."
- Please name all the brands, products, services that you "feel better about" due to their sponsorship of "XYZ event."
- Please name all the brands, products, and services that "positively impacted your consideration of the brand" due to their sponsorship of "XYZ event."
- Please name all the brands, products, and services that "annoyed you" due to their sponsorship of "XYZ event."

How can properties support the sponsor in connecting sponsorship to sales?
Utilize a best practice list.

When is sponsorship not the right answer?
Sponsorship is not the answer if you have any of the following:

- No clear objectives.
- No pre-during-post plan.
- No 360° integrations — onsite/virtual/POP.
- No time/plan to intercept with added value.
- Have no plan in general.

- No budget to activate.
- Require three years to mature and optimize.

At the time of this interview, Don was the Managing Partner, Global, at IMI International. Don has worked for IMI International since 1985, where he has personally worked with hundreds of brands in Canada and around the globe, across thousands of digital and XM programs.

Chapter 9

THE FUTURE OF SPONSORSHIP —
IS IT ALREADY HERE?

PREDICTIONS ARE DANGEROUS

Some people believe you can use the past to predict the future. Others believe the past will always repeat itself. Discuss the topic with another group, and they will convince you looking at trends is the only way to predict the future. What I will tell you is I am not predicting the future of sponsorship; pretending one can divine the future of anything is a slippery slope. I want to provide my perspective on what the future of sponsorship should be. Think of this as less of a trend watch and more as a platform for making my pitch to you, my vision of where sponsorship marketing should head over the next 10–20 years and why.

I am less concerned about being right about the next era of sponsorship than I am about helping you see what your future in the industry may look like. My hope is not legacy or fame, but I do want to inspire new ways of thinking about sponsorship. I want to motivate people to think about sponsorship from the perspective of the person on the other side of the meeting table, the sponsor. I want to help flame your passion and career ambitions for an amazing industry. If anything here contributes even in the smallest way to helping your career, I will gladly accept this discreet triumph.

I see a bright future for you and the sponsorship industry.

Perhaps I am blinded by own passion for this business. Perhaps I am an eternal optimist. Perhaps I am biased. Likely all three. However, when I consider the potential of what lies ahead, I do not want to hold back. I do not want to be restrained by what technologies exist today, because I know there will be new iterations tomorrow. I do not want to be held back by what sports or events exist today, because I know there will be new ones next week. I do not want to feel confined by cultural or societal changes, because they help create a beautiful canvas to paint what is next.

The future I see for sponsorship is built on three hopeful, if somewhat dramatic, assumptions.

People Will Still Love People

The most significant factor in driving the future health of the sponsorship marketing industry is this: human beings love to associate, connect, and bond with other people. People want to be around people. They want to make friends, share experiences, celebrate family, and create memories. This alone makes the sponsorship industry technology-proof. I maintain that no matter what amazing forms of altered reality technology can create; they will always be based on just that, reality.

The best technologies of the future will continue to be less and less about the technology, and increasingly about how they can enhance the human experience. Whereas today's smartphones distract from the live viewing experience of sports (say, people holding up their phones to take pictures/video), tomorrow they may be seamless and easily controlled by a phone's ability to respond to commands from your subconscious. The sports stadium of tomorrow could blend the live experience and technological enhancements that will accentuate, not distort, the activity.

People Will Still Support People

Regardless of geopolitical conflict, wars, terrorism, or political jockeying, human beings are fundamentally compassionate and supportive of one another. Whether it is the procurement of food for our loved ones, the protection of our neighbors, or aiding the less fortunate, we care. I know that this can be hard to reconcile if you watch or follow most newsfeeds but read closely and you will see how true it is.

Because of this, consumers propensity to support what matters to them will never die. In turn, they will have even heightened expectations of what they expect from their communities, their governments, and their favourite brands. It will no longer just be about donations or fundraising. It will be about their day-in and day-out operating principles, their public opinions, and their total contribution to society.

People Will Still Compete Against People

The spirit of competition is the foundation of many things in sponsorship. Yes, the most obvious is sports. The ideals of competition — doing your best, overcoming adversity, representing your country or community — will survive forever. I think as the world ebbs and flows, the geopolitics of sport will play a larger role than we can ever imagine. However, competition will exist between people at a different level. This may be counter to my second assertion, but the generations of people younger than me are being raised in the most competitive era of all time. Every action they conduct is now measured. How popular is their posting? Who is the first to know? What reaction did they get to their story? Who has the most followers? While amateur sports officials attempt to keep the score out of youth soccer games, those same kids will be subject to more public scoreboards and peer evaluation than you would ever find on an official soccer field. As sponsors think about the future and connecting with consumers, they will need to take this constantly pouring stream of statistics and opinions into consideration.

WHAT WILL SPONSORS WANT?

I have attempted to include here the best of what I have learned about sponsorship in my more than 20 years in the industry. My focus has been its relevance, to ensure that it is highly applicable to today's practices and for today's practitioner. I wanted it to be grounded in experience, yet forward thinking. In other words, useful and somewhat timeless.

However, the world is not going to sit still, and neither will sponsors. What they want is always evolving, maybe not as rapidly as I may like, and you should be evolving with sponsors. This is something that is constantly on my mind. My role at the agency is to primarily think about the future and how we can evolve our services to meet it as it comes. Consequently, you can imagine that much of my time is spent trying to determine what our clients and your sponsors will want in the future.

Any discussion about the future leads me to espouse my now-biased viewpoints. The conversation triggers an inner need to speculate. Some of these viewpoints are based on my interpretation and synthesis of the feedback from others, but a significant amount of me believes that certain course corrections need to occur in our sector. Here are some desires I believe sponsors *will* want.

- **Accountability:** The absence of accountability in certain pockets of sponsorship marketing must be addressed. Make goods exist in media advertising when rebates are provided if viewing audience estimates are not met; they will soon be demanded in sponsorship.
- **Data:** Sponsors will want data. Data. Data. Data. Every business. B2B. B2C. Direct. Indirect. Services. Products. Experiences. They will all hinge on data. Sponsors will become sophisticated at tracking their customers behavioural and purchase patterns. Your property will need to be a part of that mix.
- **Shares:** Yes, the word "partnership" is used by so many properties that they better be prepared for a sponsor to call them on it. If we are real partners, where are my shares? The sponsor is investing in your property, and investment means equity. Don't want to give up shares? Stop overusing the word partnership.
- **Embedded Activation:** I do not want to put myself out of business, but why is it that properties do not include activation as a core asset of their offering? It should not be an add-on. "Just for Laughs" in Montreal is now providing creative services for their sponsors. They know best how to create and distribute comedic content. Why should their sponsors look elsewhere?
- **Broadcasting Powers:** Sponsors will want to be broadcasters. The battle for content rights is becoming more intense by the day. For a property, the broadcast revenue is often still the largest driver. Sponsors are frustrated as they want to activate, but they cannot utilize the best content in real time. Something is going to break. I think it is the model of sponsorship as we know it today.
- **Total Ownership:** Red Bull does it. Nike often does it. Virgin does it. Bell has started doing it. Big brands realize that they have the resources, talent, and clout to create their own properties. These owned properties deliver precisely what the brands want in terms of fulfilling their marketing needs. They often result in

the brand owner securing secondary sponsors, managing ticket sales, doing broadcast rights deals, and securing government grants.

- **Leverage Community:** Sponsorship properties talk a lot about community, but they cannot deliver. The need to be local in an increasingly global world is a significant driver for many brands. As you watch major brands such as FC Barcelona, the NBA, and others build tours, offices, and special events in far-flung markets around the world, you can see a pattern emerging. Sponsors know their consumers want a tangible connection to the property. Properties need to figure out how to deliver it.
- **Creating Their Own Charities:** Many sponsors have causes that are near to their business heart but find that the entities operating in that sector are either disorganized, controversial, or not sufficiently focused. Businesses are not distracted, and they want to jump in and create their own, especially when they realize that today's consumer will grant them permission to do so.

WHAT WILL YOUR SPONSORS WANT?

There is one final, simple message with which I would love to leave you: talk to your sponsors. What do they want today? What do they want tomorrow?

In some cases, they will be able to articulate it clearly for you. I will warn you that in other cases they may not have the direct answer you are expecting but ask anyway. Ask them more than once. Ask more than one person inside and outside of your sponsor's organization. Trust me, the answers exist. It will just take time for them to become apparent.

That is what this book is intended to do. To help stimulate your mind so that you will know where to find the answers. To help you think a bit differently than you did before page one. To help you reframe how you deliver your property to your sponsors.

Somebody asked me if the creation of the *What Sponsors' Want* framework was a response to a particular request. It was not, really. Sometimes the best solutions are for problems that people have but were never able to articulate. I think that is why I wrote this book. In dealing with my clients and colleagues, I could sense their need for answers to questions that perhaps they have no been able to ask.

I have done my best to identify those questions and more, providing answers to those questions and more, but if you have some of either — questions or answers — please connect with me, and we can have some fun tackling them.

I look forward to hearing from you about how your new approach is working.

SCENARIOS

GOLF PROPERTY SPONSORSHIP OFFERING SCENARIO

Background

With the continued growth of the golf industry in Asia, a new Global Golf Tour (GGT) tournament has been scheduled. Although an official date has not been selected, it is confirmed that the event will take place within the next five years on a beautiful island course. Renovations to the course and clubhouse are set to be completed before then and will bring the course to GGT standards with first-class facilities. As the event is brand-new, the Local Asian Golf Association (LAGA) must work to develop a sponsorship offering and secure sponsorships well ahead of the event in order to meet financial targets.

Align on Objectives

As part of a successful future, LAGA management team has determined they need to create a comprehensive sponsorship offering to build a sponsorship portfolio that focuses on revenue generation and brand building.

Internal Assessment

An important first step in developing a lucrative sponsorship portfolio is to perform an audit of all sponsorship assets and their worth. This will include media assets, signage assets, onsite consumer engagement assets, venue naming rights, publications and collateral, and more. Analysis should be conducted to determine the value of borrowed equity sponsors will receive based on the sponsorship of specific assets.

- Understand LAGA's and the tournament's brand guidelines and goals to ensure potential sponsors are the right fit.
- Review resources necessary for implementing a successful sponsorship program: personnel, tracking systems, fulfillment systems, and financial resources.
- Review LAGA's financial goals of the tournament and determine how sponsorship will play a specific role in meeting these goals.

Possible Learnings: What percentage of revenue does sponsorship need to generate in order reach the top-line objective?

External Assessment

- Research case studies regarding golf properties/sports entering new markets to determine factors of success.
- Research sponsorship industry trends and sports sponsorship industry trends.
- Research trends in golf, such as the rise of virtual reality golf stimulators, and how fans are engaging with golf in different ways.
- Research other golf tournaments and sport properties in the Asian market, who sponsors them, how many sponsors do they have, what do the sponsors pay for specific rights, what are the attendance figures, etc.
- Build an understanding of different types of media value in the region.
- Conduct research around potential consumer demographics, attendance figures, viewership figures for GGT properties, and other sports properties in Singapore.

- What sponsorship assets are typically made available by GGT properties, and what assets can LAGA purchase/create/utilize for the new tournament to set themselves apart.
- Research organizations that meet brand and revenue potential criteria and create a list of potential sponsors.
- Which potential sponsors will help grow and strengthen the brand of the tournament?
  - How large is their audience, do they have similar characteristics, do they engage with the local market or international markets, etc.

Benchmarking Analysis

Research sponsorship programs of other GGT and LAGA properties that have potentially similar attendee demographics, reach, and size of market, which will enable comparisons across available alternatives.

- Focus on factual information: sponsorship pricing, attendance figures, demographics, viewership, etc.

Distill Findings

Determine the total revenue potential of the golf tournaments sponsorship assets and equity, and the potential value the assets would have for sponsors by assessing the information collected in the internal assessment, external assessment, and benchmarking analysis. Through analyzing these assessments, take note if there are any common themes that you can leverage when approaching sponsors.

Strategic Approach

Based on your findings, determine which tournament assets are sponsored and develop a game plan to sell these assets.

1. Determine what your sponsorship is offering.
    a. Ask yourself what is unique that you can provide to sponsors.
    b. Why will they want to sponsor you?

Idea: Leverage the lifestyle association of golf and the tightknit community that exists within golf or leverage the global opportunity for brands who are looking to expand into Asia.

2. Determine a list of sponsorship assets.
    a. List should prioritize assets by their potential worth.
    b. Ask yourself which assets are appropriate for different sectors of prospects.

3. Determine appropriate list of prospects.
    a. Need to ensure the prospect's objectives align with what you can offer.

Idea: Look at a vertical integration for a brand. Look for companies who sponsor with a variety of golf players and varying levels of golf associations in Asia. This will not only help them grow their golf portfolio but give them a seal of authenticity.

4. Properly equip sales teams.
    a. Build a creative offering that meets the prospect's needs rather than a generic list of what you have.
    b. Ensure the team knows your core offering.
    c. Allow for flexibility in the ability to offer discounts, customized packages, etc. There is no more "Bronze, Silver, and Gold" packages.

Idea: Have an intern working with your sales team who can final all information about potential prospects to ensure the sales team can focus on converting prospects into sponsors and not the time-consuming research.

5. Develop servicing plan.
    a. Once partners are obtained, you need to properly service to retain and renew these sponsors.
    b. Ensure contracts finalization is seamless, provide incredible communication, and listen to your sponsors and their needs.

Idea: Always look past year one and see how this partnership could develop in the future. Be aware of your partners business objectives and challenges and see if you can help them at all.

Design Implementation Plan

- Where can you find external help?
    o Work with an agency or research firm or hire an intern to conduct research.
    o Ensure that you have the appropriate resources at every stage in the process.

- Ensure you have dedicated resources specifically to sales team, as well as to everyone else.
- Develop a sponsorship sales schedule and funnel. This includes a workback plan with identified key dates.
    o Create goals and objectives that your team can work towards to keep them motivated.

LOSING TITLE SPONSOR SCENARIO

Background

The National Heart Association (NHA) is the largest non-profit, voluntary organization in the nation dedicated to fighting heart disease. They employ over 3,000 employees and over 20 million volunteers. They run many initiatives throughout the year to help generate revenue for the association, including runs, walks, tournaments, corporate events, etc. Each individual event has their own team and set of volunteers dedicated to managing the event, selling sponsorship, and servicing sponsors.

Aside from each individual event, the NHA has national, multiyear partners that support the organization as a whole and leverage the existing events through activation. Many of the NHA's resources, including staff, rely on these partner's contributions. Recently, NHA's highest revenue *Premier Sponsor* has informed them they will be opting out of their five-year partnership after three years into the deal. This is a significant revenue loss for the NHA. The NHA needs to find a new sponsor in order to continue all their initiatives and employ all their staff.

Align on Objectives

It is a top priority to find and sign a premier partner to a multiyear agreement and ensure that this agreement is seen through in full. NHA needs to improve sponsorship sales efforts and offering that is already in place.

Internal Assessment

NHA will quickly need to reassess their own resources and programs in order to identify how sponsorship sales can be better managed and optimized. This process will require the NHA's sponsorship team to sit in a room and establish their core offering to the new potential sponsor. Some of the items that will need to be established internally include:

- What assets does the NHA have available for a title sponsor, and how will these engage their target market?
- Asses what assets were currently available for the title sponsor, and what can be added to maximize the return on investment for the sponsor?

- o Does the NHA have any benefits or experiences for the sponsors employees?
- o What assets allow the sponsor to hit their specific target?
- o What assets allow the sponsor to hit the maximum number of impressions?

- Conduct in person conversations with all small and large decision makers of the NHA/the specific event the sponsor will be sponsoring, to ensure alignment on what type of sponsor you would like to target.

Idea: It may be worth holding stakeholder interviews or meetings with current sponsors to determine if there is a servicing gap. NHA can ask these current sponsors what they are happy and unhappy with and further improve on their core offering to potential sponsors. These current partners may be able to provide exact insights into what a potential partner may be looking for.

External Assessment

NHA will need to understand relevant trends and all environmental information available to them. This information includes but is not limited to the following:

- Information on sponsorship decision-makers.
  - o Are there brands who are currently making annual donations to the NHA, who could be brought in as a sponsor? Or decision-makers who have a personal tie to the NHA?

- Best practices in sponsorship sales.
  - o Look at who is raising the most money annually through their sponsors.
  - o How are other charities approaching potential sponsors?
  - o What do successful sponsorship pitches/packages from like companies look like?

- Relevant case studies, like other heart/health associations in comparable markets.
  - Complete an analysis of their financials to see how much revenue they are receiving from sponsors on an annual basis.

- Research sponsors already in the health cause space.
  - Research different walks/runs and seeing who their sponsors are, and how those sponsors are activating at these events to get inspiration.
  - Look at brands who are sponsoring health events.

Best practices in sponsorship sales are a great place to start. NHA may be able to find a nugget to help them quickly make a significant sale. In order to find best practices, it may be worth considering all sectors and not just the health cause market.

Conduct Benchmarking Analysis

When assessing the NHA's offerings, it is important to compare those to others of similar suit.

Distill Findings

After compiling the internal and external assessments, you next outline what you believe are the similarities between the two takeaways from Internal and External Assessment:

- Many large partners are looking for one-year deals rather than multiyear deals.
- Many partners prefer to focus on a few specific events rather than an entire organization.
- Sponsors are looking for something specific to their brand, trying to stand out from the clutter.
- Sponsors all have a set of objectives and they are willing to spend appropriately to meet all those objectives.

Strategic Approach

Develop a strategy fully focused on sales efforts.

1. Determine what makes you unique.
   a. Determine your unique selling point for sponsors, to ensure that you are giving sponsors a unique opportunity. This will give you competitive advantage in an over saturated market.

2. Develop single and multiyear packages.
   a. Develop a more concise single year sponsorship package in addition to the multiyear package already in place, ensure that you are catering each of your sponsorship packages to each prospect.
   b. Determine which assets are most important to a partner and include these in the offering in their customized package.

3. Cultivate a shortlist of prospects
   a. Identify a shortlist of select prospects who have objectives that you can solve, perhaps having an intern working with the sales team.
   b. Determine which brands would be a contender for a single year sponsorship and which you want to target for a multiyear package.

4. Identify who the key decision-makers are.
   a. Discover ways to meet their organization and personal needs.

5. Establish a relationship with the prospects.
   a. Remember that this is not only a sponsor for an event, but potentially could be the beginning of a long-term partnership. Ensure that you are making the entire process seamless and as smooth as possible. Show your prospects that you are serious and professional.

Implementation Plan

Once you have determined your strategic approach to successfully meet your objectives, you compose an implementation plan:

- Source/Determine the team who will be responsible for sponsor prospect sourcing.
  - Research information on prospects to properly equip the sales team.
- Source tools/support for the sales team during proposal/negotiation process.
  - Implement internal pricing tools, negotiation guidance, prioritization guidance, and contract advisory.
- Ensure that the team has a detailed workback schedule to ensure deadlines and key dates are met.

ARTS FESTIVAL SCENARIO

Background

Some 82 years ago, the festival in question was born as an art auction. Its original founders were a group of local painters, struggling to make ends meet. Finding customers for their art seemed impossible despite the almost universal praise they received for their creations. One autumn day, two of the artists attended an antique auction, as they were both passionate yet fiscally challenged collectors. The idea of mimicking the auction format struck them both simultaneously, as they realized the energy in the room generated by the auctioneer's ability to create a sense of excitement was resulting in many of the pieces selling for far beyond their worth.

It was only two months later they convened their first art auction and the financial windfall far exceeded their initial trepidation of attempting to organize an event, when they felt their only true capabilities in life were much more intangible. Over time the partners invited other artists to participate not only as contributors but organizers. In order to accommodate the growing number of painters who wanted to sell at their event, the collaborators created ancillary events including wine tasting, musical performances, art classes, and meal occasions. Magically it seemed that no matter what they included, it was well received and financially beneficial.

As the festival grew and expanded, two important realities set in. The organizing and executing of the event had quickly outpaced the abilities and the interest of the organizing artists. Second, the event's success was attracting requests to participate from a broad array of businesses, charities, political groups, and vendors. Everyone wanted in on the action. Solving the first dilemma would provide a mechanism to deal with the second, so a decision was made to create a non-profit organization, governed by many of the key collaborators who would now serve as a board, and then hire professional staff to manage the event. A critical mandate of this staff was to not only ensure the artists continued to have a venue for being discovered and selling their work, but also to establish policies and protocols to handle the intake of interested non-indigenous organizations.

A Crowded Pallet

Over time, the staff found it quite easy to secure sponsors. The festival was unique, the interest from corporate partners was flattering, and their demands were quite minimal. Businesses were excited to affiliate with the festival as it magically drew young and old, wealthy and poor, locals and tourists. It provided days of entertainment for families and venues for VIPs to feel important.

Despite the artsy origins of the event, its accessibility was infallible. The participating artists ranged in talent and renown providing opportunities for anyone to find something that fit their price range. For those who had no interest in art, the surrounding events provided significant entertainment. Beer gardens featured fiddlers, and acoustic bands. A bingo hall provided fun and excitement. A roulette wheel offered even more thrills.

Brands poured in. Some acting as vendors, selling their wares. Others providing financial donations in return for a better table in the VIP lounge. Companies wanting to impress new customers would commission artists to paint gifts for their clients. Businesses that wanted their employees' loyalty held company picnics onsite during the event to which they paid for every employee's family to enjoy.

The festival grounds were quickly turning into a messy canvas of signs, logos, exhibits, and messaging. It increased gradually every year, so only those who had not been onsite for a few years would even be capable of detecting the changes, but over time the staff and sponsors started to sense that something was wrong. The festival had somehow gone from being a creative celebration to feeling like a Fall fair. It was bright, noisy, and camped.

Many of the longstanding sponsors started to withdraw when new executives ascended at the company and begin to question the value of participation. While the festival staff did the best they could, the demands of unhappy partners taxed their resources and capacity. Quickly a snowball effect began to occur, as unhappy partners demanded more attention, resulting in less attention for happy partners who then became unhappy. This year the festival Board finally recognized that they were losing sponsors, and something needed to be done.

Starting with an Empty Canvas

The Board decided to strike a working committee to solve the sponsorship issue who reached out to me for some process advice.

I recommended they utilize my T180 process given that they had never attempted this before. What is beautiful about following a process is you can utilize the learnings of others to eliminate wasted steps or actions.

Don't forget this is a fictional case, so the committee that does not exist, did not actually reach out to me. The following is a summarized version of the outputs for each phase in the strategic process.

Align on Objectives

The committee agreed that they needed to completely revamp the festival's approach to sponsors. There was alignment to deal with potential short-term decreases in revenue to ensure that the right long-term solution was found.

It was determined that sponsorship and programming of the festival would no longer be distinct departments.

Internal Assessment

- Reviewed past five-year revenue to determine our 80/20 rule of sponsors. Realized that on average 15 sponsors contribute 81.1% of our revenue, five partners contribute 8.5% and 82 sponsors contribute the other 10.4% of revenue.
- Evaluated the contracts of all sponsors and identified that 78 of the 82 Tier III sponsors term their contribution as a donation, but still expect sponsor benefits.
- Conducted a survey with all participating artists to understand their comfort level with corporate partners and what they feel adds or detracts from the property.
- In-person conversations were held with a cross-section of sponsors from small to large.

External Assessment

The committee conducted interviews and meetings with dozens of similar festivals and special events in the regional area to understand their approaches. It becomes clear from this review that those events that treated sponsorship as more than a revenue source were having the most success.

- A survey was issued to all sponsor prospects from the past two years as well as lapsed sponsors to get their feedback which clearly indemnified that prospects did not see much value in sponsoring the festival. The prevailing sentiment was the festival was like a flea market when it came to corporate involvement.
- For inspiration, a review of all winning cases from the past three years of festival and events sponsorship awards competitions was conducted.
- These cases richly informed the committee's understanding of what made for great festival sponsorship programs.
- A consumer survey was conducted in the region, asking for attribute feedback on the various festivals within a two-hour drive of the respondents which showed significant issues in the net promoter scores for this festival.

Benchmark Analysis

An assessment of the festival was conducted to compare the direct competitors, indirect competitors, and best-in-class properties. This analysis focused on:

- Numbers of sponsors and tiers.
- Attendees to sponsorship revenue.
- Number of staff with sponsorship in their title.
- Clustering of the assets being offered.

Distill Findings

It was clear from all the analysis conducted that there were three core issues:

- The property had too many sponsors.
- Many of the festival's sponsors were Hospitality purchasers, exhibitors, or donors.
- The sponsorship clutter was having a negative overall impact on the brand health of the property which was resulting in declines in ticket sales, volunteerism, and media coverage.

Strategic Approach

- Need to build a path to ensure better sponsor servicing and to reduce clutter.
- Hire additional dedicated staff to service each category of sponsor.
- Individualize sponsor deals to separate top sponsors from donors.
- Build clear distinction between sponsor package and a brand who is marking the contribution as a donation and still expect sponsor benefits.
- Create a new way for companies who cannot afford sponsorship to be involved.
  - o This could include developing new compare offerings: donations, group sales, special events. Packaging those offerings. Present the new offering to partners during culling meetings.

- Build a customized package for those top 20–25% sponsors that justifies a cost increase (exclusivity, reduced clutter, improved servicing, better activation opportunities).
  - o Possibly set a high activation standard.

- Redefining what constitutes a sponsor. The tactics would be to establish partners, identify who qualifies, develop a clear definition of what is a sponsor, culling the sponsor list done through corporate reviews with each company over 18–24 months.
- Offer to renew all longstanding sponsors for one year with the caveat that things will be changing the following year with price changes, etc.
  - Important to ensure conversations between property and sponsor are smooth and contract process is seamless.
- Another strategy could revolve around sponsor servicing.

Implementation Plan

- Source work to an agency to help in contract negotiation, sponsor communication/servicing and activation ideas.
- Dedicate staff to servicing.
- Year-by-year reduce sponsor clutter rather than making a massive change in one year.
- Launch a B2B marketing plan to ensure the right type of sponsors are aware of the opportunities.

Rewriting History

If the original founders were alive today, they may look back at the evolution of their child and highlight some lessons learned that are worth recording in the annals of the festival's history. They are lessons that provide untold value for young or old properties as they are timeless.

- The 80/20 rule applies to sponsorship as well. Your property should build a new plan for the three tiers of partners. Tier I contributing 70–80% of your revenue; Tier II being 15–25%; Tier III contributing 5–15%.

- By reducing sponsors, you will be able to offset the revenue loss from eliminating the underperforming partners with rate increases you can justify with remaining partners. This can be based on providing broader category exclusivity while facilitating deeper integration with your property, that should improve stakeholder engagement results.
- In addition to freeing up inventory for higher value partners, you can leverage assets and infrastructure that previously was allocated to low value partners to other business needs such as building your brand or enhancing the participant experience. For example, signage locations that were previously used by sponsors could now be used to provide wayfinding for guests, build the star power of your performing talent, or provide a photo opportunity.

LOCAL CAUSE PROPERTY SCENARIO

Background

The National Association for Camp Counsellors (NACC) develops the education for, and national communications and PR on behalf, of camp counsellors across the country. The NACC has existed for 24 years and is comprised of provincial members who distribute the NACC's communications and education to their given province. The NACC team is split into three operational departments including: Education, Marketing and Communications, and Operations/Admin.

The NACC's governance model — provincial members owning the delivery education to camp counsellors in their province — creates struggles with ownerships of events that could generate sponsorship revenue. NACC does not have great brand awareness and their public relations has not had much success. The NACC does do a great job at generating earned media through its provincial members and camps across the nation by sharing messaging through those groups.

The main issues NACC are facing include generating sponsorship revenue and the fact they do not own education events.

Align on Objectives

- NACC needs to expand their program offerings that support the provincial partnership.
- NACC need to ideate and secure new ways to generate revenue.

Internal Assessment

- Conduct an analysis of the organizations capacity to undertake new programming and what are existing programs.
  - Determine if any could be used to generate revenue.
- Based on the organizational structure, understand the impact of the membership and what values they contribute to the national body.

Idea: Review the provincial initiatives and identify that each of the provincial members is hosting their own "Camp Counsellors Week" at various times throughout the year.

Idea: Conduct interviews with influential member provinces and ascertain whether they want the national education standard that they deliver to be highlighted; they are supportive of rallying behind the national brand.

- Evaluate existing sponsorship contracts that are in place with the NACC.
- Interview prospects to understand what they want from NACC.
  - Determine what they are looking for from the NACC as a sponsor and identify what you can offer as a property to sponsors.
- Be honest about organizational gaps and use them to identify areas for development or areas where you can have a greater impact.

Idea: Review budgets and programs of the past five years and identify a public relations and brand building gap.

o Understand the organizational mission and ensure work is on-message to build stronger brand affinity for potential partners.

External Assessment

- Assess the organization against other not-for-profits of similar size, similar mission (education).
  - o How many sponsors do these organizations have?
  - o What types of sponsors do these organizations have?
  - o What type of programs do these organizations have?

- What programs are sponsored?
- Assess the organization against other not-for-profits with provincial memberships.
  - o How do these organizations leverage their network for revenue generation?
  - o How do these organizations collaborate with their provincial members?

- Determine list of tangible and intangible assets of the organization — are there program elements that are not included that are easy to undertake?
- Identify what programs your provincial members are running — are they all having success on the same programs, are there provincially-run programs with the chance to scale?
- Identify opportunities to equity share with the provincial membership in a nationally branded ownable property.
  - o Are there examples of this in the industry or in like-organizations?
  - o What would this look like — would the equity cost be worth the risk?

Possible learnings:

- Some national not-for-profit organizations in other markets collaborate with their provincial memberships on an awareness week to generate public relations and brand awareness.
- The collective support for these national weeks expands the marketing engine powering the movement.
- Online events — measured by social aggregators — combining in-person activations (provincial) and national messaging have the power to unite across province.

Conduct Benchmarking Analysis

- When assessing your property's offering, compare it to alternatives.
- How do the number of attendees with different target demographics compare?
- How does your social following compare?
- How does overall popularity and brand perceptions compare?

Distill Findings

- Use what you have learned from the internal and external assessments to identify ways to address the objectives.

Possible key takeaways:

- Identify the need for the NACC to have an ownable property.
- Identify types of own able properties that can generate the NACC revenue and support the provincial membership.
- Illustrate that a NACC awareness week as an ownable property can address key objectives (brand building, partnership with the provinces).

Strategic Approach

Next, after looking at the distill findings, it is crucial that you develop a strategy to successfully meet the outlined objectives:

Develop an ownable property that will support provincial partners and generate revenue. The ownable property could be a National Camp Counsellors Week, which engages provincial members in allowing them to host events in their province to specifically support National Camp Counsellors Week.

In order to generate revenue, the NACC will need to research and prospect potential partners. Securing sponsorship partners will allow for revenue generation and a successful property. It is important to allow for provincial members to secure their own sponsors for supporting the event in their provinces.

Establish Your Resources

In order to create an ownable property, that continue to grow and succeed, the planning is vital. The NCCA needs to ensure that they have the proper resources dedicated to this project.

Idea: outsource a creative agency to assist in concept ideation as well as determine an execution plan.

Create A New Ownable Property

Idea: *National Camp Counsellors Week*. This week would engage provincial members in allowing them to host events in their province to specifically support National Camp Counsellors Week.

Begin Sponsorship Prospecting

- Determine what assets you have to offer a sponsor and the estimated value of these assets — are there any unique selling points for the NCCA?
- Research various organizations and companies who could be potential sponsor.
- Do their objectives, values, and mission statement align with the NCCA for a natural partnership?

- Create various sponsorship packages, for single year and multi-year partnerships for companies/brands ranging in sizes.
- Ensure that you are catering and personalizing each package.
- Create a shortlist of prospects who you will approach and start conversations with those prospects.

Sponsorship Implantation Plan

After the research and prospecting is complete, you need to ensure that you have the appropriate resources to successfully obtain sponsors

Ensure that the complete process, form initial outreaching to contract negotiations, is as smooth as possible for the prospects.

Create A Revenue Plan

Have clear goals and numbers that you want to reach, and timelines associated to them. The creation of this will ensure that the NCCA is aligned internally of what they need from sponsorship to meet revenue goals. Look just past year one and have a goal for the future to ensure the longevity of the NCCA.

MUSIC PROPERTY SCENARIO

Background

Starfest, a 20-year old music festival located in Minneapolis, Minnesota, is known as one of the Midwest's most popular spring festival experiences. A 12-year sponsor of the festival, a large bank, has a new CMO, and the festival's direct contact at this company (Sponsorship Manager) continues to suggest that they are re-evaluating whether music will fit within their sponsorship strategy moving forward.

Align on Objectives

It has been determined that it is a top priority for the Director of Partnerships at Starfest to renew this sponsor, as the amount of revenue that would be lost (at least until a potential replacement sponsor is found) could significantly damage the festival's financial health and overall success.

Internal Assessment

It is important to understand what the brand looks to achieve through its sponsorships — which may be shifting this sponsor. This type of information is typically best secured informally in this situation, since many strategic principles will want to be kept confidential by brands.

Through coffee meetings, lunches, or other chats, you might be able to learn who the sponsor's target market is, whether they want to be top-of-mind among this target, or what to build a very specific brand image, whether they want to engage employees, host B2B clients, etc.

If possible, meet with the new CMO herself, rather than just relying on information to be passed along from the Sponsorship Manager. Review past results from the bank's sponsorship of Starfest.

Possible learnings:
- The bank wants to connect to 18–34 year-olds through their passion points, and it wants to be able to offer unique experiences to high-net-worth clients.
- It worries that a music festival is not the right type of experience for its high-net-worth clients.
- Knowing what the sponsor is looking for, it is important to be brutally honest in assessing your own value proposition as a property.

- What assets and benefits that you offer could allow this sponsor to engage its target market?
  - ○ Onsite signage, brand integration in marketing communications
  - ○ Onsite experiential rights
  - ○ Unique prizes for contests

- Which assets and benefits give them a lot of visibility? Which assets and benefits give them unique experiences for employees and B2B clients?
- VIP experiences with artists.
- Tickets and experiences at year-round satellite events.
- Starfest has rights to engage artists in promoting the festival (remotely) for up to a month prior to the event, and it is not currently leveraging these rights.
- Several onsite consumer services on the event grounds, are not currently sponsored — including a barbecue food area and an evening karaoke contest.
- It is important to ask if it is obvious to current and potential sponsors that your property offers these benefits, or is there a disconnect between your property's value proposition and what others perceive it to be?
- Does the sponsor know of all the images and logo files at their disposal to use in promotions and marketing communications?
- Does the sponsor know how well your offering compares to alternatives?
- Does the sponsor understand how their experience as a sponsorship manager will be versus alternative sponsorships (sponsor servicing)?
- Among sponsors, Starfest has a perception of being a family festival, even though it has more young people in attendance than any festival in the Midwest.

External Assessment

- Look to best practices and case studies to explore new possibilities for how your property can meet the sponsor's needs.

- Look at what is winning awards and making headlines.
- Look outside of the music space, borrow ideas from sport, charity, and cause.
- What do banks look for in sponsorship, perhaps beyond what your contact told you in your interview?
- Info you might look out for:
  o Are there any new emerging media platforms that should be added to your approach for engaging your audience?
  o Are there more effective ways of integrating sponsor branding/ messaging in your property's consumer experience?
  o Are there any new ways that sponsorship effectiveness can be measured?

Possible learnings:
- Some European music festivals are now live streaming their performances and staging satellite festivals in different locations, showing the performances on a big screen.
- According to many studies on sponsorship, sponsors are increasingly feeling as though properties are not providing enough measurement and reporting to demonstrate sponsorship impact.
- Banks generally want to engage local branch staff in sponsorships.

Conduct Benchmarking Analysis

- When assessing your property's offering, compare it to alternatives.
- How do the number of attendees with different target demographics compare?
- How does your social following compare?
- How does overall popularity and brand perceptions compare?

Possible learnings:
- Starfest is one of the top music festivals in terms of onsite attendance, but its digital following is lower than a few other

festivals, and it does not offer the year-round digital platform that music streaming services can offer brands.

Distill Findings

From all the Internal/External Assessment findings, highlight what you felt were any common threads or reoccurring themes.

Possible key takeaways:

- Emphasis on "proving" that the festival engages the bank's target, and that it has appeal to this target.
- Must provide tailored opportunities to engage the bank's clients and employees.
- Must be open to the fact that the bank has specific objectives that they want to measure a certain way.

Strategic Approach

Based on the key takeaways highlighted in the Distill Findings section, build a roadmap for securing a sponsorship renewal decision from the sponsor.

- How to Engage the Decision-Maker?
- Plan appropriate timing and tactics to engage bank's CMO and Sponsorship Manager (the way in which Starfest's value proposition is presented to them).

Idea: Offer a bespoke VIP experience to not only the new CMO, but also to one of the company's key industry partners/clients.

- Present consumer insights.
- Begin with the target consumer's connection to music in general, then get into Starfest as a property within music (vs. other properties within music).

Idea: Send this report through as a landscape overview, discon-nected from a sponsorship proposal — just providing information.

Idea: Scour through information from past years' festivals to draw conclusions around how the sponsorship delivered value to the brand.

- Empower the bank to build the best sponsorship package for them.

Idea: Showcase an array of VIP experiences for the bank's high-net-worth clients that include digital engagement with artistes. skype chats, song writing session.

Idea: Propose title sponsorship of a new live stream platform, or of the evening karaoke contest (which can serve as an employee engagement opportunity).

- Ease their mind.

Idea: Offer a significant discount in rights fees in order to allow the new regime to "test drive" the property, and to free up budget for research/evaluation.

- Service, service, service.
- Ensure that the entire negotiation process, and contract finaliza-tion is as smooth as possible — demonstrating Starfest's com-mitment to sponsor servicing, communication, and fulfillment.

Implementation Plan

Source support:
- What research firm or intern can help with the consumer insights?

- What graphic designer can provide some pro bono support for mockups?
- Dedicate an office as the renewal war room for a dedicated team. Build a work back plan with key milestones.